Praise for *Finding the Words*

"Avoiding theory and jargon, Dr. Hayley Watson's *Finding the Words* is a hands-on resource for teachers and other caring adults who hope to address young people's mental health issues proactively, responsively, and responsibly. From her deep experience as a clinical psychologist, Dr. Watson presents a practical framework for understanding common problems young people are facing—and then illustrates it with sample conversations that offer constructive strategies to support young people in overcoming these obstacles. Using highly accessible language, she encourages us to act on everyday opportunities to have a positive impact on young people who are experiencing mental health challenges."

—Sheldon Berman, Ed.D.,
Lead Superintendent for Social-Emotional Learning, AASA,
The School Superintendents Association

"*Finding the Words* serves as a trusted colleague for educators, offering guidance and examples crucial for supporting students in their moments of struggle. This reliable companion empowers educators to authentically connect with students, equipping them with the words needed to navigate challenging situations and foster meaningful understanding."

—Liz Hill, M.Ed.,
Assistant Superintendent, West Vancouver Schools, Canada

"Dr. Watson's kind and open heart in the pages of this educator's guide make it possible to reach and connect with students and heal ourselves. Having strength, courage, and knowledge in all our approaches even when challenged by a student's behavior is our own healing. Always leading with the heart, Dr. Watson makes us stronger and wiser through practical and accessible guidance. In this guide, educators can find comfort in knowing that there are answers to hard questions as they navigate challenges with students as we learn and grow together."

—Maura Papile, L.I.C.S.W.,
Senior Director of Student Support Services, Quincy Public Schools

"The book beautifully encapsulates the idea that as educators, our role goes far beyond imparting knowledge; we are also responsible for nurturing the emotional well-being of our students. Dr. Watson highlights the crucial steps in self-reflection that can help students confront their inner needs and find their true selves. By making space for this self-discovery, educators can profoundly impact a student's personal growth. Every educator or supporter of education can benefit from this book."

—Scott Frauenheim,
President and Chief Executive Officer, Distinctive Schools

"*Finding the Words* is more than just a book—it's a call to action, empowering educators to engage in transformative conversations with young people facing significant challenges in their lives. Dr. Watson skillfully uses real-life scenarios to demonstrate the application of a six-part process designed to boost mental health resilience among youth. At the heart of this approach is the value placed on deep, meaningful conversations between young people and supportive adults, providing the context for nurturing the insights and skills youths need to help them navigate adversity."

—Jenny Williams,
Educational Consultant and Developer of http://wellbeingbc.ca

"I have known Dr. Hayley Watson for many years and have seen firsthand the work she delivers into the school system for both students and educators through the Open Parachute program.

Dr. Hayley has a deep, authentic passion for helping students' mental health journey and for educators to be equipped with the tools to help do and say the right thing in the moment. I believe this book will be the toolkit educators need to help students navigate some of their most challenging years of mental health. Dr. Hayley's wisdom, intellect, and genuine care for humans comes through in the words of this book. She breaks down the seemingly overwhelming subject of mental health and gives educators the confidence and the language to meet students where they are at. It gives constructive and practical examples of real-life interviews with students for teachers to draw on to prepare for tough conversations.

I believe that this book will be a game-changer for educators, who are often the first point of call for students when they are suffering. I recommend the work and balanced views of Dr. Hayley, and I'm excited for this book to go out into the world and help people."

—Jules Sebastian
Founder of The Sebastian Foundation

Finding the Words

Finding the Words

Empowering Struggling Students through Guided Conversations

Dr. Hayley Watson
Clinical Psychologist & Founder of Open Parachute

JB JOSSEY-BASS™
A Wiley Brand

Published by John Wiley & Sons, Inc., Hoboken, New Jersey.
Published simultaneously in Canada.

For general information on our other products and services or for technical support, please contact our Customer Care Department within the United States at (800) 762-2974, outside the United States at (317) 572-3993 or fax (317) 572-4002.

Wiley also publishes its books in a variety of electronic formats. Some content that appears in print may not be available in electronic formats. For more information about Wiley products, visit our web site at www.wiley.com.

Library of Congress Cataloging-in-Publication Data is Available:

ISBN 9781394187140 (Paperback)
ISBN 9781394187164 (ePDF)
ISBN 9781394187157 (ePub)

Cover Design: Thalassa Tam
Cover Image: © Anyese Khamis
Author Photo: © Thomas Pastro

SKY10065956_012624

This book is dedicated to every incredible child and teenager I had the pleasure of interviewing over the past few years, whose words form the core of this book. I am consistently in awe of your wisdom, courage, and resilience. Speaking to you gives me such hope for the future, and I know that with your voices leading the way, beautiful things will happen in our world. Thank you for being a hero in your own life and allowing that heroism to be used as guidance for others.

Contents

Contents xiii

Acknowledgments

One of my own mental health patterns is assuming that I need to do everything on my own and that I can, in fact, do things all by myself. This comes from my own childhood experience of feeling like the world was a scary place and reacting to that fear by trying to control my reality. The good news is that even with this shadow quality rearing its head my whole life, I have been constantly surrounded by people who have loved me, made me feel safe, given me clarity, reminded me of my own courage, and helped me form my own identity. Many of these people also helped me to write this book, and it truly would not have been possible without them. Bridget Kamp, my partner in crime since we were 4, you provided an educator's lens that was invaluable in clarifying my language. Tom Pastro, my partner in life and in business, you always make me and everything I do better with your (sometimes infuriatingly accurate) insights and insanely brilliant mind. Sanna Purinton, my teacher and guide, you heighten my perspective so that I can see the whole world in a single moment every time we speak. Christina Lawson, your tireless and endlessly efficient efforts in collating all of these interviews made the writing of this book feel seamless. Simon Bowen, your ability to tease out my (often chaotic) thoughts into concise and understandable frameworks gave this book shape. The rest of our incredible team at Open Parachute, you provided insights and ideas at just the right time and kept the life raft moving forward in so many important ways, which gave me the space I needed to put these words onto the page.

Finally, Thalassa Tam, your fabulous designs brought my ideas to life, and Anyese Khamis, your beautiful artwork captured the essence of conversations with young people, who are our true teachers.

Introduction

This book is unique in its approach. It is not a book about theories or analysis, it is a practical how-to handbook. It will provide you with guided conversations based on interviews with real students so that you can learn the specific language that will help you respond to the challenges your students face.

Mental health can be an overwhelming topic for educators. You hear the terrifying statistics. You know your students are struggling now more than ever. Mostly you might feel confident in your ability to help because you know your students and you're good at what you do. But right now, youth are in a mental health crisis, and sometimes you might get stuck when things are heavy or intense or on a scale you haven't yet experienced. Sometimes it's hard to know when to refer your students to a mental health professional and what you can say in those moments when there is no one else there but you.

This learning is essential for every educator, even if you don't want to speak about mental health at all with your students (which is completely understandable!). Think of it like CPR training. We aren't doctors, we don't know how to do surgery, but we all go through the training so that in the event that we are in front of someone whose heart has stopped, we can keep them alive until help arrives.

One of the hardest things about being an educator is that you are always "on." When you encounter student struggles and mental health challenges, it is on the fly, in the moment, and you often don't have the luxury of providing much more than a few words. Feeling on the spot with a student's reality and not being quite sure what you should or shouldn't say can be a stressful and challenging experience. This is part of what is leading to so much teacher burnout.

Being an educator, you are immersed in human connection, and the messiness this entails, and you are the first to see the ever-changing landscape of challenges that young people face. Even though you might not feel equipped to deal with some of the things your students are experiencing, you are. You care, and you want to help. Those are the fundamentals. You don't need to be a psychologist or a mental health "expert." All you need is a source of practical guidance that you can use to build on your already strong foundation to provide support for your students while also supporting yourself.

This book is that source. You can use the index to flip to any challenge you see occurring for your students, and in a matter of minutes, you will have an example of dialogue and language that you can draw on. This will help you move from your already strong foundation of connecting to and caring for your students to knowing precisely what to do in order to provide deep and meaningful mental health support. To provide the kind of support that builds resilience in students so they are more equipped to help themselves, and that creates a healthy boundary for you at the same time. When you know your words are helping, you are less likely to take the burden of what you hear in the classroom home with you, creating less stress in your life. These impactful conversations with struggling students will mean that you have more time, headspace, and energy to focus on teaching. And more specifically, teaching students who are mentally and emotionally ready to learn.

The information found in this book is based on my education in this field, which includes five academic degrees, my Ph.D. research into school bullying interventions, and my work as a clinical psychologist. But more than any of that, the greatest insights I have gained to advise my theoretical perspective are based on two things: First, my own therapeutic processing of the trauma that I faced in my early life, which allowed me to develop a deeply personal understanding of the theories I was presented with throughout my educational journey. By seeing my own patterns, changing some, and struggling to change others, I have become acutely aware of how our thoughts and feelings play out in the way we treat ourselves and each other on a daily basis. And second, the work I have done with schools and students over the past 20 years—some as a psychologist, some as a program developer, and some as a mentor and youth worker. Doing this work has given me a deep insight into the way mental health plays out in the real world, in school settings. The mental health challenges that educators are presented with are often confusing and multilayered, and there is usually a deficit of time to deal with the challenges of so many students in the midst of a busy school day. This is what led me to develop Open Parachute, which is a Tier 1 mental health curriculum program to assist teachers in delivering impactful mental health lessons to all of their students without needing to be a mental health "expert" themselves. Many of the teachers delivering these lessons all over the world have asked me a similar question: "If something comes up in class, what *exactly* do I say?" This book is an answer to that question, and is for all the brilliant educators out there who tirelessly (and often thanklessly) do the hard work every day to connect to and care for their students. In these pages, I hope you find the words that can help you navigate the challenges you face in your classroom every day.

What Is Really Going on with Students?

Every child is born with the wisdom to flourish. Every person inherently knows what they need to thrive. If they didn't, we wouldn't have survived so effectively as a species. And yet in today's world, many youth are struggling for a growing list of reasons. Many families face challenges that are beyond their control, and in many homes, the isolation and sudden changes of COVID exacerbated these challenges. Most students are in consistent contact with technology, and this can overwhelm and overstimulate them. While social media serves as a powerful tool for connection, it also increases many students' experiences of loneliness and decreases their self-esteem. With more and more image editing, increasing numbers of students feel ashamed of their bodies, which further diminishes their sense of self. Any student who does not quite fit in with their peers begins to see themselves as "less than," which impacts their agency and motivation to strive. There are so many ever-changing challenges that children and teenagers face in our world right now that it has become an impossible task for parents to protect them or prepare them adequately.

While this can all feel pretty bleak and disheartening, the good news is that there actually is something that we, as adults, can do to help. No, we don't have all the answers. No, we can't make their challenges go away. But what we can do is remind them that *they have everything they need to find their way to the other side of whatever they are facing*. It might not be easy, and it might take time, but they *can* learn to reflect on and understand their own experiences, and do things to actively build their support systems and support themselves. These steps will drastically improve any student's mental health, and these are things that we can coach and encourage them to do every single day.

Humans have the capacity to overcome seemingly insurmountable obstacles. This has been proven time and time again. When faced with struggle, we have the incredible ability to shift, change, and adapt to achieve greatness that we never would have imagined. When faced with 27 years in prison, Nelson Mandela cultivated the courage and open-heartedness to lead an entire nation to a peaceful revolution. When faced with starvation and isolation, Anne Frank found the wisdom to write words that would teach profound compassion to the world for generations to come. When brutally gunned down, Malala Yousafzai found the strength to speak with such a commanding presence that she started an educational revolution that gave millions of girls the opportunity to expand their minds. Each of these incredible people changed the course of history simply by *facing a personal challenge*. As they struggled, they dug deep within themselves, and in so doing, found their own unique brilliance that could help not only themselves, but the world around them.

Every one of us has within themselves that brilliance and power. We just don't always know how to access it.

And so instead of expanding to our fullest potential when we face adversity, many of us simply fall into despair and get caught up in our fears. We start to self-destruct. We are so lost in our reactions that we become disconnected from our natural internal motivation to thrive. This is what separates us from animals. Our incredible mind has the ability to make something out of nothing. So when we are connected to ourselves and the world around us, we can be courageous and compassionate beyond measure, inspiring the world to do what is right and good and fair for everyone. But when our mind is spinning away from us and we no longer have a grasp on who we are or what we're capable of, all that mental power becomes focused on *escaping what we're feeling.* At all costs.

In the classroom, this might look like daydreaming, persistent disruptive behavior, withdrawal, nonattendance, or overly dramatic responses. All of this flags a deeper issue that this student is facing.

Imagine walking along a mountain path that's clearly marked, so every time you come to a crossroads you can see an indication of the right direction to take. Maybe it takes you a while to find the correct markings, and you might start down the wrong path and have to turn back a few times, and sometimes the right path is steep and rocky. But because you know where you are going and what to look for, you eventually find your way to the top of the mountain. This is what life is like for a mind that is in tune with itself, and able to devote its full attention to the task at hand—climbing whatever mountain is in front of us.

But let's consider the alternative. Imagine that you are on that same path, but this time you are looking at your phone because your friends are messaging you conflicting opinions about where you should be going. And you are also looking at social media accounts of famous people who have rapidly leaped over mountains much bigger than this, so you're wondering where the elevator is. And at the same time, you're searching online for what the "experts" say is the correct path to take. But these experts all seem to be fighting over different sources of evidence, and accusing each other of misinformation. Your mind is preoccupied and overwhelmed. You don't even bother looking up and *trying to find your own way.* All you can think of is getting off this mountain and back into your comfy bed because the whole journey has become way too overwhelming.

When a student is in this state, you might see them becoming engrossed in social media or video games, sleeping in and missing deadlines, or focusing more on their friendship dramas than on self-care or even basic hygiene. All of these are avoidance tactics (usually unconscious) that indicate these students are overwhelmed with their reality and are trying to retreat to situations and experiences that feel safer, more familiar, and easier to resolve.

So you take the first path that leads downhill to simply get *away*, and you follow it even though you're now walking through swamplands, being bitten my bugs and getting scratched by the underbrush. You become distracted by all these new challenges. You forget that there is still a mountain that you can climb to completely change your reality, circumstances, and perspective, and you continue to go farther and farther downhill. Your desire to escape the confusion and challenge of the mountain overpowers your wisdom and trust in yourself to reach the peak. Every time you come to a new crossroad, it becomes harder and harder to take the upward path. You are less and less able to see the markings that can lead you to the summit because you are more and more fixated on the desire to get back to something you know, that feels safe. The deeper you go, the more turned around you become and the less perspective you have. It starts to feel like everything you do is hopeless and nothing is going to bring you back home.

And therein lies the problem. Our mental health suffers when we *stop looking for our own path* and trusting our own ability to find our way through adversity. We become focused on trying to find *safety* (avoiding the challenge) instead of *expanding to become a new version of ourselves that can overcome this challenge.*

This is why you might see many students lacking what we call a "growth mindset," who give up easily or who don't want to keep working at something until they master it. The more students avoid their uncomfortable thoughts and feelings about the challenges in their lives (by seeking comfort through their phone or other distractions), the more they develop a pattern of shutting down anytime a difficult feeling arises (such as feelings of failure, disappointment, or inadequacy, which are all a natural part of learning).

How Can I Help?

All of this is preventable. If students just knew that they could turn around and face their mountain. If they realized that they have all the answers within them, and that all they have to do is direct their attention in the right place, toward *overcoming the obstacles they face, instead of seeking a way to avoid them.*

We can't create a world for youth where they don't struggle. That's life. But we *can give them hope.* We can remind them of their strength. We can walk beside them so they know they're not alone, and remind them to look up and take in the glorious view of how far they have come, so their joy sparks new energy and a strengthened will to climb higher.

Change is hard. It's scary and often painful. And we live in a world that hides away from discomfort. So as the world constantly, rapidly, and drastically changes around us, most of us are not changing along with it. We are not adapting and thriving. We are freaking out. And so are our youth. Many children and teenagers are terrified, overwhelmed, depressed, anxious, and confused because they don't see a path to new heights, only a mad dash away from an increasing number of obstacles.

But students don't need to be in this state. They have the ability to create beauty in this new world. They can find joy. They can live up to their fullest potential, not in spite of the challenges they face, but because of them. Each mountain in front of them presents an opportunity to discover more of their own ability to thrive, and along with it the confidence to know they can go further, and do greater things in the world.

And we can help them do it.

You, as an educator, are in the uniquely perfect position to give your students this gift. You are connected to them every day, and they know how much you care for them. You have the perspective to see their patterns play out in their daily struggles of being "out in the world" (at school) in a way that their parents don't have access to. And you also have the ability to nudge them in the right direction every single day.

How to Use This Book

This book is designed to help you understand how to respond to students facing all different types of challenges. It will give you the language to support, encourage, and draw out the wisdom of your students so that you can maximize the impact you have, not only on the knowledge your students retain in class, but also on the people they become and the positive impacts they have on the world.

In these pages, you will hear from real youth expressing their deepest challenges and their greatest courage, strength, and resilience. Through their stories, you will learn how to help every young person you come in contact with find the same resources within them to overcome whatever challenges they face, and truly flourish throughout their lives. You will learn tools for helping students overcome specific experiences that impact their mental health, like bullying, addictive patterns, low body image, violations of consent, prejudice, and stress. The goal of this book is to give you the confidence to create meaningful change in the next generation every single day.

Sometimes you will have a student confide in you. Sometimes will find something out from a parent or counselor and are asked not to address it with the student directly for privacy reasons. For the most part, the conversations in this book are about *building skills* and can be used whether you can talk openly about a student's specific challenges or not.

With some students, it takes prolonged effort, multiple points of contact, and constant availability for them to feel safe enough to make changes that can help their mental health. Many students will display behavior that is rude, cruel, disrespectful, or it might seem like they don't care about anything. This is one of the biggest challenges as an educator, and it's incredibly difficult not to take these actions personally. But breakthroughs do happen, often when we least expect it, and simply reminding students again and again that you are here to help them will have a bigger impact than you will ever know.

As a clinical psychologist, I speak to students about their challenges regularly, so my comfort level with these topics is naturally higher than it would be without this experience. Therefore, I usually ask direct questions because I am very familiar with the types of answers I will get. You might feel comfortable having these frank conversations already, or this might seem foreign to you. Either way, the more conversations you have, the easier it gets. So be gentle with yourself and move at your own pace, knowing that any level of interest you show students about their mental health and well-being will go an incredibly long way to helping them feel safer to open up to the people in their lives who can help them when they need it most.

Thank you for listening to these brilliant young heroes. As we help them, we are also helping ourselves. Their voices will lead us all to the bright, peaceful, exciting new future that we so very much deserve.

The chapters do not need to be read in order, and you can read any chapter or group of chapters without reading anything that comes before it. I encourage you to start by thinking of a student you know is struggling, find that struggle in the index, and go to that section in the book. Use the guided conversation as a model for when you next have the opportunity to speak with this student.

Keep the book in your classroom, and grab it at the end of each day if you have any questions about your students, if there are any interactions that aren't sitting well with you, or if you find your students' behavior requires constant consequences, and nothing seems to "work." You can open the book and flip to the section that relates most to what is happening with that student. See if you can picture your own student while you read through the conversation in the chapter. Then try the language and see what happens. This book is designed to be used again and again to give you practical, usable guidance that transforms your already strong foundation of connection with your students into something that you can be confident is deeply supporting their mental health.

The more you use it, the more the pieces will fit together, and this language will become more and more natural and spontaneous. Think of this book as your psychologist friend. Someone you can call up anytime and say "My student is struggling with *x*. What can I say to them in the context of a classroom that will help?"

There are three additional Bonus Chapters that can be found at *www.openparachuteschools .com/finding-the-words* covering topic areas that are more specialized in nature ("Helping Students Who Are Overwhelmed or Having a Panic Attack"; "Coaching Students with Obsessive/Perfectionistic Thoughts"; "Coaching Students Away from Gang Culture"). If your students are facing these specific challenges, the bonus chapters will also be helpful for you to draw on.

When you have more time, you can read through Chapter 1, "Understanding Student Mental Health," to get a broad overview of why these conversations are so effective. The theory presented here is intentionally brief and is provided only *in service of the practical conversation guides*, not the other way around. This is a bottom-up approach that is grounded in evidence but presented in a format that *means* something to you as an educator. You probably don't really want your psychologist friend to give you a long-winded analysis of your student's concerns. You know them; you see them. You sometimes don't understand exactly what's going on, but you always want to help. You just want some practical guidance so you can have organic conversations with your students that you are confident will help them.

After Chapter 1, there are five sections to the book, each exploring different ways that student challenges manifest (see Figure 1.1 in Chapter 1). At the beginning of each section is a chapter that will help you understand these issues from a psychological perspective and explore the specific, structured steps you can take in conversations that will help your students thrive. You will notice some overlap between the sections, and this is because many of the issues that students face have multiple layers and can be looked at from many different angles. You will also notice that the same conversation steps apply to every student challenge, and as you read through the sections, you will see different ways that these steps can manifest, depending on the student and the circumstances. Looking for *similarities* will help you in applying this in your own communication with students.

The chapters within each section will then explore one specific challenge in more depth, with a breakdown of:

1. **Why** the challenge is happening (from a psychological perspective).
2. **What** you can do to help (applying the structured steps laid out in the first chapter of the section).
3. **How** you will do this (hearing directly from students, based on real transcripts of my 300+ interviews with youth aged 5–19 across the United States, Canada, and Australia over the past four years, interviews that form the basis of the Open Parachute school mental health program).

At the end of each chapter, you will see a "Related Chapters" section. This shows you chapters that could be similar in the types of issues that students are facing or the types of reactions they are having. You can use these suggestions to guide your process of flipping through the book instead of reading each section in the order it appears in the book if that seems more intuitive to you.

Each interview shows additional commentary to provide context about why I responded the way I did, what I was feeling, or a different response that could have been more appropriate. This is designed to help you digest and understand these conversations and identify things that resonate with you or that you would do differently, depending on your personality, personal history, and relationship with your students. I recommend reading each interview without these comments first so the flow of the discussion is uninterrupted, and then reading it again with the commentary so you can reflect on how you would apply the conversation yourself. It's also important to note for context that these interviews were all done with students that I did not know previously, and I interviewed each student once for about an hour (after first speaking briefly on the phone with them, their parent, and sometimes their school counselor). In the interviews, they were speaking on camera about their challenges, so that other students who participate in our Open Parachute mental health curriculum program can hear authentic accounts from real peers to encourage their own mental health skill-building.

I have changed all the names and some of the details in the transcripts, but the voices of students are real and they are their own. In this way, all of the learning is coming directly from the source. You will see real dialogue between myself and these incredible students, so that you can gain specific insights into youth mental health *from their perspective*. You will notice that the student voices represented here often possess maturity and wisdom beyond their years because the adversity they have faced has forced them to grow up faster than most. This is why youth who face struggles are the perfect role models that we can all learn from. They see things in a deeper way, and learn lessons that can apply to all of us.

1 | Understanding Student Mental Health

This chapter will give you an overview of how to understand youth mental health. The purpose of this chapter is to explore the theory that underpins the guided conversations that you will learn about to help you with some of the challenges that your students face. You can read this chapter first if you prefer to understand the broader perspective before diving into the guided conversations, or you can read this chapter after you have started flipping to the chapters that relate to your students' challenges and using the tips associated with each specific situation.

Shadow Qualities and the True Self

In order to support student mental health, it's important that we start to break down this concept so that we can better understand the ways that we can help. Every student is equipped with a set of qualities that lead to resilience and that help them overcome the struggles they face. The qualities that we focus on in this book are *acceptance*, *spontaneity*, *openness*, *leadership*, and *freedom of choice*. I synthesized these qualities from my research, clinical practice, and experience with student mental health. There are many ways to look at mental health, but in my experience, these qualities are the key to determining whether a student will struggle or thrive. Students turn away from these qualities toward their *shadow* qualities when they are faced with adversity and forget their natural ability to overcome whatever it is they are facing. Throughout this book, you will learn how to support your students each time they have turned to a shadow quality by reminding them how to make the journey back to their true self quality. To help you understand this concept, see Figure 1.1.

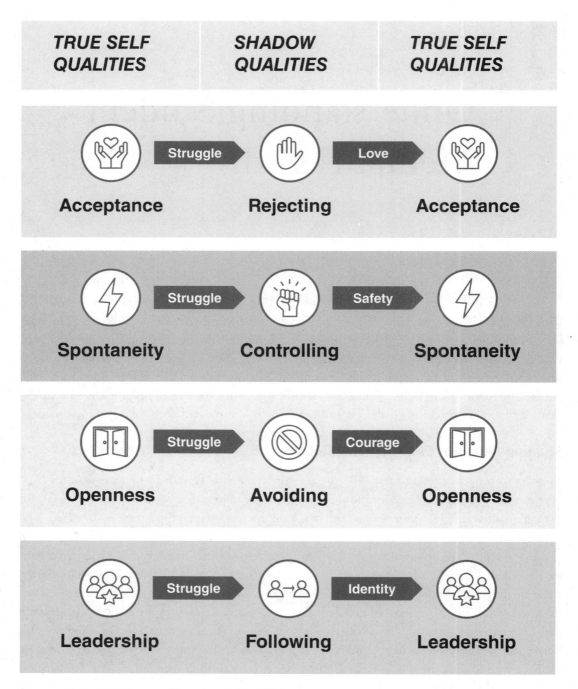

Figure 1.1   Shadow and true self qualities.

Reproduced with permission from Open Parachute.

Figure Explanations

Students can exhibit one or more of these expressions at any given time, and are always on a continuum moving back and forth between their true self qualities and their shadow qualities, depending on the challenges they encounter and the resources they have to face and overcome them.

Rejecting/Acceptance (Remembering Love)　　Children naturally accept the world around them, the people they encounter, and the experience of things not going their way. However, they move away from this acceptance and start to reject themselves and the world around them if they are repeatedly hurt by people or circumstances, or are not shown a level of acceptance by others. These experiences cause them to lose trust in their connections with others or in the world in general. Students displaying these behaviors need to know they are *loved* so they can return to a state of accepting their reality.

Controlling/Spontaneity (Remembering Safety)　　Children have a natural level of spontaneity, making decisions based on how they feel in each moment, without too much concern for getting things "right" or following a plan. However, they move away from this spontaneity and seek to control themselves and their world when they have experiences of change that are harmful or chaotic. This causes them to fear change, and become cautious with anything unplanned or unpredicted. Students responding in this way need to know they are *safe* so they can return to their natural fluid and spontaneous state.

Avoiding/Openness (Remembering Courage)　　Children are naturally open to their internal reality, and possess an incredible level of honesty in expressing their feelings, needs, and wants. However, if their emotions are not tended to when they are expressed, or they are shut down or shamed for their vulnerability, they start to avoid their feelings and any situations that trigger those feelings. These patterns also arise if children witness similar avoidance tactics in the adults close to them. Students who are in a state of avoidance need to remember their own *courage* so they can return to their natural state of openness to their own emotions.

Following/Leadership (Remembering Identity)　　Children have an incredible amount of agency, and make choices about their own actions based on what feels inherently right to them, regardless of outside influences, which is an important quality of any great leader. However, when they are not encouraged to use this agency, or are forced to bend to the will of others in ways that harm them or repeatedly work against their nature, they forget their ability to lead their own path, and instead, begin to blindly follow others. Students responding in this way need to strengthen their own *identity* to return to their natural state of leadership.

Repeating/Freedom (Remembering Clarity)   Children naturally act from a place of freedom, changing their opinions, responses, and actions based on the new information they learn in each situation they encounter. However, if they are exposed to people who are repeating the same harmful actions over and over again, they lose sight of their own freedom of expression and begin repeating the patterns they have been exposed to rather than determining the action that is best for them to take in any given moment. Students caught in these patterns need to develop *clarity* so they can see their choices and return to their natural state of freely choosing their own path instead of repeating the path that has been laid down before them.

Providing Support

Students will struggle with these different shadow qualities to varying degrees at different times, depending on a variety of factors (e.g., family/cultural patterns, biological predispositions, early life trauma, support systems, and the nature and severity of current stressors). Understanding the different categories can help you understand what is going on for students, but what is most important is seeing the *universal* ways that we, as adults, can help students, no matter what shadow quality they are turning to.

The biggest threat to students' mental health is not that they face challenges; it's that they often don't have the understanding or the motivation to *take the steps needed to overcome these challenges*. That is why the constant encouragement, reminders, and guidance of how to navigate their personal struggles, coming from a trusted adult such as yourself, is so vital in their pathway to becoming a thriving, independent adult. Building mental health resilience is a skill set, and like any skill set, it requires learning. This learning is cyclical, and therefore, I refer to it as a *learning cycle*. This means that the steps of learning happen over and over again, in various orders, and must be applied to every new situation that a student encounters in order for them to generalize these skills.

For example, if a student is struggling to learn a math problem, they will need to be guided through the steps of how to face and overcome this (e.g., change their thoughts that they aren't smart, accept their feelings of frustration, keep trying to solve the problem even if it feels impossible). If they are then faced with a friendship challenge, they will need to use these same skills, but they will need to be guided to understand how to apply them in this different experience (e.g., change their thoughts that their friend doesn't care about them, accept their feelings of rejection, keep trying to communicate with their friend to repair the relationship).

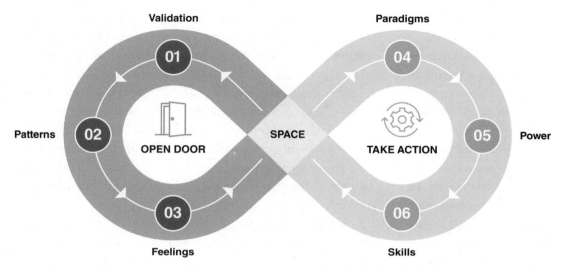

Figure 1.2   The learning cycle for building mental health skills.

Reproduced with permission from Open Parachute.

Every single challenge, big and small that a student encounters has an impact on their mental health because it affects their thoughts, feelings, and actions. Therefore, every challenge is a chance to reinforce the mental health skills that will help them in every area of their lives. This involves first *opening themselves up to see their challenges clearly*, and then *taking actions that will help them overcome these challenges*. See Figure 1.2 for an explanation of the learning cycle for building mental health skills incorporating these steps. This learning cycle will be referenced throughout this book, and you will be shown how it can be applied to each unique mental health struggle that you see in your students.

What you can do as an educator is to make *space* for students to move through the six steps of self-reflection that will help them navigate whatever struggle they find themselves in, that is, causing them to turn away from their true self and toward their shadow qualities. These steps fall into the two categories explained next.

Figure Explanations
Category 1: Open the Door.
First, we help students open the door in their own mind to connect to what is really happening for them. We can do this by:

1. **Validating** them and their experiences.
   Validation means letting a student know that what they are facing is normal, and we understand where they are coming from (e.g., "It's okay to feel nervous about the future; that is a really common response when things feel out of control") and that there is

nothing inherently wrong with them. Even if they are acting in an unhelpful way, we can validate them as a person while still discouraging their behavior (e.g., "I know you are a really good person, *and* some of the decisions you're making right now are harmful").

2. Helping them notice their own **patterns**.

    A *pattern* is any behavioral reaction (e.g., swearing, pushing, not handing in homework, leaving people out, disregarding instructions, etc.), way of thinking (e.g., not believing in their own abilities, thinking everything is someone else's fault, assuming that something bad will happen, etc.), or emotional response (e.g., feeling incredibly hurt by the unintentional actions of others, seeming not to care when they cause harm or don't follow the rules, etc.). In order to change these patterns, students first have to *notice* them.

3. Encouraging them to relate directly to their **feelings**.

    Feelings are the physical and emotional responses that a student has to their experiences. These might be in the form of emotions such as sadness, anger, confusion, or joy, or they could arise in the form of physical sensations such as an upset stomach, a headache, or fidgeting/struggling to sit still. Asking students directly about their feelings helps them to understand their own experiences better.

Category 2: Take Action.

Second, we help students take actions to help themselves, by:

4. Helping them shift their **paradigm**, or the way they are seeing things.

    A *paradigm* is a student's fundamental views about themselves and the world. For example, a student who has experienced a loving and emotionally safe environment might develop a paradigm that the world is a loving place, and that their emotions are safe to experience. However, a student who has experienced the loss or abandonment of a parent, or who has not been given a chance to express their emotions, might develop a paradigm that the world is a harmful place, and that their emotions are unacceptable. There is always a problematic paradigm underneath any mental health struggle. When it can be shifted, a student is much more likely to see a positive path forward.

5. Reminding them of their **power**.

    A student's *power* is their ability to act with agency in their own world—their ability to enact change and influence their experiences. When a student faces challenges and is able to take actions that help them overcome these challenges, their belief in their own ability to help themselves increases, meaning they have more perceived power. If we can remind them of the power they have used in the past, students are much more able to draw on that same power in the future.

6. Supporting them to use a **skill** that helps them move forward.

Skills are anything a student does that helps them cope or change their physical and emotional circumstances. This can include setting boundaries, asking for help, changing the way they think about things, taking care of their emotions, connecting with others, eating well, exercising, and getting enough sleep. Anything that positively impacts a student's mental health is a skill they can use to make changes that will help them move toward their true self, and away from their shadow qualities. When a student is struggling, they often forget these skills and need to be reminded to use them again and again.

All of these steps are needed in order for students to *move through struggles*. If we skip the steps required for opening the door in their mind, then the actions they take *won't be connected to what they truly need*. If we skip the steps required for taking action, then they *won't learn how to move forward when hard things happen*. These steps don't always happen in order, and they can also occur across multiple conversations. However, keep in mind that it all starts with *validation*, which is the first step in opening the door for a student to feel safe enough to self-reflect with you.

Something to note is that *it can often look on the surface like a student is getting worse when we encourage this level of deep self-reflection* (e.g., they become more visibly upset, they start articulating more negative thoughts, or they act out in more extreme ways). It's important to remember that this is *part of the learning cycle* and vital in the process of overcoming challenges. *If a student doesn't first recognize that they feel sad about something, they won't know that they need support to help them navigate it*. It's a bit like when we first start exercising. We usually feel tired, frustrated, and generally horrible as our body adjusts, but then eventually we gain strength and enjoy the process of exercise more and more the stronger we get. The self-reflection process is the same—it gets worse before it gets better, but *it does get better*. We just have to be patient.

This can be hard for us as adults, if we were not raised in families who engaged in open reflections about feelings. And even if we were, our culture generally holds the belief that if a child *appears happy on the surface*, we should stay away from triggering topics so as not to disturb their peace. And conversely, we are given the message that if a student appears upset when we are talking to them, then *we must have done the wrong thing* in our approach to supporting them.

However, the opposite is often true. If we avoid this deeper reflection with students, if we stay on the surface and teach students only to "regulate" their emotions rather than really understand their own internal conflicts, we can never truly help them change.

When students are getting into squabbles with classmates, acting in disruptive ways, or becoming overly emotional in class, the most common response we have as adults is to try to help them *calm down their emotions* so they can get back to whatever they are doing and stop disrupting the learning. Sometimes this means we send them to a "calm down corner" or out of the class, and sometimes it means we try to solve their problem (e.g., moving them away from someone they are arguing with) to reduce the emotional trigger. These are all very practical and useful strategies to deal with the tension of the moment. However, if we stop there and don't also help students reflect on *why they were reacting this way in the first place*, they won't learn to make more helpful decisions in the way they think, feel, and behave and will simply keep doing the same thing over and over again.

We end up always fighting the same fight over and over again in the classroom. They are stressed and overwhelmed by the workload. Their friend hurt their feelings and they don't know why. They are unmotivated and pay more attention to their phone than the learning. All of these things you can "snap them out of" or "soothe" as a short-term solution. But not only is this not effective in the long-term, it's exhausting because these are things you also deal with outside of the classroom with our own families, and this leads to educator burnout. You feel like you are running on a hamster wheel because, really, you are. You are putting out fires again and again because your students aren't being empowered to see what's driving their struggles or given the tools to change their patterns. You see the outcome of this playing out again and again, and it's confusing and distressing.

You can't be expected to be a therapist or to understand the layers of what is happening for your students. This is not the intent or expectation. What you can do is support them in returning to the truth of who they are by helping them have clarity, feel loved and safe, and find their own courage and identity.

And the fun part is that everything you learn that will help your students will also help you. These are transferrable skills for everyone involved. One of the most powerful gifts we can give to others is our own self-reflection. The more we understand and face our own challenges, the more we know on a deep level what's needed to help others. As you read this book, I encourage you to apply this learning to your own life, and by doing so, bring it off the pages so it becomes real and alive for you. That way you won't just be learning this information, you will be *living and breathing it*, which means you will effortlessly pass it on to every one of your students.

Throughout this book, you will gain a deep understanding of the mental health struggles that your students face, and hopefully, find ways of relating to your students on an even deeper level as you also reflect on your own life in and outside of the classroom. This information is designed to give you guidance on how you can intervene in simple, effective ways to point your students in the direction of growth, and remember their own strength and power, while protecting and enhancing your own mental health at the same time.

SECTION

1 | Rejecting/Acceptance (Remembering Love)

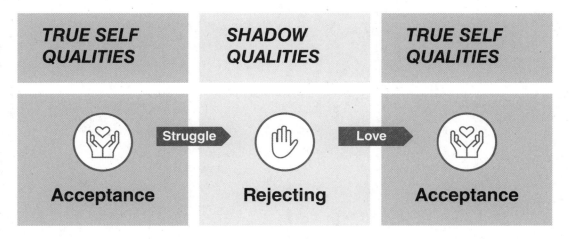

TRUE SELF QUALITIES	SHADOW QUALITIES	TRUE SELF QUALITIES
Acceptance	Rejecting	Acceptance

Struggle → Love →

Reproduced with permission from Open Parachute.

This section will focus on conversation tips for students who are rejecting *themselves* (e.g., because they have faced trauma/abuse or cultural norms that shame their gender expression) or the *world around them* (e.g., not attending school, being cruel to peers, etc.). You will learn strategies for helping students in these situations find more *acceptance* of themselves and others by reminding them that they are *loved* and *loveable*, regardless of their actions or how they are treated.

2 | Finding the Words with Students Who Are in *Rejecting* Behavior Patterns

Some of the hardest students to teach are those who are in a state of *rejection*. These are students who display aggressive and destructive behavior who seem to not care at all about themselves or others. Students who react in these ways are doing so because their trust has been broken by painful experiences in their past. When children go through trauma, abuse, and other adverse life experiences that they do not have the support to cope with, they can begin to believe that the world is an uncaring and unloving place. They do not feel love in the way they know they should, and it can be too painful to accept a world without love. So they reject it.

This rejection dominates their thoughts and actions. For example, if they are unsuccessful in their learning, they will cause disruptions to the students around them because they feel rejected by academics, their peers, and even you as a teacher. They assume the world is against them, and it is hard for them to get past this thought to understand that you care about them and believe in them.

Underneath all of this resistance and aggression is a deep, buried pain. Sometimes we know the specifics of a student's past (e.g., they come from a violent household). And sometimes we have no idea what life they have led. But one thing we can always count on is the fact that any student who rejects other people, is cruel and unkind, or refuses to engage in class or with others, has *always been hurt in a major way*. When they reject people or experiences, what they are really wanting to reject is *what happened to them*, whatever that may be.

And the saddest part about this pattern is that deep down every child who is rejecting their past harmful experiences is also *rejecting themselves*. Rejecting the part of them that was taken advantage of or hurt. They *unconsciously believe that their pain and vulnerability are a weakness that (on some level) caused the trauma to occur.*

This is why students who have grown up in traumatic environments often appear aggressive and cruel and seem to be lacking in empathy, gentleness, or softness. Their anger serves as protection, masking their pain by *rejecting all parts of themselves and others that can feel this pain.*

In order to shift out of a state of rejection, students need to be guided in connecting to the pain that lies underneath their anger, and we can help this by letting them know that *their pain is seen and honored.* When we provide this space for students, they can drop the resistance—even if it's just for a few moments. In those moments when their guard is down, they are able to feel *accepted* and *loved*.

It will take a lot of this acceptance and love to shift cycles of rejection, and that is why students who are reacting in this way need long-term relationships. *Staying connected and accessible to students, even when they lash out or become dismissive,* is vital to helping them change their perception that the world is against them. Their reactions are not personal. It's not because we haven't done enough or because they don't care. It's because *they do care and it scares them.* A child who has learned that people can't be trusted will naturally pull away when they get too close to someone. Their frame of reference for closeness is one where that closeness will always be taken away or violated in some way.

The goal when we are supporting students who are in a state of rejection is to simply show up again and again *and again*. To accept them as they are in each moment, even when they are acting poorly. To see past their harmful behavior to the pain that is underneath it. To remind them that *they are so much more* than what they are showing on the outside and that no matter how much they push back, *there are people who won't disappoint them or hurt them.*

If you don't have the chance to engage in a direct conversation with students who are in a state of *rejection*, you can simply provide consistent validation and *notice them* every chance you get. If they come to class for the first time in weeks, tell them you're happy to see them. If you see them making *any kind of effort*, tell them you appreciate it. If they act out, let them know you see their pain. You can still set a boundary, while also telling them that you care (e.g., "what you are doing is not okay, but I know you have your reasons, and I'm really sorry you feel that this is the only option"). Students who are *rejecting* need to feel *acceptance* from others, even when they are acting in harmful ways, so they can learn to *accept themselves* and the world around them. It's important to remember that we can *accept the student* while not *accepting their actions*.

By approaching them with this perspective, you are opening the door to a deeper conversation with a student when the opportunity arises. This deeper conversation will naturally occur when they feel *loved* and *accepted*.

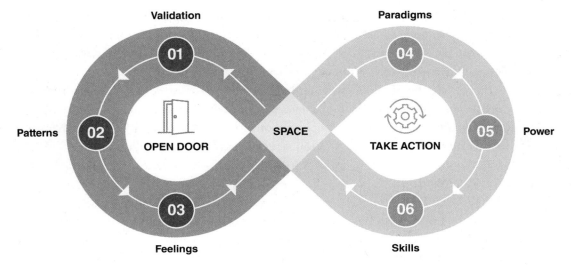

Figure 2.1   The learning cycle for building mental health skills.

Reproduced with permission from Open Parachute.

What Can I Do to Help Students Who Are Rejecting?

Your goal is to make *space* for students to move through the six steps of self-reflection, shown in Figure 2.1, that will help them move *away from rejecting and toward acceptance*. These steps fall into the two categories explained next.

Figure Explanations
Category 1: Open the Door.

1. **Validating** them and their experiences.

    Validation means letting a student know that what they are facing is normal, and that we understand where they are coming from. When a student is rejecting, it's important to use language like "I understand that feeling," or "I get why that upset you," or "I know you're a caring person, even if you get angry sometimes." This shows the student that you are on their side, and you see past their unhelpful actions to the person they are underneath.

2. Helping them notice their own **patterns**.

    A *pattern* can be any behavioral reaction, way of thinking, or emotional response. When students are rejecting, we want to help them notice their own reactions by asking questions in a nonjudgmental way that invites honest self-reflection (e.g., "I wonder what you were feeling that made you act that way," or "When I think that people don't care about me, sometimes I lash out. Were you having any thoughts like that?").

3. Encouraging them to relate directly to their **feelings**.

    Feelings are the physical and emotional responses that a student has to their experiences. When students are rejecting, they are likely feeling sadness, pain, and shame. These feelings might be buried really deeply, so you may need to start with helping them first identify the embarrassment, frustration, or even giddiness that is on the surface for them.

Category 2: Take Action.

4. Helping them shift their **paradigm**, or the way they are seeing things.

    A *paradigm* is a student's fundamental views about themselves and the world. Students who are rejecting usually see themselves in a negative light because of the harm that they have experienced. If we can show them *our* acceptance of them, this can help them to change their viewpoint (e.g., "I see that you are a really caring person and you feel things deeply" or "What happened to you is not your fault").

5. Reminding them of their **power**.

    A student's *power* is their ability to act with agency in their own world—their ability to enact change and influence their experiences. When a student is rejecting, we can help them remember their power by pointing out every tiny step they take in the right direction, rather than focusing on how far they still have to go (e.g., "I noticed you only got angry for 10 minutes this time, and yesterday you were angry for the whole class. I really see you making an effort!").

6. Supporting them to use a **skill** that helps them move forward.

    Skills are anything a student does that helps them cope or change their physical and emotional circumstances. Students who are rejecting often need to practice the skill of *accepting love from others*. Reminding them of their positive connections can help them practice the skill of trusting those around them (e.g., "Do you have a close friend who cares about you?" "I notice that your classmates really love your sense of humor.").

These steps can help your students understand their own worthiness, and overcome the impacts of their past trauma to shift out of harmful patterns. The chapters that follow in this section will give you examples of how you can support students in various *rejecting* patterns so that you can find the words to say in those moments when an aggressive or cruel response from a student can throw you off balance.

3 | Encouraging Students Who Are Disengaged from School

This chapter will give you tools for responding to students who are not attending school, not paying attention in class, not doing their school work, or not applying themselves to the best of their ability. Students exhibiting these behaviors are *rejecting* school and/or learning, and you will learn language that can help them move toward an *acceptance* of themselves and their learning environment.

WHY Do Students Disengage from School?

Students disengage from school because they are in a state of *rejection*. (See Chapter 2 for a deeper explanation of *rejecting* behavior.) Often this is because they doubt their ability, fear rejection, or assume that any success they achieve will be taken away from them. There are often other layers of trauma in their past as well, which have caused them to feel unaccepted and unworthy of love. The more they reject school, the harder it becomes to learn and to fit in with their classmates, causing them to fall further and further into this cycle. Often this behavior is misidentified because we assume that students simply don't care or are being disruptive to get attention. It's always important to question *why* a student is disengaged from school and reflect on what else they might be rejecting.

WHAT Can I Do to Help a Student Who Is Disengaged from School?

Students who are disengaged from school need to be given a space to explore the pain that lies underneath their behavior. If they feel accepted and know that their pain is seen, they can begin to accept themselves and therefore the world around them.

HOW Will I Have a Constructive Conversation with a Student Who Is Disengaged from School?

Fiona told me that she did not like going to school, and often skipped class. Through our conversation, she was able to express her sadness and the struggles she has faced at school and uncover her pattern of using anger and apathy to mask her more vulnerable feelings.

The following is a transcript of my conversation with Fiona, showing how the six steps of the learning cycle, shown in Figure 3.1 (validation, patterns, feelings, paradigms, power, and skills), play out in the messiness of a regular conversation with a student who is expressing disengagement from school. See Chapter 2 for a deeper analysis of using these steps with students who are *rejecting*.

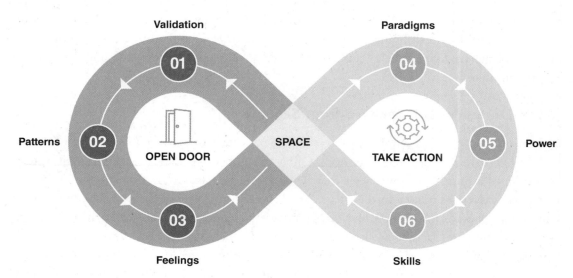

Figure 3.1   The learning cycle for building mental health skills.

Reproduced with permission from Open Parachute.

Interview with Fiona (Age 14)

F: I don't really go to school that much. Like, cuz like I usually skip school to hang out with my friends.

H: And why don't you like school? *(Patterns)*

> This felt to me like Fiona was trying to get a reaction from me. Whenever a student does this, it tells me there is a lot going on under the surface, and *I try to focus on being curious, with a really open tone.* This can help open the door to deeper reflection and dialogue.

F: It's boring.

H: Hmmm. Have you had any negative experiences at school? *(Patterns)*

> I suggested the possibility of negative experiences because *I always assume that anger and apathy come from a place of pain.* This is a really great way to show love and acceptance to a student who is resisting learning—*showing that you know there is a reason why they are acting the way they are signals that you have not rejected them even if they are rejecting you.*

F: Mm, not really.

H: No? (Patterns)

> Note that I asked this question again. Often students who are disengaged will have an aggressive front and it may take more than one probing question to help them open the door to their own self-reflection.

F: Well, at my old school, yeah.

H: Do you wanna talk about that? I would love to understand. *(Patterns; Validation)*

> Simply saying "I want to understand" is a great way to validate a student who is saying or doing things that are not in their best interest.

F: Well, this one kid at my old school, like he called me a freak and then I got so mad at him. I started swearing at him, and then I walked outta the school and spat on the door, and then I, yeah, started walking away. And I never went back to that school ever since.

H: I'm so sorry you went through that! I understand why you would have such a big reaction. Why do you think he called you a freak? *(Validation; Patterns)*

Often when a student rejects school, it is because they have been rejected by their peers and this is too painful for them to face. If they share this experience of harm with you, it can be really helpful to ask "why" they think their peers have rejected them. This can uncover their false beliefs about their own rejection (generally, deep down, they will think that the rejection is their fault).

F: I don't know cuz I haven't been to school in like a while and then like, I didn't really like talk to the other kids cuz like, I don't know.

H: Hmmm. Does it feel like they were a bit different than you or it was hard to, like, connect with them? *(Validation; Patterns)*

I suggested how Fiona was feeling here in order to help normalize her experience. Students can be ashamed of the way they feel, and if they hear us say it first, it can help them reflect on their own feelings more easily.

F: Yeah. Um, I don't really like, I keep to myself a lot. I don't talk to a lot of people that much. I think there's a lot of people like that, but people sometimes don't understand. Sometimes it's hard to come out, like it's hard to like talk to people, you know? It's like hard to like say stuff.

H: I really get that. And so do you feel like they wouldn't understand you? *(Validation; Patterns)*

F: You know what, some people have like different problems. Like some people struggle with throwing stuff and you don't know what they deal with on a daily basis.

H: Yeah, definitely. And what are some of the things that you struggle with on a daily basis? *(Validation; Patterns)*

Students often talk about "other people" because that's much easier to reflect on than themselves. When I hear this language, I always try to gently bring the focus back to their own experience.

F: Um, getting out of bed because like it's so comfy and I just wanna sleep there all day. Not move it's like so comfy.

H: Yeah, it's nice to feel comfy. Is that different from how you feel when you get up? *(Valida-tion; Patterns; Feelings)*

As soon as Fiona mentioned a *desirable* feeling, I took the opportunity to reflect on the *painful* feelings she most likely feels that are causing her to disengage from school.

F: Yeah, like, um, I don't know. I just get really paranoid for some reason. I don't know why. Like really like nervous, like when I talk to people.

H: Yeah. You're being so brave right now. I'm really impressed. *(Validation)*

F: Thank you. I really appreciate it.

H: Um, what kinds of things do you worry about when you're talking to people? Do you worry that people judge you? *(Patterns)*

I suggested a common thought that can lead to social anxiety (being judged) because it's usually easier for students to affirm something that has already been said than respond to the open-ended question "What are your thoughts in that moment?" (This is true for all of us—it's really hard to notice our own thoughts unless we practice it a *lot!*)

F: Yeah, like if someone judged me and I'm worried if I say like the wrong thing.

H: And do you think that sometimes you're feeling worried or shy, but then what comes out is anger? Do you think that ever happens? *(Patterns; Paradigm)*

I was hoping that I could help Fiona see that she was using aggression to cover over her pain, to shift her perspective of herself as a "bad kid" (which is naturally how a student who is disengaged from school will feel because that is how the world labels them).

F: Yeah, sometimes like something like that, you know, because like I have anger issues, I get really mad easily if I like lose something, I'll trash the whole house and like I'll start like getting really fucking mad. Like really mad. Like I'll start like terrorizing everything just to find one thing that doesn't even like mean anything.

H: That makes a lot of sense. Like we get angry on the outside because we're feeling something else underneath. Do you know what you might be feeling underneath the anger, like sad or scared? *(Validation; Patterns; Feelings)*

F: Uh, no. Um, I don't know. I just get really mad cuz like my brother, he calls me names and like, that's what gets me mad too. And like, I just, I don't like when people call me names, like I have to say something back. I don't wanna stand there and like look like a pussy.

H: Do you think on the outside sometimes it looks like you don't care? *(Patterns; Paradigm)*

F: No, I don't really care. Like, it doesn't really matter. Like, you know, it's really hard. It's hard to trust people nowadays. Like there's a lot of fake people.

H: I really get that. It's hard when people hurt you. Have you ever had anyone who made you feel really safe? Who you could trust? *(Skill)*

> I chose to ignore Fiona's comment that she doesn't care because I know deep down every child does care. I switched the focus here to helping her remember the love she has in her life, so she could practice the skill of trusting that love. If I were able to talk to Fiona again, this would be a great comment to pick back up on (e.g., "I remember you saying that you don't really care about people. I would love to hear more about why you feel that way.").

F: Like, there was this one teacher that was really nice to me and I miss her. She like made me smile and like, she was so nice. Like, but then I switched schools and went to high school.

H: Tell me about that, what did the teacher do that was so awesome? *(Skill)*

> Again, here I ignored Fiona's comment that she had to leave this teacher because I wanted to focus on helping her remember the love she experienced. I could have also added in a comment of validation about how hard that must have been here, and that would definitely have helped Fiona feel more "seen" by me. If I could talk to her again, I would definitely bring this up (e.g., "Leaving that teacher must have been really hard. Do you want to tell me more about that?").

F: Um, she used to like, take me outta class so I didn't have to do my work. And like, she used to, like, we used to like just sit down, play games, like do a little bit of work and then play more games and like, yeah.

H: So it sounds like she took an interest in you and actually formed a connection to you. *(Skill)*

F: But then by the end of the year, that's when I started getting more in trouble. That's when I started skipping school. Like I stopped caring about like the teacher, what she's gonna say.

H: That sounds hard. I wonder if school was feeling really hard, or maybe it felt really overwhelming? *(Validation; Patterns)*

F: It felt overwhelming and like, I don't know, I just like have really bad like, communication skills. Like it's hard for me to like say something to someone, even a teacher. So like, I don't like that. That's probably one of the main reasons why I didn't go to school cuz like it was pretty hard for me and like, I don't know, I didn't like feel like I belonged there kind of, like I just felt left out.

H: That's something that so many people feel. And I think a lot of people wouldn't be able to say it as well as you did. What are some of the things that made you feel left out? *(Validation; Feelings)*

F: I don't know. I just like always feel like the third wheel, like, I don't know. Sometimes when I'm at school, they treat me like I'm different. And like sometimes I feel like I'm left out and maybe it's because I'm rude to them too.

H: That's a good insight. I really appreciate you sharing that. So do you think maybe you're rude because you're feeling left out? *(Validation; Feelings; Patterns; Paradigm)*

F: Yeah. Cuz like my emotions are all over the place, throughout the year.

H: Definitely. And what are some of the things that . . . why do you think they treat you differently or like how do they treat you differently? *(Patterns)*

F: Mm. You know what, sometimes I struggle with my work and when the teacher comes to me and like, if I ask for help, I feel like everyone's watching me and like, I don't feel comfortable there. Like, that's what I mean by like overwhelming cuz like that's one other reason why I don't want to go to school cuz I feel like everyone's watching me. And like, that's what I mean by different cuz like, some people like, you know, like have a hard time learning and stuff like that.

H: Definitely. You said that so well and it's exactly what happens. People don't know and then they're watching you and they look at you like you're dumb. And do you find it hard to learn sometimes? Is that a struggle for you? *(Validation; Patterns)*

F: Yeah. Like the teacher doesn't really explain it well to me cuz like they just explain it once. And plus I've like hearing problems with my ears and like I can't really hear well. Like I've been like that ever since I like was a baby.

H: That's really hard! And if no one knows that, then they judge you, which is so, so hard. What do you wish that people thought about you? *(Validation; Patterns)*

F: Um, I wish my classmates knew I'm not a mean person. Cuz I'm not like, yeah. I'm not really a mean person. I'm really nice, but like I'm just mean because I feel all those things.

H: Right. That makes perfect sense. Anyone who feels those things would act that way. It's fantastic that you can see this because seeing what you want gives you the power to make it happen, to help your classmates see who you really are! *(Validation; Patterns; Power; Paradigm)*

Even though Fiona didn't tell me about anything she had done to help herself, I could remind her of her power by letting her know that *seeing what she wants* is a powerful step in making a change. Fiona's reflection of the fact that she is mean because she's feeling overwhelmed was exactly what I was hoping she would get to. Even though a conversation like this might not change her behavior right away, seeing herself in a different way is an important first step.

This type of conversation will help your students feel accepted and worthy of love, so that they can stop rejecting their own pain so fiercely. Notice how much time I spent trying to understand Fiona's experiences and struggles. Just asking those questions with openness and curiosity is such a gift to students who are disengaged. It's what helps them start to build back the trust they lost.

Related Chapters

Chapter 4, "Supporting Students Who Face Abuse and Domestic Violence"; Chapter 5, "Coaching Students Who Bully or Are Aggressive/Violent"; Chapter 12, "Supporting Students Who Self-Harm"; Chapter 14, "Encouraging Students Who Are Depressed or Apathetic"; Chapter 22, "Supporting Students Who Are Bullied"

4 | Supporting Students Who Face Abuse and Domestic Violence

This chapter will give you tools for responding to students who have been abused or mistreated at home or who have witnessed the abuse or mistreatment of others. Students who have been through these experiences will sometimes exhibit erratic, aggressive, or self-sabotaging behavior, which comes across as a *rejection* of themselves or others. You will learn the language that can help them move toward an *acceptance* of themselves and an understanding that they are not to blame for their experiences.

WHY Does Abuse and Domestic Violence Impact Students?

Students who have faced abuse or domestic violence are often in a state of *rejection because they are trying to reject the experiences they have had*. (See Chapter 2 for a deeper explanation of *rejecting* behavior.) They feel rejected by the people closest to them, and they therefore assume that everyone will hurt them in a similar way. They turn away from the *acceptance* of others as a way to protect themselves. Deep down they also often think that *they are to blame for their mistreatment*, so they are also in rejection of themselves, which is why their actions can be incredibly self-destructive. It is easy to misinterpret their behavior to mean that a student is simply lacking positive initiative. However, it's always important to reflect on how they might have been treated in the past that could cause them to react in this way.

WHAT Can I Do to Help a Student Who Has Faced Abuse or Domestic Violence?

Students who have faced abuse or domestic violence need to be guided in connecting to the pain caused by their experiences, and be shown that these experiences are *not their fault*. This is a way of accepting them without judgment because we are informing them of the *reason why they are acceptable* (e.g., they are not to blame for what happened to them). This helps students because it allows them to *acknowledge the harm,* which means they can *separate themselves from it.*

HOW Will I Have a Constructive Conversation with a Student Who Has Faced Abuse or Domestic Violence?

In my conversation with Nolan, he disclosed domestic abuse, a fact that I had already been informed of by his school counselor. If his counselor had not already been aware, I would have still had the same conversation, followed directly by reporting this incident. It's important to remember that while mandating reporting is absolutely necessary, you can also *really help* a student in these situations through your own conversations with them. Through our dialogue, Nolan was able to reflect on the fact that what happened to him and his mother was *not his fault* so that he could begin to *accept* himself more fully. If you know about a student's situation (e.g., you are told by the school counselor or a parent) but the student doesn't disclose it to you, the same steps apply. You can still reinforce the belief that they are not to blame for things that happen to them *even if you don't directly discuss what those things are* (e.g., speak in general terms about "hard things" rather than one specific hard thing).

The following is a transcript of my conversation with Nolan, showing how the six steps of the learning cycle, shown in Figure 4.1 (validation, patterns, feelings, paradigms, power, and skills), play out when a student discloses abuse and you are communicating with them before or after a counselor (or whomever else you are mandated to refer the student to) arrives. See Chapter 2 for a deeper analysis of using these steps with students who are *rejecting.*

Interview with Nolan (Age 11)

N: Um, my dad abused my mom and I always . . . I helped my mom because like she was scared.

H: I'm so sorry that happened. It's a really hard thing to go through. Did you see the abuse? *(Validation; Patterns)*

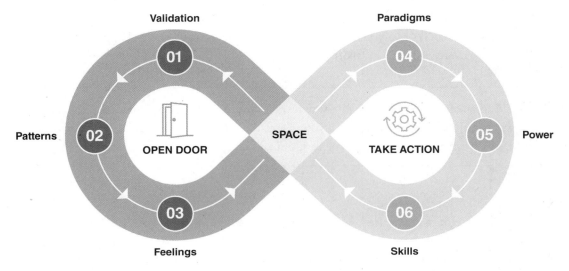

Figure 4.1   The learning cycle for building mental health skills.

Reproduced with permission from Open Parachute.

When a student discloses abuse, our first priority is always to help them feel loved and safe. My tone here was very soft, warm, and concerned. It would have been good for me to also add "I'm really glad you told me about this." And if I didn't already know that a counselor was fully aware of the situation, I would have added "Now we can work together to make sure you're safe," which leads into what I could have said at the end of our conversation: "Your safety is my No. 1 priority, so I'm going to take you to the counselor who can help us further with this."

N: I saw him like, always just yell and curse and I saw him always like punch her in the face in her arms and he always used to like, pull her hair and slap her.

H: That's really scary. I'm so sorry you went through that. How did you feel when you saw that? *(Validation; Feelings)*

When a student says something really intense like this, I always ask about their feelings. This helps them feel seen and cared for, and it also gives me space to feel what I'm feeling as well (which is usually similar to what the student felt!).

N: Scared. Um, really like sad and mad.

H: That makes sense. It's really, really scary. How old were you when this happened? *(Validation; Feelings; Patterns)*

> I asked Nolan about his age here as a way to help him reflect on how impactful this situation was for him. If we face abuse at a young age, this can shape the way we see the whole world, so I was setting the stage to speak about this later.

N: Probably like, four, or three.

H: And those feelings, that scared, sad, mad. Where do those feelings go? Do they stay with you? *(Feelings; Patterns)*

N: Um, yeah, because it's like all these years and I just like keep on reminding myself like that it happened.

H: And do you think sometimes when you get mad and sad now, it's a little bit about those feelings? *(Patterns; Paradigm)*

> I was hoping that Nolan could shift his perspective in terms of how he understands his current feelings. Often students who have been abused are incredibly confused about their emotions because their early experiences have not been processed fully (which leads to complex emotional reactions). I was hoping to give him a new perspective that could help him understand, and therefore, love and accept himself more fully.

N: Um, probably.

H: Makes sense. When we see something that's so scary and so hard like that, those feelings do stay with us, and when we go through something like that, sometimes our mind can tell us things that aren't true. Like we start thinking it's our fault, or we think we've done something wrong. Did you ever get like, thoughts like that? *(Validation; Patterns)*

> Notice that I suggested this thought by saying "we" to normalize the fact that all of us internalize our trauma. I did this to help Nolan feel accepted and less alone, so that he could be honest with me.

N: Yeah, because like, it just hurts to like, have that like vision in my head.

H: Yeah, it's devastating and it's important that you know there's nothing you could have done to stop that. It is not your fault. It is never the fault of the child ever. When we're young, we can't do anything. Do you know that? *(Validation; Patterns)*

> When a student shares a story about being harmed, I always make sure that somewhere in the conversation I explicitly tell them that it's not their fault. They will always think this on some level, and this is an incredibly important mindset to help them shift.

N: Deep down, not much, but I always like felt like it was my fault because I never really like, had a chance to help. Like really help.

H: And you were a child. We can't help our parents when we're little and it's really important that you know that it's not your fault. There's nothing you could have done. Do you believe me when I say that? *(Validation; Patterns)*

N: . . . (Nolan looks down and doesn't say anything, and starts to tear up.)

> I definitely teared up here too when Nolan did. When a student becomes visibly upset, it's normal to have your own emotional reaction! While this can feel vulnerable, and sometimes even unprofessional, our own emotions are actually a powerful tool of connection and communication. (As long as we don't let them derail the conversation!)

H: It's hard to believe that, isn't it? That might be why you get so mad. . . .. Is there anything that helps you remember that it's not your fault? *(Validation; Patterns; Skill)*

N: Probably, um, my grandpa, cuz he helps me push through.

H: And what does he do that helps? *(Skill)*

> The skill I was trying to help Nolan explore here is the skill of *identifying exactly what help he needs and wants from others.* This can be a challenging thing to do when our trust has been violated by others, so it is an important skill to focus on.

N: I just like the vision of him. Like I can just like hear him like, just saying like, you could like, keep trying.

H: And does your grandpa love you a lot and, and know that you're a really good kid? *(Skill)*

N: Mm-hmm.

H: And what are some of the things that he says to you? *(Skill)*

N: He gives me lots of encouragement and it makes me feel really happy.

H: That's fantastic. And do your friends also help you when you're feeling upset and angry, and you think things are your fault? *(Skill)*

N: Yeah, my best friend, he just like, like calms me down and hugs me. And like he tells me to like take deep breaths and like just, "It's okay," and stuff.

H: Amazing! And how do you feel when he does that? *(Skill; Feelings)*

N: Really like, happy cuz like, I actually have like a friend.

H: And when your friend tells you those things and he's supporting you, does that help you not think that things are your fault? *(Skill; Paradigm)*

N: Yes.

H: That's amazing. It's so hard to change those thoughts, and you are finding ways to do that! That's incredible. Do you want to find your friend now so he can help you with that? *(Validation; Skill; Power)*

I chose to ask Nolan to use his skill in the moment because what he shared with me was so heavy. Coming back to a skill to use *right now* is a great way to transition these conversations, and it's helpful to remember that you have this tool up your sleeve. Talking about heavy topics with students feels less overwhelming when you know that after you open the door to reflection and give them space to connect to their feelings, you can guide them in *supporting themselves with those feelings*. This is how you are helping them build resilience! If I had a chance in future conversations, I would bring up this skill with Nolan every chance I got. This is a great way to keep reinforcing the depth of his learning without needing to have a heavy conversation each time.

N: Yeah!

This type of conversation will help your students remember that their experiences of abuse or domestic violence are *not their fault*, so they can work on *accepting* themselves. This conversation can help to free them from their own *self-rejection*. Even if they never disclose what happened to them, you can use the same language (e.g., "Sometimes we go through hard things and we think they are our fault, and it's important to remember that it's never our fault if other people hurt us or the people we care about.").

Related Chapters

Chapter 3, "Encouraging Students Who Are Disengaged from School"; Chapter 5, "Coaching Students Who Bully or Are Aggressive/Violent"; Chapter 12, "Supporting Students Who Self-Harm"; Chapter 14, "Encouraging Students Who Are Depressed or Apathetic"; Chapter 16, "Communicating with Students Who Have Faced Loss"

---

5 | Coaching Students Who Bully or Are Aggressive/ Violent

This chapter will give you strategies for responding to students who are being cruel or unkind to others (e.g., causing physical harm, relentlessly teasing, leaving others out, spreading rumors, etc.). Students acting in these ways are *rejecting* others as a reflection of their own self-rejection, and you will learn vocabulary to encourage them toward more *acceptance* of themselves and others.

WHY Do Students Act with Aggression or Bully Others?

Students who are violent, aggressive, or bully others are in a state of *rejection*. They are rejecting the people they are hurting as a form of self-protection from their rejection of themselves. (See Chapter 2 for a deeper explanation of *rejecting* behavior.) We may never know where their anger comes from, but we can be sure that it will always have come from some sort of struggle they have faced in the past that caused them to feel unlovable or unacceptable (e.g., they were bullied themselves or deeply hurt by a peer or family member). The feeling of rejecting themselves is too painful, so they project this feeling into others (believing *someone else* is unlovable and unacceptable and punishing this person for their own self-loathing). This is usually unconscious and always an act of desperation. When we see this behavior, it's common to think that students are simply cruel and uncaring, so it's vital that we stop and think about why they are treating others in this way.

33

WHAT Can I Do to Help a Student Who Is Being Aggressive or Bullying Others?

Students who are being aggressive or bullying others need to be reminded that they are separate from their actions. That *they are acceptable even if their actions are not.* This will help them start to see their own patterns and understand how they can make different choices.

HOW Will I Have a Constructive Conversation with a Student Who Has Been Aggressive or Bullied Others?

Travis let me know that he recently beat up a fellow student. Through our conversation, he was able to notice his own pattern, reflect on where it comes from, and find an example of a time he made a different choice. Helping him notice his own positive choices was a crucial step in helping him *accept himself* in this moment so that he could move forward. It is advisable to wait until a student has calmed down after an incident before attempting a conversation like this, so that they are no longer overwhelmed with emotions and are more able to consciously reflect.

The following is a transcript of my conversation with Travis, showing how the six steps of the learning cycle, shown in Figure 5.1 (validation, patterns, feelings, paradigms, power, and skills), can unfold with a student who has been aggressive or violent toward others. See Chapter 2 for a deeper analysis of using these steps with students who are *rejecting*.

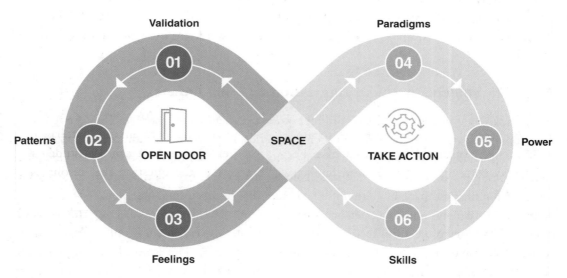

Figure 5.1   The learning cycle for building mental health skills.

Reproduced with permission from Open Parachute.

Interview with Travis (Age 14)

T: A couple weeks ago I got into a fight with a kid and beat him up real bad.

H: I'm so sorry that happened! Sometimes when we get really angry, it's because we are reminded of something else that makes us angry or feel sad. Do you think that happened? *(Validation; Feelings; Patterns)*

> Notice how I immediately opened with a suggestion of *why* he did what he did. This sends the conversation in the direction of self-reflection and acceptance, and opens the door for everything that follows. This was not an open-ended question (such as e.g., "What were you feeling?") and I use this approach of suggesting a possible answer as a way of helping to guide students in their self-reflection. An open-ended question about feelings can seem overwhelming (they may have never thought about how they feel, or even know how to answer that question). If you offer a suggestion, it allows them to either agree with you and then you can go deeper with it, or correct you and then you can explore the alternative. Either way, it helps them start the process of self-inquiry.

T: Um, yeah, he said something and it sounded exactly like what my dad used to be like. And it just set me off. So, yeah.

H: That's really hard! What did he say? And what was going through your mind? What did you feel? *(Validation; Feelings; Patterns)*

> I asked three questions at once here, which is typically not the most useful approach (although sometimes it can help students by giving them options of how to respond). I tend to do this because I struggle to move slowly (due to my own anxious patterns!). Asking just one question would have been great here, but as you can see, students are very forgiving and will often just answer the part of the question that resonates with them.

T: So, he, I don't know why, like he called me a "failure" and kicked me and it instantly, like, you know, I just lost it.

H: Definitely. And what did you feel in your body? Like, did you just go blank? Like, what was actually happening in you? *(Validation; Feelings; Patterns)*

> I really went into the feelings and physical sensations a lot here because I wanted Travis to
> see that his reaction came from a place of total overwhelm. I was hoping that this would
> help him see that *he was not a bad person*; he just made a bad choice when under stress, a
> choice that he could change if he learned to cope differently with his stress response.

T: I was kind of, not really, but I was kind of picturing like, this is me with my dad, you
know? But yeah, it really isn't. So I was taking all this out on this random kid for
no reason.

H: Totally. And it's so true. That's exactly what we do. We forget, we get taken right back
there to a place where we were hurt before. And then what, what happened in that
moment? Did you just get overwhelmed? Did you, you know, did you lash out then?
What was that like? *(Validation; Patterns)*

T: Yeah, so basically like in the moment he said it, my whole body was just fueled with
anger, like, you know.

H: Yeah, I totally get it. And so then what did you do? What was the outcome? *(Validation; Patterns)*

T: I hit him a couple times. Like he wasn't really expecting it either, so I felt really bad. Like
after I realized, like once I calmed down, I've just hit this random kid for no reason
basically.

H: That's really hard. But I see you only hit him a few times, which is better than if you kept
going! What did you do then to try to help yourself shift out of that? *(Validation;
Power; Paradigm)*

> Here, I was trying to shift Travis's perspective of himself. I could tell that Travis knew
> his actions were not okay, so he didn't need me to press that point; what he needed was
> to see himself in a positive light so that his shame didn't block his ability to self-reflect.
> So the paradigm shift I was going for was "I can make positive choices." I was hoping
> this would also help him remember his power to make more positive choices in the
> future.

T: Well, I just, I just left, you know. I just left, tried to be around no one.

H: That's great! And have you ever had a situation where you started feeling angry and you
noticed, I know I'm gonna snap here. *(Validation; Power)*

I was fishing here, and it paid off. *I do this a lot when I'm talking to students—fish for any examples of their brilliance.* It's something I was taught as a psychologist to teach to parents as well. We call it "catch them doing good" because whatever we pay attention to (whether positive or negative attention) is reinforced. I wanted Travis to think of a time when he made the right choice *before* lashing out, so that he would see himself as a person who is capable of responding in a helpful way to his own stress response.

T: Um, a couple weeks ago. No, I think it was last week. Um, someone was, I'm just gonna say mean to my friend. And yeah, so I got really angry and the teacher obviously saw that and I was like, can I just go for a walk? And then, yeah.

H: That's really significant. What were you thinking that helped you make a different choice? *(Validation; Power; Skill)*

Now that we had an example to work with, I wanted to hone in on exactly *what Travis did* (what skill he used) so that he could remember to use that same skill next time.

T: I was getting really angry. So, like, I just thought like, why would I be exactly like my dad when I hate him so much? You know?

H: Wow. That's such a powerful statement. . . .. I'm amazed you thought of that in that moment! And so what did you do? Like how did you contain yourself? *(Validation; Skill; Power)*

I was floored by how insightful Travis's statement was. I literally nearly burst into tears, and he could see that. I personally think that showing true emotions like this is helpful (as long as the conversation doesn't get derailed by our emotions, or the student feels like they have to console us in some way). But when a student's insight takes your breath away, tell them! This is a powerful validation of their wisdom.

T: I really don't know. It just happened. Usually I don't have that self-containment, but, yeah, I just did.

H: It's incredible that you did that! Do you think the situation a few weeks ago where you beat up the other kid helped you reflect on how you react? *(Validation; Skill; Power)*

> Again, I'm digging for a skill here to help Travis see what he did to achieve this positive result. I could have suggested anything (e.g., did you take deep breaths, think about the outcome you wanted, etc.) the purpose was to get him to think "what *did* I do, anyways?"

T: Yes. I basically like, I was thinking "why would I do this to just this random kid?" And then, yeah, so I told the teacher and I left.

H: And so did acting in this way of restraining yourself, did that make you feel good about yourself? Cuz that really is an incredible thing to do. *(Validation; Feelings)*

> I wanted Travis to reflect on what it *feels* like to make a positive choice, so that he could see the positive benefits of that choice, not just for others, but for himself too. I wanted this feeling to be a *motivator* to help guide him to make a positive choice in the future.

T: Yeah, it just made me feel so good.

H: Awesome. And have you ever talked to anyone else about this? *(Validation; Skill)*

> I was hoping to help Travis remember that he has a support system of people who care about him. If he could remember even just one person who had shown him love, that could help him *feel more loveable* and therefore, encourage him to act in a way that is in line with this.

T: Uh, yeah, I talked to a counselor.

H: That's so great you did that! And did they help you? *(Validation; Skill)*

T: Yeah, it just made me feel so good that, um, there's finally someone to talk to. Like obviously I could talk to my mom and my brother and my sisters, but my sisters are a bit young. My brother doesn't live with us currently. And you know, my mom's very busy.

H: Yeah, definitely. And do you feel confident looking forward in your ability to keep being the person you wanna be and keep resisting going to that place of aggression? Cuz I see your ability to do that. You're not an aggressive person; you just get mad sometimes. *(Validation; Power; Paradigm)*

I wanted to bring back the paradigm shift here of separating *Travis as a person* from *his actions*. Saying this explicitly can be really powerful—if a student hears that someone whose opinion they respect (e.g., an adult in a position of authority) sees them in a certain way, this can really influence how they see themself. If I was in regular contact with Travis, I would say this to him as regularly as possible to counteract the negative messages about who he is that he has clearly received from others.

T: Yeah. Like, oh, I don't really know. . ..

H: Do you think you'll feel more confident walking away, now that you've done it once? *(Power)*

Travis was clearly uncomfortable with my comment. This showed me that he didn't see himself in this way yet. Discomfort is actually a positive thing in these conversations! Changing our frame of reference is incredibly uncomfortable. But even though I know how powerful these moments are, I still find it hard to see someone else's discomfort. (I have strong people-pleasing tendencies!) So I rushed into the next statement here. If I could do this over, I would pause for longer here or say the same statement again about the difference between *him* and *his actions* so that I could reinforce this new paradigm even further.

T: Yeah, I guess it's easier to do it once you've already done it. So, like instead of losing my cool and stuff, it makes it easier to remember like, "Oh, but what about when I did this instead of lashing out? You know, I'll just do that this time."

H: That's such a great way to think about it. And so when you think of the next time someone triggers you, what do you think you're gonna do? *(Validation; Skill)*

T: Hopefully the good option. You know, try to keep my calm and if I can't, you know, go to where I can calm down.

H: I believe you can do it. And honestly, the first time is the hardest. Always. So you definitely can continue making that choice. And if you don't, that's okay. You just keep trying. You just learn. *(Validation; Power; Skill)*

This is an important thing to express to students when you are asking them to change. They won't get it right all the time! We don't want to set them up for feeling like a failure, so reinforcing the message that "all we can do is keep trying" is more helpful than "you will now do the right thing every single time from now on."

Delving into a specific aggressive experience with a student like this and exploring *why* they reacted the way they did will help them understand their own patterns and feel more accepted and loveable. Looking for examples of times when they made a different choice will also help students see more of their own internal positive qualities. This conversation can help students accept themselves more and have less pent-up aggression to take out on others.

Related Chapters

Chapter 3, "Encouraging Students Who Are Disengaged from School"; Chapter 4, "Supporting Students Who Face Abuse and Domestic Violence"; Chapter 22, "Supporting Students Who Are Bullied"

6 | Helping Gender Diverse Students Feel Included

This chapter will give you strategies for responding to students who are gender diverse and are experiencing community values, religious perspectives, or cultural norms that are eliciting feelings of shame and *self-rejection*. You will learn techniques for having a supportive conversation that helps students in these situations to find *acceptance* for themselves, even when they don't feel that same acceptance from others.

WHY Do Many Students with Gender Diversity Struggle So Much?

I won't attempt to unpack *where* gender identity originates from. Instead, I am focusing on *why students who have questions about their gender often struggle more than others* because that is what is most relevant in a classroom. In essence, they struggle because they are different from their peers in a pretty major way, and often their peers and even adults can be cruel or insensitive about these differences. It is common for students to internalize these messages and reject themselves in the same way that others have rejected them and in the ways that they feel unseen in society in general. (See Chapter 2 for a deeper explanation of *rejecting* behavior.) This perpetuates a cycle of feeling "wrong," which then exacerbates confusion about who they are and where they belong. Sometimes students who are gender diverse and experiencing rejection are misinterpreted as being aloof/detached or overly emotional. It's important to remember that these responses are a *normal reaction to being constantly rejected for who they are*.

WHAT Can I Do to Help a Student Who Is Gender Diverse and Struggling to Feel Accepted?

Students who are gender diverse and are facing challenges as a result of this need to be reminded that they are acceptable and loveable *just as they are* and be helped to find people who can accept them fully and remind them of this regularly.

HOW Will I Have a Constructive Conversation with a Student Who Is Struggling with Their Experience of Gender?

In my conversation with Dannie (who was born a boy, visually looked masculine, and was wearing a name tag that said "she/her'"), she started talking about her experiences with gender. My goal in this conversation was to help Dannie feel seen and accepted and also to uncover any self-rejecting patterns. Not all students who are gender diverse reject themselves, but many do because of the way they are treated. Exploring this can help them see their pattern of internalizing these messages so they can make space for more self-acceptance.

The following is a transcript of my conversation with Dannie, showing how the six steps of the learning cycle, shown in Figure 6.1 (validation, patterns, feelings, paradigms, power, and skills), can be used to support a student who is gender diverse and struggling with a lack of acceptance by others. See Chapter 2 for a deeper analysis of using these steps with students who are *rejecting*.

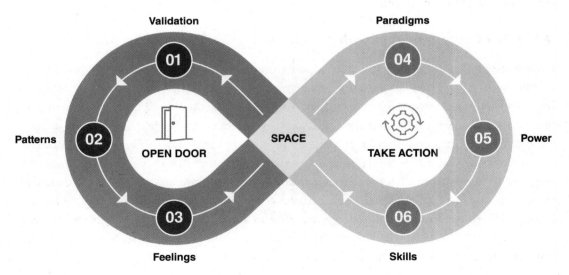

Figure 6.1   The learning cycle for building mental health skills.

Reproduced with permission from Open Parachute.

Interview with Dannie (Age 14)

D: I always felt not right as a boy, I didn't fit into the like the tough, manly man sort of thing, and I wasn't really like the other stereotypical, I wanna say boys and like what it means to be a boy. I felt more in line with more of the girly and feminine stuff and I was like, well, maybe I'm one of those.

H: Girly stuff can be fun! And do you think that gender norms, in general, are quite damaging and problematic? *(Validation; Patterns)*

> I immediately asked about gender *norms* here because this is always an element of the struggles a student will face if they are gender diverse, and it is something that I can relate to (even though I can't relate to *being* gender diverse, I can relate to the *feeling* of being put in a box because of my gender). This is a great tool for helping students feel seen and heard—find any way that you can *relate to their feelings* so that there isn't a sense of "otherness" between you and them.

D: They significantly are damaging, yeah.

H: Um, do you wanna tell me about your experience of being a boy, sorry being born as a boy, and feeling like you didn't fit into the stereotype of what it means to be a boy? Tell me about that. *(Validation; Feelings; Patterns)*

> Note that I said "being a boy" and had to immediately correct myself to "being born as a boy." I felt really bad about this slip-up, given that Dannie was literally wearing a nametag that said "she/her," but because my tone was warm and Dannie could tell I was genuinely interested, I was forgiven. This is an important thing to remember—students are forgiving when they can see we genuinely want to respect and support them to the best of our abilities. It can feel like a minefield to have conversations about gender if we are not used to them, but having the courage to *try* is what helps students learn to trust the world and their place in it.

D: Well, it felt kind of like being exiled. Couldn't really talk to anyone cuz you would have nothing to talk about.

H: Hmmm, that is hard. Do you wanna give me an example of that? *(Validation; Patterns)*

> Asking for an example is usually a good way of encouraging more reflection because it can lead to an exploration of feelings and patterns and then specific skills that can be used to cope with the situation.

D: Um, there'd be a group of boys that would be talking about like football or they'd be talking about this like one game. And I would not play sports very much, and the game was too themed away from what I would like.

H: And so what did that feel like for you? *(Feelings)*

D: Um, it felt horrible cuz I wasn't able to make many connections to people. I ended up only having two or three really close friends by the end of elementary school.

H: Yeah. And so was part of that process for you, just sort of that questioning of like, "Where do I fit?" Was that kind of a little bit what was happening for you like, "I know I don't fit into that category," and then trying to figure out for yourself where you did fit? *(Validation; Feelings; Pattern)*

> What I'm trying to do here is find common ground, trying to connect to the *felt experience* that Dannie went through, even if I don't directly understand the specifics. I was rambling a bit because I wasn't sure what Dannie was feeling. In other situations that I can relate to more directly, I can usually be more concise. Remember, it's the intention that matters the most! I was hoping that if I could uncover a way to understand Dannie on a deeper level, this would help her feel validated.

D: Yeah, it was really hard to find where I did fit, and I couldn't think about where I would fit for a big chunk of time.

H: Yeah, absolutely. And so what kind of thoughts did you have about yourself when you thought that you didn't fit into this male category? *(Validation; Patterns)*

> I asked about Dannie's thoughts because it is safe to assume that any student who doesn't feel like they belong in their peer group (for any reason) will think self-rejecting thoughts. I wanted to uncover these thoughts so I could support Dannie to change them.

D: Well, I kind of started to hate myself, if that's the right word. Um, I felt like, well, I should, I probably have to. It's what I was born to be. It's what I've been raised as; I should fit. Because at the time, um, I only figured out transgender existed later.

H: Absolutely. I really get that. It's normal to feel that way when we think we don't belong. Was anyone mean to you about the way you wanted to express yourself? *(Validation; Patterns)*

Even though I don't understand what it's like to be questioning my gender, I do know what it's like to have self-loathing thoughts, and these thoughts are very common. Again, here I am working on relating to Dannie's *thoughts*, not her *unique experience*, and this can really help a student to feel accepted. Hating yourself is a thought that can lead to self-harm or suicidal thoughts. In this case, Dannie's counselor was in the room with us, but if she wasn't I would have reported this to her directly after.

D: Um, here, not so much. I have my group of friends and I don't really go places without them around the school, so it's kind of hard for someone to get an insult in. I also somehow appear threatening to people and they leave me alone.

H: Yeah. . . . And so at your previous school did that happen? *(Patterns)*

I didn't address Dannie's comment about appearing threatening to people, mainly because I wanted to get to the bottom of where the self-hatred was coming from, and I assumed that kids must have been mean to Dannie at some point to create those beliefs. I do often ignore comments like this that will take the conversation off track when I have only a short time to talk to a student, so that I can focus on helping them find their own power in the midst of their negative thoughts. If I could talk to Dannie again, I would like to circle back to this comment and ask more questions about it because there will be more to uncover here about the way she sees herself.

D: Yeah, the boys were cruel. I hated myself. I felt ridiculously depressed. And the moment I moved, I started to feel a little better about myself. I still feel kind of depressed every now and then, and pretty much every day.

H: Hmm. What's that like? What do you mean when you say you feel depressed a little bit every day? *(Validation; Feelings)*

> Any time a student says anything about being low or depressed or really sad a lot, I always ask direct questions about it. Partly to help them explore their feelings to open the door for finding actions that can help them, and partly to find out if a referral is needed. I did confer with the school counselor after our conversation because a comment like this (as well as her comment about hating herself) shows that there is a lot she might need support with.

D: I just feel like a hollow feeling. Just like a feeling of like emptiness and I'm just not quite there.

H: Yeah. Understand that feeling. That's really hard. Do you think you took in the message that the boys in your last school gave you? Do you think that's a bit where that depression comes from? Like how do you think that impacted you? *(Validation; Pattern; Paradigm)*

> The paradigm shift I was going for here was to help Dannie see that being mistreated can lead to self-hatred, just to plant the seed that the self-hatred *came from somewhere*, and can therefore be shifted.

D: Um, yeah, I started not being able to trust anybody. Like there's still things some of my closest friends don't know about. . ..

H: Yeah, I get that. Is there anyone you feel you can be yourself with? *(Validation; Skill)*

> I wanted to help Dannie identify even just one person that she felt support by. It is a really important skill to remember this when we have negative thoughts about ourselves! If I could talk to Dannie again, I would ask her more about how she can open up in her friendships (e.g., "You mentioned that you don't tell your friends everything. What are the kinds of things that you feel uncomfortable saying to them?").

D: I do talk to my family because they are quite open and accepting of everything. So I can talk to my mother about things. I can't really talk to my siblings. Yeah. Um, one because he barely understands what this is, and the other one can't talk.

H: I'm glad you can talk to your mom! That's so important. Do you ever consciously change your thoughts? Like when you find yourself going into those self-doubt places, do you ever try to remind yourself "it's okay to be who I am"? *(Validation; Skill; Power)*

Here I honed in on helping Dannie see that even though she didn't feel like she could connect to lots of people, she *could* connect to her mom, and doing that is a very powerful tool that she could use in the future. I then started fishing for more skills that she has used in the past that could help her in the future.

D: Um, I do see myself repeatedly fall back into the pit of self-doubt and hatred, but I always claw myself back out again.

H: That's fantastic that you can shift out of it. . . .. How do you do that? *(Validation; Skill; Power)*

I probably could have gone deeper into the feelings here and shown more empathy, but I really wanted Dannie to see her own power, and I was worried that if I focused on how sad it was that she felt so low, she would not leave the conversation feeling any lighter. This could have just been my own desire to make her feel "better" so is not necessarily the best option here. I could have instead just simply said something about how hard that must be, and that might have been a really helpful space of acceptance for her.

D: I do that by like talking with my friends and reminding myself that I am right. I am who I want to be.

H: That's great! And so how do you tell which friends are the ones who you can really be open with, who will support you? *(Validation; Skill)*

D: Well, it's more like a visual thing. I can see that they're more open and accepting and not like, these are the boys, you can't mess with us.

H: Yeah. So you've got a really good sense of people now of who's gonna be open. That's a really important skill! *(Validation; Skill)*

Related Chapters

Chapter 13, "Helping Students Who People-Please"; Chapter 14, "Encouraging Students Who Are Depressed or Apathetic"; Chapter; Chapter 18, "Supporting Students Who Are Negatively Impacted by Gender Norms"; Chapter 19, "Guiding Students to Make Healthy Choices on Social Media"; Chapter 22, "Supporting Students Who Are Bullied"; Chapter 24, "Helping Students Who Face Prejudice"

SECTION

2

Controlling/Spontaneity (Remembering Safety)

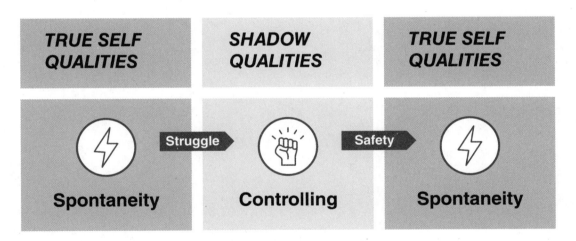

Reproduced with permission from Open Parachute.

This section will provide conversation tips for students who have controlling patterns within *themselves* (e.g., anxiety, panic attacks, obsessive thoughts, disordered eating, etc.) or toward *others* (e.g., rivalries/conflict with peers). You will learn tools for helping students with these patterns become more *spontaneous* in their interactions with themselves and the world around them by reminding them that they are *safe*, even when their mind is telling them otherwise.

7 | Finding the Words with Students Who Are in *Controlling* Behavior Patterns

Students often react to challenges by trying to *control* their circumstances or their own internal experiences. This is a natural response to feeling that aspects of their life *are out of their control*, and especially if these out-of-control elements appear dangerous, harmful, or chaotic. When we are seeking to control things around us, what we really want is to *stop ourselves from feeling uncomfortable feelings*. We think that if *we* do the right things or if *other people* do the right things, then we won't feel lost or sad or lonely. This is in essence an *anxious* reaction. The more fearful we are of our feelings, the less we are able to roll with the ups and downs and adapt to changes in the moment. We get more and more tense and less and less fluid in our reactions to things that are unexpected or unplanned.

You will most likely have noticed that after COVID lockdowns, your students in general started to appear more *anxious* and less *resilient* (less able to adapt to changes and challenges). This is, in part, because the experience of lockdowns was frightening on many levels for students. Their world changed in a way that they couldn't control, and for many of them, this was a painful, lonely, and scary experience. After going through something like that, it is natural that the mind starts *to seek out more control* (in an attempt to ensure that something like this doesn't

51

happen again). This is because the future and the unknown start to feel scary, and changes (no matter how minor) start to seem unmanageable.

This is the same process that happens to students who go through any challenge that makes them feel out of control and overwhelmed. Some examples of controlling behavior are perfectionism, disordered eating, and bossing friends around. But no matter what the *reaction* looks like, if we can identify that it is coming from a student seeking to control their circumstances or their experiences, it can help us understand how best to respond. A student who is trying to *control* their reality needs to know they are *safe* so they can become more *fluid and spontaneous*.

If you can send the message to all of your students that no matter what they are feeling, those feelings are *safe* and it's okay to feel them, this will help them let go of their desire to control themselves or the world around them in an attempt to block these feelings out. When students know that you *accept their feelings*, they will be more open to exploring a deeper conversation when the opportunity presents itself.

What Can I Do to Help Students Who Are Controlling?

Your goal is to make *space* for students to move through the six steps of self-reflection, shown in Figure 7.1, that will help them move away from their controlling behavior and toward spontaneous actions. These steps fall into the two categories explained next.

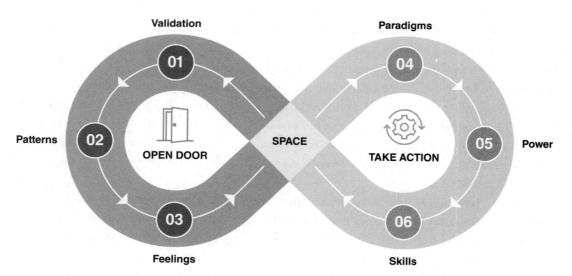

Figure 7.1 The learning cycle for building mental health skills.

Reproduced with permission from Open Parachute.

Figure Explanations
Category 1: Open the Door.

1. **Validating** them and their experiences.

    Validation means letting a student know that what they are facing is normal and that we understand where they are coming from. When a student is controlling, it's important that our language helps them feel safe and reminds them that they are okay (e.g., "What you're feeling is very understandable, given what you're facing," or "I really get that feeling; I feel it sometimes too!").

2. Helping them notice their own **patterns.**

    A *pattern* can be any behavioral reaction, way of thinking, or emotional response. When students are controlling, we want to help them *pay attention to the reasons they feel the way they do* (e.g., "Do you think you're feeling extra on-edge because you have a test coming up?" or "That sounds like a really hard situation, so it's normal if you're feeling overwhelmed."). This can help their feelings seem more *understandable* and therefore less out of control.

3. Encouraging them to relate directly to their **feelings.**

    Feelings are the physical and emotional responses that a student has to their experiences. When students are controlling, they are often overwhelmed by their feelings and physical sensations. If we can help them notice these feelings and sensations for what they are, this can help them feel less of a need to control their experiences (e.g., "What do you notice in your body right now?" or "What do you feel in those moments when things seem a bit out of control?").

Category 2: Take Action.

4. Helping them shift their **paradigm**, or the way they are seeing things.

    A *paradigm* is a student's fundamental views about themselves and the world. Students who are controlling are often misinterpreting their own stress responses as being a signal that something terrible or dangerous is happening. If we can help them identify their own reactions to stress, this can help them to see things more clearly (e.g., "When we feel stressed, it's normal to think negative thoughts, and that usually makes us feel even more stressed. Do you think you do that sometimes?").

5. Reminding them of their **power.**

    A student's *power* is their ability to act with agency in their own world—their ability to enact change and influence their experiences. When a student is controlling, we can help them remember the power they have to accept their feelings, instead of trying to control them, by reminding them of times they have done this in the past (e.g., "Have you ever been able to help yourself face feelings like that? Even if it was something small that you were dealing with?").

6. Supporting them to use a **skill** that helps them move forward.

   Skills are anything a student does that helps them cope or change their physical and emotional circumstances. Students who are controlling often need to practice the skill of *soothing themselves*, so they can focus on their own stress response (which is something they *can* control) instead of trying to change the world around them (which is *impossible* for them to control, and this focus only increases their levels of anxiety). Using language like "What helps to calm those feelings down?" or "What strategies usually help you when you're feeling like that?" can remind students to focus on soothing themselves.

These steps can help your students connect to their experiences, so they can let go and become more *spontaneous* in their responses to the challenges they face. In the following chapters, you will see examples of how these steps can be used in conversations with students who are displaying different types of controlling behavior so that you can guide them toward greater resilience and adaptability.

8 | Supporting Students Who Are Worried, Anxious, or Stressed

This chapter will give you strategies for responding to students who have been diagnosed with anxiety or who simply show signs of being stressed and worried (e.g., about schoolwork, friendships, or extracurricular activities). These reactions are a sign that students are trying to *control* their reality by making sure everything goes the way they think it needs to go. You will learn tools for having conversations that can help them become more comfortable with *spontaneity* in their daily lives.

WHY Do Students Experience Worries, Anxiety, and Stress?

Students experience anxiety (that can take the form of *worries* or *feelings of stress*) because they are not comfortable with the way they feel, and their mind is trying to *control* those feelings by coming up with *reasons why they feel the way they do*, and *ways that they can "fix" this* (e.g., "I am feeling scared . . . that must be because I have done the wrong thing, and I should be perfect so that this feeling goes away."). (See Chapter 7 for a deeper explanation of *controlling* behavior.) Anxiety isn't the feeling of fear itself; it is the *mind's reaction to that fear*. Anxiety can also be triggered as a response to other feelings like sadness or loneliness (e.g., "I'm feeling lonely . . . that must be because I'm unlikeable; I should have said something different so that people would like me better."). The anxious mind of a student will invent any number of things that they *should have done differently in the past* or that they *should do differently in the future* as a way to *control the way they feel in the present.* An anxious student can sometimes appear avoidant, timid, or give up easily when things are hard. It's essential to keep in mind that these behaviors usually signal an underlying pattern of struggling to cope with challenging feelings.

WHAT Can I Do to Help a Student Who Is Experiencing Worries, Anxiety, or Stress?

Students who experience anxiety, worries and stress need to be reminded that their *emotions are okay to feel*, and that they can interpret and relate to those feelings in a different way that helps them feel much *safer.* The safer they feel, the more an anxious student is able to be *spontaneous* and adjust to things occurring in the moment, rather than *reacting to each change as if it were a threat.*

HOW Will I Have a Constructive Conversation with a Student Who Is Experiencing Worries, Anxiety, or Stress?

Jasmine told me about her experiences of stress about school work, and in our conversation, she was able to explore the feelings and physical sensations that caused her mind to panic and try to control her reality. This helped her reflect on the fact that *she is safe even when she thinks she isn't.* She was also able to identify helpful strategies she has used in the past, and skills that can help her in the present.

The following is a transcript of my conversation with Jasmine, showing how the six steps of the learning cycle, shown in Figure 8.1 (validation, patterns, feelings, paradigms, power, and skills), can be used with a student who is anxious, worried, or stressed. See Chapter 7 for a deeper analysis of using these steps with students who are *controlling.*

Interview with Jasmine (Age 12)

J: Once I, um, had a test and it was like really, really important and I had to get all the questions right. So I was extremely nervous and I, like didn't wanna go to school, but I just reminded myself to try my hardest and that everything would be fine.

H: Awesome. That's so good. So what it was like when you were in that space where you felt like you couldn't go to school? Before you realized you could remind yourself that everything would be fine? *(Validation; Feelings; Pattern)*

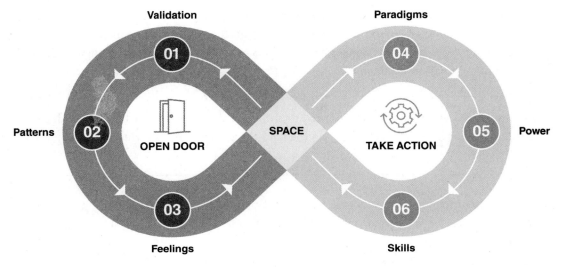

Figure 8.1 The learning cycle for building mental health skills.

Reproduced with permission from Open Parachute.

> This is common when anxious students are talking about challenges (especially younger ones). Jasmine knew the "right" thing to do (think a positive thought) because she had been told to do this when she struggled, and so she wanted to show that she did the right thing. I started with helping her dig into the "problem" a bit more so we could open the door for her to see that it's okay to simply feel what she feels.

J: Um, so it was just like, my mind would think, "Oh, I'm gonna do extremely bad and I'm going to get a bad grade and I'm gonna have to stay in sixth grade." And that just, those thoughts turned into feelings. And that turned into like pain.

H: Yes. And you said that really well. Can you explain a bit more what happens for you? What thought turned into what feeling and then did that turn into a physical sensation? *(Validation; Feelings; Pattern)*

J: So like me thinking, um, that I was gonna do bad turned into like me feeling really anxious and nervous and not wanting to go to school, and then that turned into stomach pain.

H: Oh. And it's so intense how that happens, hey? That's really hard, but you have a lot of insight into this. It's amazing that you can explain it that well, because most people don't understand those steps that happen. And do you get any other negative thoughts about school in general? *(Validation; Patterns)*

> Because it was clear that Jasmine wanted to show me that she had resolved her struggles, I wanted her to know that reflecting on the hard things is just as powerful as using skills to help herself.

J: Um, sometimes, like this week, we had to split up and so my mind was telling me, "Oh, I'm not gonna be with my friends," or "I'm gonna be with a teacher and she might be rude, or he might be rude and I'm just gonna really miss my family and wanna go home."

H: Yes. That's so normal to think those thoughts. And what about, do you get any negative thoughts when people are being loud around you, like you were saying before? *(Validation; Pattern)*

> I brought up a situation that Jasmine had told me about previously on the phone. This is a good technique to help students see *how different aspects of their life and patterns fit together.* Even if you don't see an obvious link, you can always just ask the question "Do you think X relates to what you're saying here?"

J: Um, yeah. Sometimes when I'm in class and everyone's yelling or talking, my mind just starts like, feeling really full and stressful and like I start getting a lot of thoughts. Like one might be, um, "Oh, this day is gonna be really hard, really long, and I'm not gonna be able to get my work done because my mind is focusing on all those kids that are talking and not on the teacher."

H: Totally. And what do you do to help yourself? *(Validation; Power; Skill)*

> I chose to jump straight into how Jasmine could help herself. I definitely could have spent more time exploring her patterns and feelings, but this was at the end of a longer conversation, so I didn't spend much time opening the door to her self-reflection. If I was able to talk to Jasmine again, I would definitely ask more questions about her feelings so that she has more chances to reflect on her anxious patterns and know that she is able to cope with her feelings more than she realizes.

J: So when that happens, I just remind myself that I have a lot of family members and people that are always gonna be by my side, and I just always take deep breaths and I let myself know that I will get through it and the day will be better and it's not gonna be long, and that those negative thoughts are not true.

H: That's awesome. And how did you learn to do that? *(Validation; Paradigm; Power)*

> Jasmine had clearly learned these skills in the past, so I could help her *reflect on her paradigm shift* rather than needing to present her with a new perspective. If she had not shared this insight, I would have focused on helping her see that she has the power to choose not to believe her anxious thoughts.

J: Well, I actually have a therapist at school and she helps me out a lot. My mom helps me out a lot too. She's always there when I feel really nervous or anxious. And so, that's how I remember that I have a lot of people that taught me things and that will always be there.

H: Amazing. That's so great. And so, are there any other things that you do to help yourself sort of deal with feeling nervous on a day-to-day basis? *(Validation; Skill; Power)*

> It's really important for anxious students to know that they have the power within them to support themselves, and while other people can help, they *don't always need them.*

J: Um, so sometimes I just go somewhere quiet or just, um, go somewhere that I like or do something that I like. If I go somewhere quiet, I might just sit there, take a few seconds to breathe and remind myself that I'm so lucky for everything I have, and then I might just go downstairs and do what I like to do.

H: Amazing. And what are some of those things that you like to do? *(Validation; Skill)*

J: Well, if it's not, if it's a good day outside and it's not that cold, I might just put on my roller blades and go roller blade outside or get my bike, or just go to my desk and, um, do some art.

H: Amazing. Great. Um, can you remember when you had the negative thought about like, you know, "Things are gonna be really bad," and then you started getting upset and then you had a stomachache, can you tell me what is the thought that helps, and then what do you feel, and then what happens in your body? *(Validation; Pattern; Power)*

> I wanted to circle back to the first thing Jasmine mentioned, where she spoke about using a positive strategy to help when she gets in the cycle of thoughts/feelings/body sensations. It felt like the right time to help her reflect on what helped, and how her thoughts might have also changed the way she felt in her body.

J: So when I like tell myself that "Everything's gonna be all right" and that, um, "I have a lot of people with me that will always be there," I start feeling a little more better and more, um, calm and my stomach pain slowly starts to fade or go away. And then, um, I remember that I am really lucky to be here and I am all better most of the time.

H: Wow, that's amazing that you can help your body with your mind so much! You have so much wisdom about this. What advice would you give to other kids who might also get anxious? *(Validation; Power)*

> When students have clearly learned some skills already, I often ask this question about *how they would help others* to reinforce their own power (both to help themselves and to help others).

J: Um, the No. 1 tip I give everyone is just always to believe in yourself and always remember that everything will be fine and you'll always get through it, not by yourself, but with someone else.

H: That's amazing. I hope everyone gets to learn from you! *(Validation)*

This type of conversation will help your students reflect on their own anxious patterns and realize that they are *safe* even when their mind is telling them otherwise. This will help them let go of their desire to control the moment by *fixing or changing themselves or others*, so they can respond to situations with *spontaneity* instead of seeing all changes as a threat.

Related Chapters

Chapter 3, "Encouraging Students Who Are Disengaged from School"; Chapter 13, "Helping Students Who People-Please"

9 | Guiding Students Away from Peer Rivalry

This chapter will give you strategies for responding to students who are trying to *control* their relationships, which will look like constant conflict, drama, and rivalries with others. You will learn conversation tools to help encourage students with these patterns to become more *spontaneous* in their interactions with others.

WHY Do Students Get into Rivalries with Peers and Siblings?

Students get into rivalries because they are feeling insecure in their relationships and are trying to *control* how other people act so that they can feel more loved. (See Chapter 7 for a deeper explanation of *controlling* behavior.) This behavior often begins at home in their dynamics with siblings or parents. When young children perceive that they are not getting enough attention, this can make their relationships feel threatened. Children have very little power in their world, and so they often try to *control* the people around them to give them the attention they crave (they have not yet built up the skill set to know how to *ask* for what they need). When children start trying to control the people around them, this usually backfires because their behavior is often aggressive or cruel. Parents, siblings, or friends often respond by rejecting them or getting angry with them, which makes the child feel even more unloved, and keeps them in this cycle. The more they try to control others, the less loveable they feel, and the more they seek to control their relationships. Students can show these same patterns of cruelty or domination in class, and it's important to remember that underneath these behaviors is simply a desire to feel supported/connected and a lack of healthy strategies to help themselves with this.

WHAT Can I Do to Help a Student Who Is in a Rivalry with a Peer or Sibling?

Students who are in rivalries need to be able to *connect to their own feelings* as well as *reflect on the feelings of others* in order to understand that it is safe to *let go of control* in their relationships. This requires self-reflection and perspective-taking, and often it can help them to reflect on *where these patterns first originated from.*

HOW Will I Have a Constructive Conversation with a Student Who Is in a Rivalry with a Peer or Sibling?

My conversation with Brooke started because I knew she had been involved in some friendship issues where she had felt jealous and was trying to control her friends (her mom gave me this information). During our conversation, Brooke was able to explore her feeling of being unloved at home when her brother was born and how that caused her to want to *control* the attention she was getting from her parents. This led to a reflection that a similar pattern might be playing out with her friends. We uncovered that *feeling unloved* is a trigger for Brooke so that she can reflect on this feeling more in the future.

The following is a transcript of my conversation with Brooke, showing how the six steps of the learning cycle, shown in Figure 9.1 (validation, patterns, feelings, paradigms, power, and skills), might play out in a conversation with a student who is experiencing a rivalry. See Chapter 7 for a deeper analysis of using these steps with students who are *controlling.*

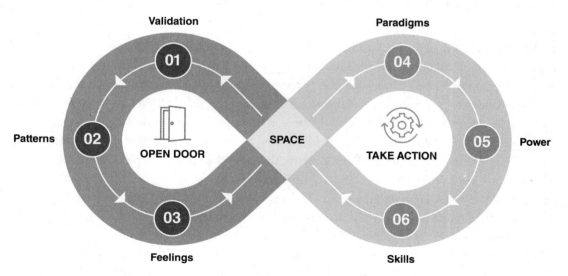

Figure 9.1 The learning cycle for building mental health skills.

Reproduced with permission from Open Parachute.

Interview with Brooke (Age 11)

H: You have a younger brother, right? Can you tell me what it was like when he was born? *(Patterns; Feeling)*

> I asked about Brooke's family because I suspected that her desire to control her friends was a pattern that she developed at home. Sibling rivalry is so common that it is usually a good area to explore to help students identify their dynamics with peers.

B: Um, I grew up in, um, a townhouse. So three stories, just my mom and my dad. Um, and I thought that was amazing, but then a little brother came along. Which wasn't the best, you know? Um, there was a funny thing I said to my mom when he came, I said, "Can you go back to the hospital?" No. I actually said that, I did, but then I felt so bad afterwards *(laughs)*.

H: Yeah, I'm pretty sure every big sibling thinks that! But people think, "I'm not supposed to say that" but it's a really normal thing to feel right? What do you think made you feel that way? *(Validation; Feelings; Patterns)*

> I mentioned the fact that *we think we're not supposed to say things like this* as a way to validate Brooke's reaction (she was laughing and clearly uncomfortable with what she had said to her mom).

B: Because I didn't wanna share mom and dad's love. Like I didn't want them to love him as well as me. My mom and dad like, were there for me. And then when he came, and I was like, "Why are you giving attention to him?"

H: Totally. And that's exactly what happens, right? And cuz in some ways it makes us feel like we have less love, right? Or we have less of our parents' attention. What was that like for you? *(Validation; Feelings; Patterns)*

B: I definitely felt jealous about it. Um, but he was a cute, younger brother, so I guess there was that too. Um, I guess our friendship did kind of come together like later as he grew up, but we're still brothers and sisters, so there's still always like that connection with brother and sister.

H: Yeah, I totally get it. And so before you realized that, "Oh, actually this is okay," do you remember what you did when you were feeling that way? Like a lot of the times when we feel that way, we might yell at our parents. We might act out, we might, you know, struggle in school. There might be all these things that we do, even though we don't really realize that's why we're doing. Do you remember what you did? *(Validation; Feelings; Patterns)*

> It's common for students, especially when they're young, to jump straight to *how things changed in a positive way* rather than reflecting on their unhelpful patterns. I wanted to make sure we didn't skip over exploring her pattern of thoughts and actions when she was feeling jealous because this would open the door to reflecting on skills that can help her when she feels this way in the future.

B: Yeah, I kind of didn't like my brother. I didn't want my parents to like him and I kind of was ignoring him sometimes. Um, and sometimes I would do things to get him in trouble, and I thought that would make me feel happier that he wasn't the favorite one. It was just like really annoying for me. Like, I would tell him like, "Go play with your toys" or "Go play with mom and dad." Like, "I'm busy. I wanna play by myself" and stuff. And he would usually walk off or he'd keep nagging me or something. I didn't know it was because he just wanted to play with me.

H: Yeah, we do things like that when we're feeling upset! That's amazing that you figured out it was because he wanted to play with you! How did you figure out that's how he felt? *(Validation; Skill; Power)*

> Here, I really wanted Brooke to reflect on how she was able to *empathize* with her brother, and how powerful of a tool this is. The skill of empathy is a hard one to use when we're feeling jealous, and is something she will need to use in the future.

B: Well, I think one day. . . . Okay, so he didn't like going downstairs, uh, to the basement where the toys were. And I was fine with doing that because I was used to playing with myself. And so I said, "Why don't you go there by yourself?" He was like, "I'm too scared to, can you come with me?" And then I realized that if he can't go there by himself, maybe he doesn't like playing with himself. Um, I realized that he needed a friend.

H: That's such an amazing thing to realize! Do you spend time thinking about things like that? Did it just occur to you? Were you talking to a parent? Were you writing about it? Like how did you actually come to that thought? *(Validation; Skill; Power)*

> Whenever students share really wise thoughts like this, I want to help them identify *where the thought came from* so they can repeat their strategy. I totally went overboard with my rapid-fire suggestions here because I was so excited. I could have just suggested one or two things!

B: Well, usually when I'm playing with myself, I get time to myself and sometimes I'll think about things, like "Why does he keep nagging me about this? Why doesn't he just go play with his toys like I do?" And then I also asked my mom and I was like, "Why does he keep annoying me?" And she was like, "Well, you are used to having no siblings. Maybe he just wants to play with you." And I thought that was basically what he was doing because he kept asking for me to play with him.

H: Amazing. That's so great. So sometimes you sit and you think while you're playing, and then sometimes you ask your mom. Um, and so what changed for you once you realized that? How did things change for you at home? *(Validation; Power; Skill)*

> I asked "What changed?" to help Sadie further reinforce how helpful it was that she made this change.

B: I definitely play with him a lot more. He's a bit happier when he's around me.

H: Beautiful. That is so cool. And now how do you feel about your parents' love for you? Can you feel that it's still there now? That it won't go away just because they love your brother? *(Validation; Paradigm; Feelings)*

> I was going for a big paradigm shift here, which is a really tricky thing for students to feel— that they are loved even when they are getting less attention.

B: I kind of, you know, got used to it. Uh, they love us both the same, or at least, it, it's what they say. Um, but sometimes it's a little hard. Like sometimes I'll want to get him in trouble. But like, I've gotten used to it by now. So, um, yeah, I guess it's okay.

H: Yeah. It's a tough situation! Do you think sometimes that feeling of sharing love is also hard with your friends? *(Validation; Feelings; Patterns; Paradigm)*

> Brooke's answer to this showed me that she is still struggling with *not feeling loved as much as she wants to be loved*. I didn't go into this here because I wanted to move onto the paradigm shift that I really wanted her to see, which is the connection between her pattern with her brother, and how she is treating her friends. If I could speak to Brooke again, I would go back to this and explore *what being loved feels like to her* (e.g., "I really understand that feeling you were talking about the other day, about how it's hard to remember people care about us. Can you tell me more about what that's like for you?") so that she could notice this more in her life and realize that she *doesn't have to control people in order to be loved*.

B: Uh, so me and my friend used to be like, always together. But then she had another friend and she was better friends with her than me. So it was kind of bringing back memories for when I was jealous of my brother. And I got mad at her and stuff.

H: That's so good that you realize, "Oh, I feel the same way with my friend as I did with my brother." So you can maybe think about how your friend is feeling, in the same way you thought about how your brother is feeling, right? *(Validation; Feeling; Patterns; Skill; Power)*

> It's important to note here that Brooke could identify this pattern in herself *after we opened the door* by exploring her feelings and experiences with her brother, and I suggested the link. If I had asked Brooke about her friends right off the bat, she probably would have struggled to see that this experience was bringing up memories about her brother.

B: Yeah.

> Here, the conversation got interrupted and went in a completely different direction, so I never had a chance to really help Brooke reflect on this pattern, but at least the seed was planted! If I had the chance to speak with her again, I would pick back up where we left off, and maybe ask "Have you thought any more about what your friend might be feeling about being caught between her two really good friends?" to help her understand that her friend's actions *do not mean she is not loved* (similar to the realization she is working on about her parents and her brother), which would help her become less controlling in the friendship.

This type of conversation will help your students explore *what is driving their controlling behavior* so that they can start to better understand their own feelings and the feelings of others. This will help them feel *safer* and more *secure* in their connections so they can let go of their desire to control the attention they are getting from others.

Related Chapters

Chapter 5, "Coaching Students Who Bully or Are Aggressive/Violent"; Chapter 13, "Helping Students Who People-Please"; Chapter 27, "Supporting Students Who Experience Intergenerational Trauma"; Chapter 29, "Responding to Students Who Share Stories of Parental Conflict and Separation"

10 | Talking to Students about Unhealthy Eating Habits

This chapter will give you strategies for responding to students who have been diagnosed with an eating disorder (e.g., anorexia or bulimia), or who simply exhibit behaviors of restricting their eating or overeating as a way to *control* how they feel. You will learn the language you can use to help students with these patterns become more *spontaneous* in their response to their own hunger signals.

WHY Do Students Have Disordered Eating?

Students have disordered eating patterns because they are trying to *control* the way they feel through what they ingest. (See Chapter 7 for a deeper explanation of *controlling* behavior.) This occurs when things happen in a student's life that feel chaotic and painful, and they are seeking to find some sense of power in the situation. Both restricting and bingeing/purging are ways that a student tries to *change their emotional experience* (e.g., "I don't want to feel sad so I will feel hungry instead") or match what they are feeling in their body to how they feel in their mind (e.g., "I feel gross, so I will affirm this by making my body feel gross too."). Exercise can also be used in a similar way ("I have to burn off all of the food that I eat in order to feel ok in my body."). There are degrees of severity with these patterns, and because of cultural pressures (e.g., social media, body image norms), many students will have at least some sort of unhealthy relationship with food. Others will have serious, life-threatening versions of this. In these cases, the act of restricting or bingeing/purging never really works to make a student feel better, but instead of stopping and trying another approach, often their mind will double down and keep going with the pattern in more and more intense ways in a *never-ending search for control*. It can be easy to misidentify students with disordered eating as simply being picky or health-conscious in their eating/exercise habits. If you are concerned for a student's safety or well-being because of their eating habits, always refer them to a mental health practitioner (before or after you speak to them). Often these behaviors go unnoticed, and this means that students are not getting the help they need.

WHAT Can I Do to Help a Student Who Has Disordered Eating?

Students who have disordered eating need a space to notice *the feelings underneath their patterns* and find other ways of relating to these feelings in a healthy way (rather than trying to control them, change them, or get rid of them). They need to see the power they have to make different choices and the positive outcomes that can be gained from treating their body with love and respect.

HOW Will I Have Constructive Conversation with a Student Who Has Disordered Eating?

Going into my conversation with Tazzie, I knew she was struggling with eating challenges (she and her mom had both told me this previously on the phone). When she brought up a really hard experience she had when she was little, I used this as an opportunity to help her reflect on *how this painful experience might be part of her pattern of eating struggles*. During our conversation, Tazzie was able to express some of her intense feelings and reflect really clearly on her pattern of *trying to control those feelings through bingeing*, as well as identify skills she has used in the past and can continue to use in the present to help her relate to her feelings in a healthy way.

The following is a transcript of my conversation with Tazzie, showing how the six steps of the learning cycle, shown in Figure 10.1 (validation, patterns, feelings, paradigms, power, and skills), can be used with a student who is showing signs of disordered eating. See Chapter 7 for a deeper analysis of using these steps with students who are *controlling*.

Interview with Tazzie (Age 15)

T: When I was in grade eight, my mom moved away and I wasn't quite aware that she was gonna move away. . . .

H: That's a really hard thing to go through! How did you respond to that? Cuz it would make sense that you felt really awful in that situation. *(Validation; Feelings; Patterns)*

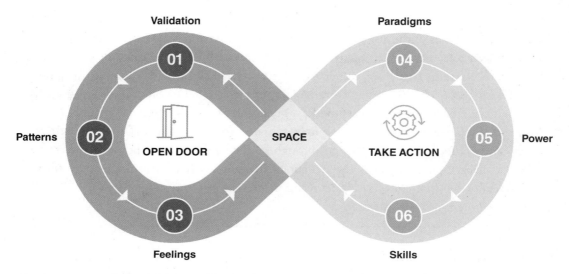

Figure 10.1 The learning cycle for building mental health skills.

Reproduced with permission from Open Parachute.

I wanted to make sure Tazzie felt validated in her response to this major trauma so that we could open the door to helpful reflections.

T: Um, I think that abandonment and that, I kind of felt like, "Oh, that's my mom and she's left me." And like, "Where's the love in that?" And I didn't feel like I had any love from that. And I think that I kind of got into a darker path from not feeling loved. And, yeah, I think that's how it all kind of went downhill.

H: Thank you so much for sharing that. Yeah, it's really hard. And so, what was the dark path that you went down? *(Validation; Patterns)*

T: Um, yeah. I was wearing a lot of baggy clothes and hoodies and I'd walk home with my like hoodie over my head. I wanted to be really antisocial and the way I was treating people was more of a, kind of a nasty way.

H: Yes there's a lot of teenagers that go through that. And so what was happening in your relationship to your body? During that time, you know, did you also struggle with body image issues or eating issues? Cuz often when we try to hide our bodies, we stop treating them well. *(Validation; Patterns)*

I changed the focus of the conversation to be about eating and body image because I had already been told that Tazzie was struggling with this, and I assumed that these struggles must have come in part from earlier experiences that had been challenging for her. I could have also explored Tazzie's comment about being cruel to others, and if I got the chance to talk to her again, this would be a great thing to explore (e.g., "I would love to hear more about what was happening for you when you were acting out toward others. That can be a really hard thing to go through!"). There are always options of where to take a conversation, and this is the benefit of being a teacher—you might have more chances after the first conversation to bring up new angles and suggest new patterns as you notice them in your students.

T: Yeah, I would eat so much shit and I would go like, cuz my parents, when my parents would stay at the farm or I'd have a night to myself or I would have a day to myself, I'd just buy heaps of junk food. I would eat lots of Reese's peanut butter cups. They would be like my favorite thing I would eat. So many of them. And there'd just be like all these wrappers in my drawers and everything. So I would definitely eat a lot.

H: Yeah, that's a really normal reaction. So do you want to talk a little bit about that? Like what prompts the desire to have a binge, what are the feelings, and then sort of the outcome of it? *(Validation; Patterns; Feelings)*

I asked about her feelings to help break down the pattern and open the door for a paradigm shift in understanding herself better. I also told her that her reaction was "normal," which is important for students to realize because they are often ashamed of their patterns and this prevents them from reflecting on them.

T: Um, basically the emptiness and feeling sad and lonely. It was a good feeling to eat and it tasted good, and you know, it was my favorite thing to eat and it made me feel good. Um, I don't really know what to say because I've never really thought about that. Like, you know, there's so much like you just wanna get out and, yeah, you just have that like emptiness feeling in your chest and everything. And I feel like, yeah, eating was definitely to subsidize for that.

H: You said that perfectly. And this is the whole point, we don't think about it. That's why, you know, it's such a struggle for people. It's like nobody's talking about it. Um, okay, so then, what have you now learned about it? How do you cope with that feeling now? *(Validation; Patterns; Skill)*

> I wanted to validate the fact that Tazzie hadn't thought about this before (most of us don't think about these patterns in ourselves because we have not been taught to!).

T: Um, I think I just remember back to what it feels like after I binge eat and just that feeling of like looking at yourself in the mirror and you're like, "This has actually hurt my body more than what I was going through." Just think back to that.

H: Beautiful. That's such a powerful realization! So how did you feel after you binged? *(Validation; Paradigm; Feelings)*

T: Just looking at myself in the mirror and thinking how pathetic I was to do that to my body and to just like think, "Oh my, God, you're so fat and blah, blah, blah." And "Look what you've done. Look what you've eaten. Like look at the garbage. Like that's disgusting." Like so you'd really beat yourself up, and then the cycle would continue, right? And I would be like, "Look how disgusting, what's in this food. That's disgusting. This is now in your body. Therefore you are disgusting."

H: That's so hard. And do you think on some level you were feeling disgusting before, like that was that feeling of like, that loneliness and abandonment making you feel unlovable and therefore you were sort of almost like trying to confirm the fact that you are unlovable? *(Validation; Pattern; Feelings; Paradigm)*

> I was trying to help Tazzie have a paradigm shift to see why she was bingeing, so I suggested what I thought was going on (that her bingeing was reinforcing a belief she already held about herself as being unlovable).

T: Uh, I don't think I thought I was disgusting before I would eat, but afterwards definitely. Yeah. Before it was just like, "There's so much emptiness here. Let's try fill it up."

H: Yeah, totally. That makes sense. And so at what point, how did you change that? *(Validation; Power)*

> Tazzie let me know that my suggestion was off base, and corrected me with her perspective on the pattern. This often happens, and it's a good reminder that being "wrong" doesn't matter. The fact that we are engaging in a reflective dialogue with a student allows them to use our reflections to more accurately understand their own—either because we are right on and it resonates with them, or because we suggest something that doesn't resonate, which allows them to correct us in a way that is more accurate for them.

T: It wasn't until my stepmom told me, "I think you have a problem." Like "You're binge eating." And I was very defensive at first and I was like, "No, that's not me. I'm not doing that." Like "I'm not binge eating." Cuz I thought that was such an embarrassing thing. Um, it was only when she did that and I came to terms with it, I was like, "Right, this isn't probably correct. I should probably stop with the Reese's butter cups."

H: Yeah, it's so hard to get that kind of feedback. It's amazing that you took that on board! What helped you do that? *(Validation; Skill; Power)*

> I wanted Tazzie to identify exactly what she did to help listen to this feedback because this is an incredible skill that will help her a great deal in the future.

T: Um, yeah, well, like I said, I just tried remember back to the feeling and "do you actually wanna do that? Because like it feels good eating it, but you're not gonna remember how it felt when you're eating it after you're done. And is that, you know, reward of the taste and the feeling good enough for the disgust?"

H: Totally. And that's a huge transition. So do you remember when that changed for you and what prompted that to be able to get that level of insight? *(Validation; Paradigm)*

> Because Tazzie was talking in the past tense and had clearly already had a powerful paradigm shift, I was able to ask about what helped her get to this shift so that she could reaffirm it for herself in the present.

T: Um, I think grade nine was the year where I started to come into myself a bit more. Yeah. I think just the age and, yeah, knowing who I was a bit more.

H: And so what were some of the things that helped you realize that, you know, you are lovable and you can be yourself and you're not empty? *(Power)*

> I probed here with basically the same question because Tazzie was doing what a lot of us do—forgetting the role of *her own effort and skills* in changing patterns and chalking it up to simply "maturing with age." I wanted her to see that *she did something to help herself* so that she could remember her own power to do the same thing again.

T: I don't know what it was; I think it was just like the time, like just growing up. I think as time passes and, you know, you get more independence and more responsibility and you find who you are and, you know, you get a job. So you have money to spend on what clothes you want to buy and, you know what I mean? It's more easy and to be yourself that way.

H: Beautiful. So even though it sort of probably just seemed like time was passing, I'm sure that you had an active role in that. You know, how did you empower yourself in that? Like, did you start to, you know, decide "I want to be a healthy person, I want to love myself"? Like do you remember ever making choices like that? *(Validation; Power)*

> Because I was repeating the same question so many times, I tried to validate Tazzie at the same time with my tone and my language so it didn't feel like a reprimand (e.g., "You should know what you did"), but more of an affirmation of her brilliance. Simply one word like *beautiful* can validate a student enough to keep the door of self-reflection open. Note that my persistence paid off, and Tazzie did start reflecting on her incredible choices!

T: Yeah, I took up boxing at the start of grade nine. And I think boxing's really, really great for, um, issues and how you feel inside. It's just so motivating and it gives you such a good feeling. I know it really hurts at the time you're doing it, but it's actually really great just to get that feeling out.

H: Beautiful. Um, that makes a lot of sense. Because then you would've been able to have the experience of "what I feel like after boxing" versus "what I feel like after eating." *(Validation; Power)*

T: Yeah. Yeah.

H: What about painting? Did that also. . ... *(Skill)*

> Tazzie had told me previously on the phone that she loved to paint, so I brought this up to help her see that it was a therapeutic skill.

T: Yeah, painting. I was never really good at art when I was a child. And I'm still not amazing, but I just grew such a love for it because when I was in grade nine, I got put into an art class and my teacher, he just inspired me so much to do art and I got so much love from it and I had so much love to give to it and so much time to give to it.

H: Awesome. And do you find that art can be therapeutic? *(Validation; Skill)*

T: Yeah. Um, art for me is really therapeutic, and painting because you don't have to be good at it. You don't have to be amazing. You don't have to be Picasso, but you don't really think about anything else when you're painting and you can, like. . ... Paints are so tangible and fluid and you can just create whatever you want on a blank canvas and it's so therapeutic for me and I actually love it so much.

H: Beautiful. Yeah. So what about the relationship between feelings and painting? Like, if we talk about when you had that empty feeling and then you wanted to fill it, like, how do you feel when you paint? *(Validation; Feelings; Skill)*

> I brought up "feelings" here because I wanted Tazzie to reflect on the specific way that art might help her with her emotional struggles. Some students will have a lot of insight into this, and some will have never thought about how their creative expressions relate to their feelings, and that doesn't matter. If we plant the seed and ask the question, we open the door for them to reflect on how creativity can be a therapeutic form of emotional expression. This also helped bring the conversation back full circle, to enable us to finish with reflecting on how her own actions helped her deal with the struggles she shared at the beginning of the conversation.

T: Um I don't try to paint my feelings. It's not something I do to express my feelings. It's something I do to feel calm and relaxed and get away from my feelings. And it's not that I don't, um, solve my problems. It's not that I bottle away my feelings, it's just that it's nice to get away from them and just have a break from them. And painting is a really great option for that.

H: Yeah. That's awesome. I love what you said about how you just sort of get a pause from your feelings. So when you are processing your feelings and relating to them, what does that look like for you? Do you journal, do you think about things? *(Validation; Skill)*

> Trying to "get away from my feelings" is a red flag for me because it usually means students have a pattern of *disconnecting from themselves*. I was a bit "leading" in my question here, making the assumption that Tazzie *did* come back and reflect on her feelings, and didn't simply try to escape them. I wanted to reinforce that the process of *relating directly to her feelings* is just as important as getting a small break from them so they aren't so intense.

T: Yeah, yeah. I do a lot of writing and, um, I don't really tell many people about that cuz I'm scared people are gonna find my journal. Yeah, I think it's so important and you get so much more clarity if you write it out and you know, you look at it and you're like, "Oh, that's what I'm feeling. And that's why that person did that." And you know what I mean? You see how it is and sometimes in your head it's all kind of like, you know, messy and bubbling around, and so just to see it on a piece of paper, you get so much more clarity.

H: Yes! I definitely get that. It sounds like that's an awesome tool for you. *(Validation; Skill)* This type of conversation will help your students identify the feelings they are trying to *control*, and feel *safe* in exploring those feelings directly rather than trying to change or escape them through their eating habits. This will help them see the potential to make a different choice when these feelings arise, and shift their pattern of punishing their body for their emotions.

Related Chapters

Chapter 12, "Supporting Students Who Self-Harm"; Chapter 15, "Guiding Students Who Are Caught in Addictive Patterns"; Chapter 18, "Supporting Students Who Are Negatively Impacted by Gender Norms"; Chapter 19, "Guiding Students to Make Healthy Choices on Social Media"; Chapter 20, "Supporting Students with Low Body Image"

3 | Avoiding/Openness (Remembering Courage)

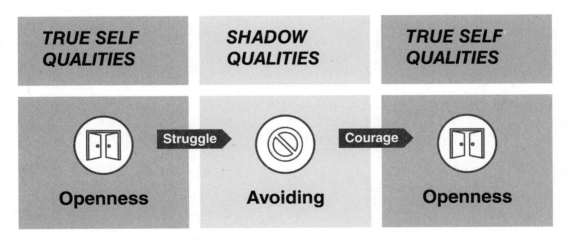

Reproduced with permission from Open Parachute.

This section will provide conversation tools for students who have patterns of avoiding *emotions* (which results in depression/apathy or self-defeating behavior like addiction and self-harm), who are avoiding *conflicts* through people-pleasing, or who have faced a loss or suicide and are avoiding *speaking about* or *processing* their experiences. You will learn strategies for helping students with these patterns become more *open* to their feelings and needs by reminding them of the *courage* they possess to help themselves make changes.

11

Finding the Words with Students Who Are in *Avoiding* Behavior Patterns

A common reaction to overwhelming emotions is to *avoid* those emotions altogether. The world we live in shows students many examples of this, so it is a common pathway for them to take. Most of us avoid uncomfortable conversations, use food/alcohol/caffeine/technology to numb our feelings, and put off actions that we know will help us, but that cause us to feel uncomfortable in the moment (e.g., exercise, therapy/self-help practices, boundary-setting). Of all the shadow qualities, avoidance is probably the most prolific and normalized (even glorified!) in our society.

Students who are avoiding their emotions might react in similar ways to the behaviors they see in the world around them (e.g., using caffeine to avoid tiredness; using social media to avoid boredom/insecurity), or they might take avoidance a step further and harm themselves, form strong addictive habits, or give up/retreat from the world in the hopes of avoiding their uncomfortable feelings. Any action that *takes us away from discomfort in the moment* is an avoidance tactic, and like all behaviors, avoidance falls on a spectrum. On one end of the spectrum, a student might avoid feelings of boredom for a few minutes by using a device but is also able to put it down and reflect on how they feel; on the other end of the spectrum, a student might be unable to experience boredom at all, and is *constantly* on their device, becoming extremely distressed anytime they are asked to put it away.

It's important to note that sometimes, avoiding painful feelings can be a *helpful* strategy. For example, if someone is being unkind to us, avoiding them can be a healthy self-protective response. However, the challenge arises when avoidance becomes an *unconscious habit*. If a student avoids discomfort, they will feel relief in the moment, and this becomes an alluring choice to make in the future. They will then get into the habit of seeking this path of least resistance, often losing sight of the long-term impacts of their actions.

The hormones that naturally flood the adolescent brain cause them to be more drawn to immediate pleasure, more likely to take risks, and less likely to understand the long-term implications of their behaviors. These are necessary brain changes because teenagers need to be incredibly risk-averse and think of the world in a moment-by-moment way in order to face the transitions needed to become independent in an adult world. However, this means that avoidance patterns in teenagers can be much more intense and harder to break.

What is needed is for students to find the *courage* to become more *open to their own emotional experiences*. It takes a great deal of bravery to face discomfort in the moment and to *feel* the pain of an experience rather than pushing it away. Every student has the courage to do this, but they have often forgotten or don't realize how important it is for them to stop habits that block out their emotions. It's important to remember that a student who is in an avoidance pattern is probably unaware of what they are doing and needs coaching to be able to see the impacts of their actions and to start taking steps toward facing their fears.

If you can help all of your students reflect on the avoidance patterns that are so common in our culture and the importance of facing discomfort in the moment in order to make choices that help us in the long run, this will help them begin to reflect on these patterns in themselves. Using an "exercise" metaphor can be helpful (e.g., *it hurts in the moment, but if we keep doing it then in the long run we feel healthier and happier in our bodies*). When you lay the foundation of this perspective, your students will be ready to dive deeper with their own self-reflection when you have time for a longer more private conversation.

What Can I Do to Help Students Who Are Avoiding?

Your goal is to make *space* for students to move through the six steps of self-reflection, shown in Figure 11.1, that will help them move away from *avoiding* and toward *openness*. These steps fall into the two categories explained next.

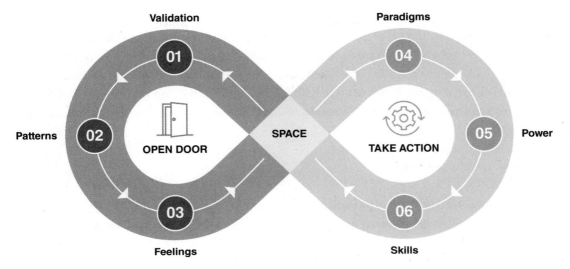

Figure 11.1   The learning cycle for building mental health skills.

Reproduced with permission from Open Parachute.

Figure Explanations
Category 1: Open the Door.

1. **Validating** them and their experiences.

    Validation means letting a student know that what they are facing is normal and that we understand where they are coming from. When a student is *avoiding*, it's crucial to help them understand that there is nothing wrong with feeling how they feel and that even if their reactions are unhelpful, they do not mean there is anything fundamentally "wrong" with them. Phrases like "It makes sense that you would feel that way" or "It's normal to feel scared/sad when hard things happen" or "When I feel sad, I often find it hard to talk about it too" will help students to open up to the emotions they are avoiding.

2. Helping them notice their own **patterns.**

    A *pattern* can be any behavioral reaction, way of thinking, or emotional response. When students are avoiding, we want to help them speak directly about their challenges and identify their avoidance patterns. This helps them to see what is needed in order to break these habits (e.g., "Do you think your choice was in line with your values, or was it going against them?" or "I really hate letting people down so I try to please them even when it's not what's best for me. Do you think you have any of those patterns too?").

3. Encouraging them to relate directly to their **feelings.**

   Feelings are the physical and emotional responses that a student has to their experiences. When students are avoiding any situation, person, or experience, what they are really avoiding is *the way these things make them feel.* So, any exploration of feelings provides a pathway to changing these patterns (e.g., "What did you feel in your body when you went through that?" or "What do you feel like in those moments? Can you describe it to me?").

Category 2: Take Action.

4. Helping them shift their **paradigm,** or the way they are seeing things.

   A *paradigm* is a student's fundamental views about themselves and the world. Students who are avoiding are usually not aware that they are caught in these patterns. It is vital that they develop an awareness *of why they are in an avoidance pattern* and the *impacts of their actions.* This shift in perspective helps them see exactly what needs to change (e.g., "It makes sense that you would shut down like that because you had lots of examples of other people responding the same way. How do you think that pattern impacts you?").

5. Reminding them of their **power.**

   A student's *power* is their ability to act with agency in their own world—their ability to enact change and influence their experiences. When a student is avoiding, we can help them remember the courage they have shown in facing their feelings in the past, and this will encourage them to draw on this same courage in the future (e.g., "Have you ever faced your feelings in a healthy way in the past?").

6. Supporting them to use a **skill** that helps them move forward.

   Skills are anything a student does that helps them cope or change their physical and emotional circumstances. Students who are avoiding often need to practice skills for facing their feelings in a healthy way, which requires an incredible amount of courage. Reminding them of strategies that help them do this can really help them become more open (e.g., "It is a really great skill to talk about your feelings. Do you feel comfortable sharing some things with me?" or "Can we explore what you're feeling that's making you want to do that?").

These steps can help your students identify their patterns of *avoidance,* and recognize their own capacity for *courage in facing their feelings in the moment* in order to take actions that help them in the long term. In the following chapters, we will explore different manifestations of avoidance behaviors in order to help you guide your students away from these harmful patterns.

12 | Supporting Students Who Self-Harm

This chapter will give you strategies for responding to students who are self-harming (e.g., cutting or burning themselves—often on the arm or upper thigh—picking at their lips or fingers, pulling out their hair, or purposefully causing damage to themselves in any other way). These behaviors are a signal that students are feeling emotions that they perceive as being too intense for them to cope with (e.g., emptiness, sadness, loneliness), and they are seeking a distraction from their experiences (i.e., *avoiding* them). You will be provided with language you can use to support a student who is self-harming to find more healthy ways of opening up to and expressing their feelings.

WHY Do Students Self-Harm?

Students self-harm because they are feeling painful emotions, and they have no safe outlet for those emotions. Usually, students who are self-harming also feel like they can't talk about what they are going through that is causing them pain (either because they feel shame about it or because they are worried about what will happen if they tell people the truth). This causes their painful feelings to become more bottled up and increasingly intense. Many students discover that they can *avoid the pain of their overwhelming emotions in the moment* by inflicting physical pain on themselves (*physical* pain makes more sense and can feel more manageable than complicated and layered *emotional* pain). (See Chapter 11 for a deeper explanation of *avoiding* behaviors.) Their minds are desperately seeking to get away from their experience of emotional turmoil, and this desire is so strong it *overrides their innate human instinct to keep themselves safe*. This pattern can lead students to inflict more and more physical pain on themselves because they can become desensitized to the sensations and need increased intensity to distract themselves from their emotional pain.

WHAT Can I Do to Help a Student Who Is Self-Harming?

Students who are self-harming need support to identify the thought and behavior chain that is leading to their self-harm so they can start to become more *open to the feelings that are driving these reactions*. This will help them to *recognize the courage they possess* to resist self-harming and express their emotions in a safer way that supports their long-term well-being.

Part of your support for a student who is self-harming will always be providing a referral to a counselor or mental health practitioner and letting them know that you need to tell someone else to keep them safe. Once this has happened, you can further support them in the ways that you communicate about their experiences reflected in this chapter. Sometimes it can be hard to identify students who are self-harming because they hide their patterns. This is why it is so important that we bring conversations about self-harm into the school setting. Other times, students can speak openly about their self-harm, and it can seem like they are just attention-seeking. It's vital that we take all self-harm seriously and keep in mind that whether a student is hiding it or showing it off, these actions are an indication that there is deep, buried pain that needs to be addressed.

HOW Will I Have a Constructive Conversation with a Student Who Is Self-Harming?

Going into my conversation with Emma, I knew that she had been self-harming because I saw the scars on her wrists. I also knew she was seeing a therapist and that her therapist knew about this self-harm (I was told this in advance) so I didn't need to give her a referral. If you suspect a student is self-harming, you always want to connect them to a professional who will provide them with a "safety plan" to make sure they know how to help themself stay safe if they feel the urge to self-harm. But you can also have a very supportive, helpful conversation with them before or after you refer them. During our dialogue in this conversation, Emma was able to identify the thoughts that led to her self-harm and *explore the feelings that she was trying to avoid*. She was able to openly discuss the challenges that led to her harmful reactions and *recognize the courage she had already displayed in finding alternative soothing strategies*. This gave her a sense of support and confidence for the work that she was already doing with her therapist.

The following is a transcript of my conversation with Emma, showing how the six steps of the learning cycle, shown in Figure 12.1 (validation, patterns, feelings, paradigms, power, and skills), can be used with a student who is self-harming. See Chapter 11 for a deeper analysis of using these steps with students who are *avoiding*.

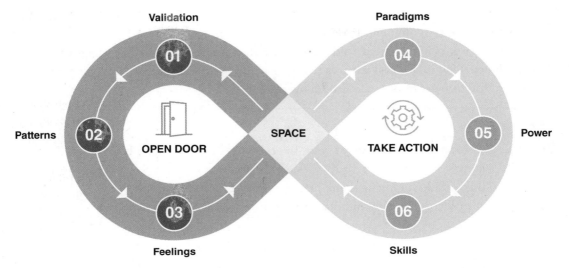

Figure 12.1 The learning cycle for building mental health skills.

Reproduced with permission from Open Parachute.

Interview with Emma (Age 12)

E: I see my dad every other week for dinner cuz there's issues with him. So I don't really stay at night anymore. I mainly just go there for dinner sometimes.

H: Can you tell me a little bit about what, what are some of those issues? What have been those struggles with your dad? *(Patterns)*

> When a student mentions a challenge like this, my first response would usually be validating (e.g., "I'm sorry you had to go through that."). Because Emma and I had already been speaking about this issue earlier in our conversation, I went straight into reflecting on the issue. However, it would have been great if I had also validated her here.

E: Um, I have to act completely different, and I can't be myself when I'm there. He treats my brother badly and yells at him most of the time and everything. And then if the dog goes up and like just to sniff some food or whatever, he'll smack her on the snout. And I always feel like it's a bad thing cuz you shouldn't do that.

H: Definitely. I'm so sorry that you had to go through that. Has your dad been mean to you ever? *(Validation; Patterns)*

> Because of Emma's comment, I was concerned about potential abuse in the home, so I asked a direct question about it. Students will usually not tell us about abuse unless you ask them directly, and it is vital if we ever suspect harm is being caused, that we report this to a mental health practitioner who can follow up.

E: He's never been mean, but like if I want to go home, I call mom and he's always like, "I can't do this anymore." Um, last Christmas he told me that um, Santa Clause would get confused and I wouldn't get any presents that year if I went home.

H: Hmmm. I'm sorry. And how did that make you feel? *(Validation; Feelings)*

> I wanted Emma *to connect with how she felt* about this experience so that she could start to face those feelings in a healthy way.

E: It made me really feel sad and upset because I didn't want to stay cuz I didn't feel comfortable staying. I was upset and I just really wanted to go home to my mom.

H: Yeah, that makes sense. And when we're in those situations, it's normal to start having kind of negative thoughts about ourselves or about the situation or about other people. What were some of the negative thoughts that you had? *(Validation; Patterns)*

> I made the assumption that Emma had negative thoughts in this situation because any child would. This helped to validate her experience so she felt safer to reflect (it's easier to admit something about yourself if you know that other people experience it too).

E: Like I thought, "Oh, no, I'm not gonna get anything this year. And my dad's gonna be mad at me if I keep saying I want to go home. Mom won't pick me up because dad won't let me call her." And at that time, I didn't have my phone.

H: Definitely. And so how did you get yourself out? Like did you have to stay there that night? What happened? *(Power)*

> Because the experience Emma was sharing sounded so hard, I wanted to bring in a *recognition of her courage* and the *power she had to help herself* so that this could be part of her memory of this event, making the memory less traumatic because there was less of a feeling of *helplessness*.

E: I did have to stay the night and I didn't . . . I think I went to bed around two, one in the morning cuz I couldn't get to sleep.

H: Yeah. And then what happened after that? Did you sort of tell your mom, "Look, I don't wanna stay there anymore"? Like, how did you help yourself? *(Power)*

E: I did tell mom and then in the end we did tell Dad and said, I just don't want to anymore. I'm getting older and these things kind of happen.

H: Good for you. That's really brave. Was that scary to do that? *(Validation; Power; Feelings)*

> I wanted to *explore Emma's feelings* in taking this step so that she knew how courageous she is capable of being.

E: It was scary. Cuz I felt like that, if I said anything to like to the school about dad or like I told mom, I feel like, it would always get back to him in the end.

H: Yeah, I get that. And then when we're holding all that in, that's when we can start doing things that are self-destructive. Did you do anything like that? *(Validation; Patterns; Paradigm)*

> I was fishing because I already knew that Emma was self-harming. I was going for a paradigm shift where she could see that her self-harm was a direct result of painful experiences and not knowing how to cope with them. This realization gives students the awareness needed to make different choices with their pain.

E: I started cutting myself with a sharpener blade, and lately, I have used my nails. And I've been scratching myself to the point where it's pus or blood coming out. So there's a scar left.

H: I'm sorry to hear that. That's really hard. What were you feeling when you did that? *(Validation; Feelings)*

A disclosure of harm like this always need a referral to a mental health practitioner who can help in an ongoing capacity. In this case, I knew that Emma was working with a therapist who was aware of her self-harm. If I wasn't sure that a professional was involved, I would have still have had the same conversation, and simply ended with connecting her with the school counselor by saying, "I need to tell someone else now so that we can keep you safe. Would you like me to tell the school counselor, or do you have a psychologist that you are seeing outside of school that I can talk to?" I asked Emma about her feelings here because I wanted to explore *why* she was self-harming so that we could figure out what strategies she could use to relate to these feelings differently.

E: I was feeling really upset and alone and that no one would help me. So I thought that if I hurt myself, it would make the pain of me feeling alone and by myself go away.

H: That's exactly why we hurt ourselves, isn't it? And why did you think that? *(Validation; Patterns; Paradigm)*

I used "we" language to validate Emma's experience, to show that it is a *common human experience* to be unkind to ourselves. I have personally never cut myself, but I *have* done things that harm myself (e.g., drinking to avoid my feelings, eating too much or too little due to body image struggles, thinking cruel thoughts about myself, etc.). Emma clearly had already made the paradigm shift to *understand why she was self-harming*, so I focused on exploring and reinforcing this awareness.

E: Well, I was just thinking if I'm upset and I hurt myself, maybe my pain for me being upset will go to me hurting myself.

H: Hmmm, and how did it feel in that moment? *(Validation; Feelings)*

I wanted Emma *to explore her feelings* as much as possible, to build up the skill of facing those feelings in a healthy way (by talking about them with me).

E: Uh, when I first started cutting myself, it did hurt and everything. And then the more I did it, the more I got used to it.

H: And in the moment, did it feel helpful or did it not feel helpful? *(Feelings; Patterns)*

> I was trying to lead Emma to a paradigm shift that *what helps her feel better in the moment is not good for her long term*. I used the language "helpful" versus "unhelpful," rather than identifying behavior as "good" or "bad," so that she could reflect on her actions with less shame.

E: It felt helpful, but then the more I did it, the more I realized that I didn't need to do it.

H: Yeah. And so there's a really big difference between something that soothes us in the moment and something that's actually good for us in the long run, right? *(Validation; Paradigm)*

E: It did feel good at first because my friends were doing it with me [self-harming], and I'm like, if I have people doing it with me, it's gonna feel better. But then the more I did it, the more I realized I can put my trust in my mother and the school counselors.

H: Yeah, and it's a really big problem, isn't it? Cuz if you're doing something with your friends, like that feels good. It feels like it's the right thing. So it sort of can trick us a little bit in that way, right? *(Validation; Feelings; Pattern)*

E: Yeah, so I wasn't the first in my friend group to start it. I can't exactly remember, but once I found out they were doing it and they said it makes them feel better and happy, I thought that if I tried it, it would make me feel better. At first it did, but then as time got on and I kept doing it, I didn't feel better. It just made me feel worse.

H: Totally. And what's the negative impact of cutting? How did it make you feel worse? *(Validation; Paradigm)*

> This is an important issue to point out—if we don't talk to students about self-harm (why it happens, the negative impacts, and how we can help ourselves make better choices), then their information will come from their friends or online sources that will give them a completely different picture. Asking students direct questions like this about self-harm (even if it feels uncomfortable) can help them truly understand this issue and have the tools they need if they are tempted by this pattern.

E: It hurts you and that you think it'll make you feel better, but in the end, it really doesn't. It just leaves scars on you.

H: Absolutely. And so how did you learn to stop? *(Validation; Power)*

> Since we had explored Emma's feelings a lot and given her time to reflect, it seemed like the right time to shift the conversation toward the skills she could use to help herself.

E: Well, I learned to stop by talking to my mom and the well-being counselor at my old school because I realized talking to someone does help and that they can actually help you.

H: That's so good! And when was the first time that you started talking? *(Validation; Power; Skill)*

> I wanted Emma to *verbalize exactly what she did* when she first reached out so that she identified her own courage and could draw on the same skill again.

E: I started talking to my mom a couple of times after I had done it, and she started to tell me like, "Sweetheart, you don't need to do this. Just come talk to me or your stepdad." So I did. And then in the end I got the help at my old school that I needed.

H: Amazing. That's so awesome that you were so brave and told your mom. And how did that feel? *(Validation; Power; Feelings)*

> I wanted Emma to *explore how her soothing strategy feels* so that she could remember the power of this skill when she is faced with overwhelming feelings again in the future.

E: It made me feel really good about myself cuz I knew that people cared about me now and that I can actually talk to someone without being like, without feeling like I didn't need to.

H: Absolutely. And can you describe the difference between the good feeling you get when you're talking to someone versus the sort-of-good feeling you get when cutting? *(Validation; Paradigm; Power; Skill)*

> I wanted Emma to say this aloud to really highlight the choice she made and the power of that choice.

E: The good feeling I get when talking to someone is that actually they can help me and they can get me to stop and they can help me with my dad and my issues. But with cutting, it just puts me in self-harm and my mental health.

H: What a great insight! *(Validation; Paradigm)*

> We ended the conversation here, but if I had a chance to speak with Emma again, I would check in with her about how she is coping. When a student discloses something that concerns their safety, it's important that we show them how serious it is and that we really care about them. You want to be careful not to let anyone else overhear your conversations to protect their privacy, but asking directly about an issue they have raised with you in the past is a helpful way of reminding them that help is available (e.g., "How are you doing with your counselor—are they helping you to keep you safe?" or "I'm so glad you shared that with me the other day. I really care about keeping you safe, so if you're struggling and your counselor isn't around, you can always come talk to me, okay?").

This type of conversation will help your students connect to their own *courage to openly face their challenges* and identify their own thought/behavior chains that lead to self-harm, as well as the impacts of hurting themselves physically. This will help them directly face and explore their feelings so that they have less of a need to avoid those feelings through physical pain, and are more able to choose healthy soothing strategies that support their long-term well-being.

Related Chapters

Chapter 10, "Talking to Students about Unhealthy Eating Habits"; Chapter 14, "Encouraging Students Who Are Depressed or Apathetic"; Chapter 15, "Guiding Students Who Are Caught in Addictive Patterns"

13 | Helping Students Who People-Please

This chapter will give you strategies for supporting students who choose their behavior in order to seek validation from others (e.g., not sharing their opinion when it differs from that of their friends, sacrificing their well-being to achieve academic success to please their parents, etc.). You will learn strategies you can use in conversations in order to help students with these patterns to become more *open* to their own needs/wants and less *avoidant* of disappointing others.

WHY Do Students Develop People-Pleasing Behaviors?

Students people-please in order to be validated by others. Usually this is because they have developed a pattern of silencing (or *avoiding*) their own emotions, believing that their emotions are not valid or are a burden to others. (See Chapter 11 for a deeper explanation of *avoiding* behaviors.) *Emotional avoidance* is a very common pattern in our culture, and many adults have learned to dismiss their own emotions. When these adults are around children (e.g., because they are close members of their family) who display strong emotions, it is natural for them to treat these children's emotions in the same way they treat their own. This is of course unintentional, but it can often create a belief in children that *their emotions are not valid*, which makes them feel invalid as a person (e.g., if what I'm *feeling* is wrong, then *I must be wrong*). They then start *looking for other people to help them feel better about themselves*. Because no one other than the student is hurt by these patterns, they are usually not addressed or noticed by others, and this cycle can continue for their whole lives. People-pleasing behavior is often missed as a mental health challenge in school settings because it can look like "good" or "kind" or "easy-going" behavior. It's important that we probe under the surface and help students reflect on whether they feel like they *always* have to be good and kind and easy-going. This is a sign that they are not able to face the fear of disappointing others, which can lead to many other harmful patterns and dynamics.

WHAT Can I Do to Help a Student Who Is People-Pleasing?

Students who are people-pleasing need to be helped *to understand where their patterns come from*, and be encouraged to be *courageous in prioritizing their own feelings,* and becoming more *open and connected to their own* impulses rather than constantly looking outwards for guidance.

HOW Will I Have a Constructive Conversation with a Student Who Is People-Pleasing?

During my conversation with Terry, they (Terry is nonbinary) started talking about being lonely as a child. By exploring this feeling and the patterns that accompanied it, Terry was able to reflect on their people-pleasing tendencies in a safe space so that they could reflect on the thoughts that led to this pattern as well as identify ways that they could work on prioritizing themselves more, even though this scared them. Terry had gone to therapy before, so had a great deal of insight about this already. I chose this interview so that you could see the level of

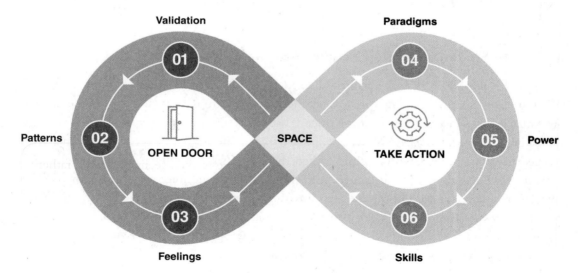

Figure 13.1   The learning cycle for building mental health skills.
Reproduced with permission from Open Parachute.

awareness that students are capable of having with the proper long-term guidance. When talking to a student who has had less practice with this way of thinking, the conversation strategy is the same, simply the *content of the student's reflections* will stay more on the surface.

The following is a transcript of my conversation with Terry, showing how the six steps of the learning cycle, shown in Figure 13.1 (validation, patterns, feelings, paradigms, power, and skills), can be used with a student who is caught in patterns of people-pleasing. See Chapter 11 for a deeper analysis of using these steps with students who are *avoiding*.

Interview with Terry (Age 17)

T: So I have two half-siblings and three step-siblings. Um, I was very close with my half-siblings growing up, but of course when they grew older and became more mature, I kind of got left behind. And because my step-siblings, we were like closer in age, but they were closer with each other than they were with me.

H: And how did that feel for you growing up? *(Feelings)*

> Because I didn't know where this conversation was going to lead, I started with an exploration of feelings, as a way to open to the door to a reflection that could help Terry.

T: Oh, it felt very alone. I always had a hard time connecting with people, and I always yearned and longed for that sibling relationship. And whenever I thought I had it [with my step-siblings], there was always something that reminded me that it's not as close knit as they had with each other.

H: Totally. Do you have an example of something that reminded you like that? *(Validation; Patterns)*

> I asked for a specific example in order to help Terry relate to their feelings directly, rather than talking in general terms, so that we could get to the core of their experiences.

T: Um, like they would go to their mom's house during the week and then come to their dad's house with me for the weekend, and they would have stories about the week and what it was like at school and like, "Oh, remember this thing?" Like it was something that I couldn't connect to.

H: Definitely. And in that situation, what were the kinds of thoughts that you started thinking about yourself or about the world or . . .? *(Validation; Patterns)*

> I asked about Terry's *thoughts* as a way to help them further identify their patterns of reaction to the feeling of loneliness.

T: During that time, like especially when high school started, I felt very alone. And I didn't have good self-esteem or confidence, so it kind of hit me with, like, I am not worth anything unless other people are paying attention to me sort of thing. And so being disconnected from my siblings, it was, it didn't help. It really like, it made me just believe even more that I was alone and that like nobody understood me. Um, and although I didn't realize it at the time, it really did play into my self-esteem and my sense of worth.

H: That's such a powerful thing to understand about yourself! And can you describe that feeling of being like close to someone physically, but feeling disconnected from them emotionally? Can you describe what that's like? *(Validation; Feelings)*

> Based on Terry's last comment, it was clear to me that they were very self-aware, so I knew that I could explore deeply with them and ask questions about *how they experience* their own emotions. With a student who had less insight into themselves, my question would have been slightly simpler (e.g., "What did it feel like to be all alone like that?").

T: Like being next to someone and being completely distant from them is so bizarre.

H: Makes sense. And did that cause you to react in some way? *(Validation; Patterns)*

> I didn't know what Terry's reactions were yet, so I was fishing to understand what pattern might have played out as a result of their feelings of intense loneliness.

T: Yeah, it really made me latch onto lots of other people. Whether that would be healthy or unhealthy connections and relationships.

H: Totally. And that's such a common thing to do; I had the same pattern when I was growing up. Was that in class, like with friends, with family, like what did that look like? *(Validation; Patterns)*

> I mentioned my own experience to help validate Terry and make them feel safe in their self-reflection. This is a good example of how a self-disclosure can just be simple, a throwaway line that doesn't make *my experience* the focus of the conversation, but that helps a student feel less alone.

T: Um, I remember in school I was the good kid, the one that nobody had to worry about, and that turned into perfectionism. I became obsessed with being perfect, and if something I did wasn't right or if it just didn't look or feel the way I wanted to do, I would begin to hate myself and hate everything that I did and question everything.

H: Totally. And so the validation is like a band-aid, isn't it? It's almost like a replacement for the true connection that we really need, right? *(Validation; Patterns; Paradigm)*

> I wanted to reinforce to Terry the perspective that their pattern of people-pleasing was directly related to feeling lonely and wanting to escape that loneliness.

T: Yeah, it was a short-term solution for a long-term problem. And in that moment it was really rewarding hearing about how much of a quiet kid I was and how I was like, I wasn't troublesome. Like I was the good kid and it was, it felt great.

H: And that wasn't really what you needed, was it? What was it replacing, being validated by all those people? *(Patterns; Paradigm)*

T: Well, I always found it silly when people told me that confidence came from within and that, but you do have to put the work in to love yourself.

H: Awesome. That's so wise! And so what were some of your limiting beliefs or thoughts that were really contributing to this pattern of seeking validation from others, instead of putting the work in for yourself? *(Validation; Patterns; Paradigm)*

T: While I was at therapy, um, one of the things that came up was that my core beliefs were that I was worthless, um, that I wasn't good enough, like I'm pathetic, small, weak, et cetera.

H: And so, what started happening for you when you started realizing that you had these thoughts? *(Patterns; Paradigm)*

When students have been to therapy, they often use a lot of psychological language like this. (FYI, *core beliefs* are simply beliefs that we hold about ourselves and the world that our central to our sense of self.) When students start talking in these kinds of terms, I try to come back to more simple language about thoughts and feelings, so that the conversation doesn't become too abstract and philosophical (which is another way we can avoid directly relating to our feelings!).

T: I'm still working through that process. Um, but I think realizing the problem of me craving that validation from other people and putting their needs before my own. I think that in itself was a big step for me and I want to be able to say, "no." I want to be able to tell people that I am there for them and I will support them, but I also want to make my mental health a priority.

H: Awesome. That's such a fantastic realization! And so what does it actually look like to you to prioritize yourself? *(Paradigm; Skill)*

I asked about what it "looks like" to help Terry identify a *specific skill* they can use to help with this behavior change.

T: It's listening to other people about their problems, but it's also me telling them, "Hey, I am like not feeling it right now. Like I just need to go sleep or eat or something. Like I can't do this right now."

H: It's huge and it sounds simple, doesn't it? But it's a really big thing to do. What does it feel like for you when you think of doing that? *(Validation; Skill; Feelings)*

I asked Terry how it feels to think about doing this, to help *them imagine the positive outcome* of taking that step, to help with motivation.

T: It feels refreshing, like it's one less of a problem that I don't have to think about. Because when people tell me their problems, I like get invested, like I worry about what will happen to them, if they'll be all right. So putting my stance of, "I'm not feeling it right now, can we talk later?" It's refreshing, but on the other hand, I feel like it's me letting my friends down, me not being a good friend.

H: Totally. And I think that's a really important point because how does saying "no" actually help you be a more supportive friend? *(Validation; Paradigm)*

> I wanted Terry to reflect on this paradigm shift more (that *setting boundaries can feel unkind, but is actually better for everyone*) as another motivation tactic.

T: It's like a cycle. If I focus on what I want and my needs, then I can help them with what they want and what they need. And if I don't prioritize what I need, then I can't help with what they need.

H: Absolutely. And so now what are the things that you do to consciously give yourself that space? Do you say things to yourself? Do you do things for your well-being? Like what are the things that you do to remind yourself that your needs are valid and you need to take up space in the world and those kinds of things? *(Validation; Skill; Power)*

> I suggested a few ideas of skills that Terry might have used because I wanted them to *see how courageous they have been in the past*, again to encourage motivation.

T: It's difficult. I'm still trying to like remind myself that I'm allowed to take up space, which has been a thing that I've struggled with a lot, um, that I am allowed to speak up.

H: Totally. And did anyone ever tell you to be quiet or that you were taking up too much space, or was it more subtle? *(Patterns)*

> I took this opportunity to dive back into exploring Terry's patterns, to see if they had more reflections on where they were developed.

T: It was more subtle. I think because of the way I was brought up, taking up space was just a thing I wasn't allowed to do. There were a lot of subtle hints that I was taking up space or that I was being too much.

H: It makes sense that you developed that pattern then! You have so much insight into this. It's just always a practice to keep reminding ourselves to be brave and do it even when it feels scary, isn't it? *(Validation; Skill)*

I wanted to end with a further reminder that Terry simply needs to keep being brave. They clearly know what they need to do, and just need support in nudging them along their path of growth. Because we had to end here, I didn't have time to further explore Terry's last comment. If I could talk to them again, I would pick back up with this train of thought to help them reflect more on their pattern of not wanting to "take up space" (e.g., "you mentioned a really powerful insight, that you felt like you couldn't take up space as a kid. That's a really hard thing to feel! I would love to hear more about that if you want to share.").

T: Yeah.

This type of conversation will help your students remember they have the *courage* to prioritize their own needs, and be *open* to their own feelings, even when it's scary. They will also be able to more clearly see where their people-pleasing tendencies come from, so that they can understand that these patterns *do not make them a bad person*, and can be changed if we work on them.

Related Chapters

Chapter 6, "Helping Gender Diverse Students Feel Included"; Chapter 14, "Encouraging Students Who Are Depressed or Apathetic"; Chapter 21, "Helping Students Stand Up to Peer Pressure"; Chapter 27, "Supporting Students Who Experience Intergenerational Trauma"

14

Encouraging Students Who Are Depressed or Apathetic

This chapter will give you tools for communicating with students who are showing signs of depression, low mood, or apathy (e.g., seeming to not care about things they used to care about, appearing flat or emotionless, lacking a sense of purpose or zest for life). While you, as an educator, are never tasked with changing these patterns in your students (this is the job of mental health practitioners), there are still many ways that you can help these students thrive. In this chapter, you will learn the language that can help students in depressive cycles become more open to themselves and the world around them.

WHY Do Students Get Depressed and Become Apathetic?

Students become depressed and apathetic because they feel hopeless about making positive changes in their lives. This often happens when they have learned to *avoid* their emotions rather than facing and moving through them. (See Chapter 11 for a deeper explanation of *avoiding* behaviors.) When emotions are avoided for an extended period of time, they often get bottled up and become too overwhelming to connect with at all. This leads to a numbness and a sense of helplessness or a feeling of being lost and like it's "all too much." When a student gets into this helpless state, *everything* starts to feel too hard. They can start thinking that *nothing will ever change* and feeling like they are just *going through the motions* rather than really living a full life. Because

103

they are disconnected from their emotions, even things that are inherently joyful won't break through the haze because they aren't able to feel and connect to the excitement of the moment. This cycle can bring students into a more and more disconnected state, making it harder to see anything but the doom and gloom of life. Depression, like anything, falls on a scale of severity. It's helpful to remember that a student who has been diagnosed with severe depression has a much heavier burden and most likely, more biological and environmental reasons for their depression, but the *underlying patterns are similar* to a student who is apathetic about their school work. Suicidal thoughts are a natural extension at the extreme end of this—if a student is seeking an escape from their feelings that seem so overwhelming that they can't see any other way out, it is not uncommon for thoughts about suicide to arise. These thoughts should always be taken extremely seriously, and a referral should be made to a counselor or other mental health practitioner to support a student with these patterns. Students who are depressed can often appear angry, uncaring, sloppy, or unfocused. It's important to always look deeper at any behaviors like this that seem self-destructive because there is likely a depressive pattern underneath.

WHAT Can I Do to Help a Student Who Is Depressed or Apathetic?

Students who are depressed or apathetic need support to *open up* to their own feelings and remember that they have the courage to face those feelings. Often students who are depressed forget all of the things they do to help themselves and need to be reminded of the impact of their own self-care strategies in order to motivate them to use these strategies regularly.

HOW Will I Have a Constructive Conversation with a Student Who Is Depressed or Apathetic?

In my conversation with Abby, she told me that she had started to feel sad a lot when she was younger. This is often how a student will explain a depressed state. During our conversation, Abby was able to explore her feelings and notice her own patterns that have been keeping her stuck. She was also able to reflect on her own past courageous acts and the skills she already possesses to help herself. We ended with a focus on inspiration for the future, which will help Abby see herself and her future differently, remembering the agency she has to make changes in her life and the possibility that she has the potential to feel differently. It's important to note that if Abby had mentioned anything that made me concerned for her safety, I would have asked her directly if she was thinking about harming herself (e.g., "Do you ever think about harming yourself?" or "Have you had any thoughts about doing something to hurt yourself?"). If she answered in the affirmative, I would have taken her to a mental health practitioner at the end of our conversation. All the other elements of our dialogue would have remained the same so that I could show her that *other adults also want to support her through this*, not just her counselor.

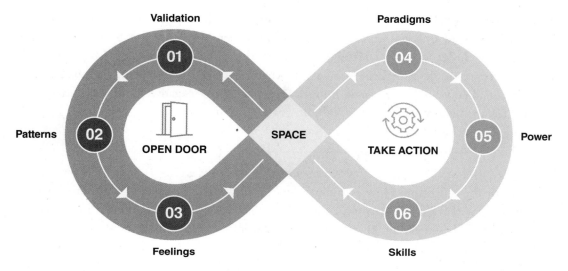

Figure 14.1 The learning cycle for building mental health skills.

Reproduced with permission from Open Parachute.

The following is a transcript of my conversation with Abby, showing how the six steps of the learning cycle, shown in Figure 14.1 (validation, patterns, feelings, paradigms, power, and skills), can be implemented with a student who is depressed or apathetic. See Chapter 11 for a deeper analysis of using these steps with students who are *avoiding*. Another part of my conversation with Abby can be found in Chapter 24, "Helping Students Who Face Prejudice" so you can see a bit more context about where some of Abby's depressive thoughts might have come from.

Interview with Abby (Age 15)

A: Um, at around like maybe like 11 or 12, yeah, I don't know. Just one day I started feeling sad a lot.

H: I'm sorry you went through that. Do you want to talk about what happened? *(Validation; Patterns)*

> I didn't know where the conversation was going, so I was opening the door here for Abby to share a bit more with me.

A: Um, well, uh, well, I think my mom noticed it and my dad, cuz my dad's a mental health nurse, so he noticed it and my mom noticed it. And then I went to a lot of people like psychiatrists and therapists. Um, like a lot since then, from then to now. But like it's kind of all been the same. Sometimes it's been like really bad. Sometimes it's just like normal.

H: And so can you describe a bit more about what it felt like for you? Did you start getting low mood and didn't want to do things? Were you having negative thoughts? Did you feel numb? Like what was it like for you? *(Feelings; Patterns)*

I started asking about her actual *experience* of depression, which is helpful in opening the door for reflection. How a student *thinks and feels* is a better way to get to know their reality than simply learning about a diagnosis they have been given. I made suggestions here based on my knowledge about depression, but I could have just as easily said something more general like "What thoughts and feelings did you have during that time?"

A: A lot of lack of motivation. Like I would say "no" to everything and I would stay in my room all the time. Um, there was a long time where I wouldn't get excited about anything and I think that's kind of like stayed cuz I don't get like overly excited even for the things I would find really exciting before.

H: Hmmm . . . do you have any examples of that? *(Validation; Patterns)*

Asking about *examples* helps bring the conversation to a specific situation, which will make it more of a personal reflection, leading to the specific skills she could use to help herself. Also note that simply saying "hmmm" can be a powerful tool to validate a student and make them feel safe—it's a sound that acknowledges that you're listening and you want to hear what they have to say.

A: Um, a lot of times. Because when I was younger, I loved food a lot. Like I would always eat leftovers of other people's food. And then, um, when I started getting like low mood and stuff, um, people would say like, "Oh, I have this food for you," or "You wanna go get some food? Do you wanna eat this person's leftover food?" And I would just say "no." Or I'd be like, "I don't care."

H: And so it sounds like you felt like an "I don't care," like numb, kind of just blocking everything out, is that right? *(Validation; Feelings)*

Another tool for validation is to repeat back or clarify what a student is telling you as a way to show you are listening and you really want to understand their experience. When a student has low mood, often their responses can seem flat and unemotional, and using tools like this to tease out their experiences can be a helpful way of supporting them to explore and express their own feelings.

A: Um, yeah. At first it was a lot of like blocking other people out. And then, um, just like thoughts like, oh, you know, "They didn't care about me." But that probably came from blocking people out.

H: Yeah. Absolutely. And what other thoughts did you have*? (Validation; Patterns)*

This was a great insight that Abby had here (that she was thinking people don't care, but this was actually a result of her keeping them at bay). This was creating a cycle of isolation that could be a major part of her depressive patterns. I totally missed the gravity of this insight when she said it. I do notice that when a student is depressed, I find it harder to catch the full meaning of what they are saying because their tone is flat and I personally struggle to fully connect when I'm faced with that. You will find certain patterns are harder for you to connect to than others, and that's okay! Reflecting on how you feel when you're talking to students with different challenges can help you learn more about what you find the hardest so that you can support yourself with you are dealing with those issues in your class. If I was able to talk to Abby again, I would bring her insight up again (e.g., "You had such a great insight the other day that I only realized when I was reflecting on it after. You said that you think people don't care but they're just keeping their distance because you're blocking them out. Can you tell me more about that?").

A: Um, I don't know. They kind of just like came and went. Um, probably a lot of, like, "They don't understand me."

H: And why did you think they didn't understand you? *(Patterns)*

Asking "why" questions is a helpful tool to assist a student in going deeper with their reflection if they are giving short answers like this. It's important that your tone is warm and curious when asking these questions so the student doesn't feel put on the spot, but knows that you are genuinely interested in exploring their mind with them.

A: Um, well, I don't know. I think cuz with my parents, when you talk about some-thing, they would tell you things like you need to do. I mean, obviously they like said that I could have help from other people, but they always said it was mostly up to me. And, um, it was like a cycle. Like I would have to go and seek help, but I didn't have the motivation to seek help, which would just like, it would just like keep going.

H: And what did that feel like? That cycle . . . can you describe what it was like? *(Patterns; Feelings)*

I chose to focus on the *cycle* here, instead of asking questions about the family pattern that she shared because I really wanted her to reflect on *what specifically happens for her* in her depressed state, so that we could target the best ways to shift things for her. But it would have been great to also validate what she said about her family here (e.g., "I get why that didn't feel very supportive to you."). If I had the chance to talk to Abby again, I would explore her family's patterns more, so that she could see where some of her thoughts were coming from (e.g., "I would love to hear more about how you felt like you had to do it all on your own when you were growing up. Do you want to share that with me?").

A: Um, it was like, just repetitive. It's what my life has been feeling like since then. Just like, wake up, go to school, come home, do some chores, homework, go to sleep, and then just over and over again. But then once in a while maybe have like a birthday party or like you go on a holiday and you just go back to it.

H: And so do you feel like there's not that much joy or there hasn't been that much joy in your life? *(Feelings)*

A: Yeah, there's definitely moments, um, where I am very happy. Like, I'm not like sad all the time, especially with my friends. Like I'm rarely feeling down around them. Um, but if I'm like just alone and I'm just sitting and it's just quiet and nothing's going on, then I hate that. That's why I have, I have my music; I have like movies and stuff.

H: Yeah, definitely. And I think a lot of us can relate to that. It's hard. It's really hard. And it's almost like all the feelings come back when we're on our own. What is it like for you? What happens? Do you get anxious? Do you feel a rush of feelings? Do you feel really sad? *(Validation; Feelings)*

Here, I chose to validate Abby by speaking in "we" terms because I could tell she was feeling hesitant to share. I personally have never been diagnosed with depression, but I can definitely relate to times when I have felt overwhelmed, lonely, and down when I was on my own. This kind of language lets a student know that they are not alone in their experiences, which helps them feel safer to self-reflect. I also gave her a few *examples* of things she might have gone through in my question here, again to help her feel more validated in what was happening for her (e.g., if I said it first, then clearly, she's not the only one who has experienced it).

A: I mostly just feel like really sad. Like it used to be like a thought would come in and I would just be like, "Okay, yeah, cool." And then it started being like, a thought would come in and I would like dwell on it for a while until I got distracted. It was always like I would think about something until I got distracted.

H: And what kind of a negative thought? *(Patterns)*

A: Just like, um, well, I've always feared, probably like, feared the future and like what's in store and like how, like what am I gonna do when I leave school? Like, am I gonna finish school? Just people always say that I'm always like down to earth and in the moment, that's cuz I only feel safe when I'm in the now, in the present.

H: Yeah, I get that. And what do you feel when you start thinking about the future? What happens? *(Validation; Patterns)*

Abby shared a really powerful self-reflection here, so I knew that continuing to ask questions and validate her was the right approach. She wanted to self-reflect; she just needed a bit of guidance to get there!

A: I just get really nervous, really anxious. Just like, I don't want to think about it at all.

H: And what do you feel in your body? Do you get tense? *(Feelings)*

A: Um, I usually get really sweaty hands and, um, yeah. When I get really anxious, I just like freeze up and I just sit really still, I guess.

H: Definitely. And what kinds of thoughts come up? Like do you think, "I don't know what I'm gonna do, something bad might happen, I don't like the future"? Like what are your thoughts that come up? *(Patterns)*

A: Mostly just like, like a lot of, like "nothing will be the same." I think I've been thinking about that a lot. Like "nothing will be the same as like what's happening right now." Like there'll be things that are similar but like nothing will be the same.

H: And why does that feel scary for you? *(Patterns; Feelings)*

Again, I used the "why" question here to help her get to the heart of what her fears were. Sometimes we call the deepest fear that we hold about ourselves or the world a "core belief," and to be able to tap into that deep belief can really help in the self-reflection process. Once we name a belief, we can start to see what's driving it and what might help us to let it go.

A: Um, I think cuz of the fact that nothing can be the same. There's always an opportunity for something bad to happen and I won't be prepared for it.

H: Definitely. And have you had experiences, like when change was a negative thing for you? *(Patterns)*

Bingo! Because Abby identified a really deep fear ("I won't be able to cope with change."), I assumed that she must have had *an experience that caused her to believe this.* Most of our fears come from direct experience, and I was hoping that if I could help her identify what experiences she had that led to this belief, she could start to see that those experiences were in the past and didn't have to dictate her life in the present or future.

A: Um, I think when I was younger, changing schools, um, it was, I mean, it would've been hard for like any, anyone to change schools. I've been to about five schools, or six. Um, and then just like, just changing all the time and having to relearn names, having people learn my name, making new friends and like not getting bullied and stuff like that.

H: And so what did you start to associate with change? *(Patterns; Paradigm)*

I was trying to help her get to the bottom of the *connection* that her mind made between (1) the *experience of so many changes,* and (2) *her inability to cope.* That seemed to be the core of where her patterns were stemming from, and if she could really see this, it could lead to a big paradigm shift for her (e.g., "My thoughts come from something that happened and don't mean there's something wrong with me," which is what our mind assumes when there is no alternative presented). I could have also added a validation of her experience here (e.g., "That sounds hard."), which would have helped her feel even more seen and heard.

A: Just like bad things to happen.

H: And so do you think that's where your mind goes now? *(Patterns; Paradigm)*

A: Yeah, definitely. That's where it goes. Definitely.

H: And that's really normal. That's absolutely normal. That's a trauma response. That's what happens when our brain starts learning from our past experiences and then starts predicting more of the same. And what happens when your brain goes there? Cuz it's . . . we go into a little bit of a fight or flight response. Like we either freeze or we start lashing out and getting angry or we get really overwhelmed or we try to get out of the situation. What's your response when you start getting in that panic? *(Validation; Paradigm; Patterns)*

Here, I am giving her specific psychological knowledge to help with her paradigm shift, but I could have just as easily have said something simpler, for example, "It's really normal to have thoughts like that. How do you react when you have those thoughts?"

A: It always depends on like where I am. Most of the time I freeze and I just shut down completely. But if I'm with, um, people who I'm really comfortable around, like my friends, I will usually get pretty angry. But I've always been like a calm person. Like people need me to be calm. And so when I get angry, I immediately follow it with like a joke or something to like ease the tension.

H: Yeah, definitely. I get that. So do you feel a little bit like you have to kind of keep your emotions in? *(Validation; Paradigm; Patterns)*

What she just shared is really powerful. This is a people-pleasing pattern, which is often linked to depression (we *avoid our own feelings* in order to *influence the feelings of others*). I wanted to help her to reflect on where this comes from and how it contributes to her low mood (a further exploration of people-pleasing behaviors is found in Chapter 13, "Helping Students Who People-Please").

A: Yeah, like, um, at home, there would be an argument and I would, um, shut down or freeze up and get really angry, and I'd usually end up like in my room crying.

H: Definitely. I really get that. And so do you think that kind of, that freeze response or bottling things up, do you think that ends up making you feel more sad because you can't express what you're feeling? *(Validation; Paradigm; Patterns)*

> I was hoping that Abby could have the paradigm shift to see another layer of where her low mood might be stemming from—when she bottles up her feelings, this actually leads to *more of a sense of overwhelm when those feelings come rushing back in.*

A: Yeah, I think so.

H: And is it a little bit like when you are alone, that's when all those feelings come back? *(Patterns; Paradigm; Feelings)*

> Here, I was linking back to what she said earlier, and helping her to reflect on *why* she feels so overwhelmed with emotions when she is alone.

A: Yeah.

H: And when you're there, do you think about it or do you kind of try to push the feelings away? *(Patterns)*

A: Um, just instantly push it away. Just, yeah.

H: And why is that? *(Patterns)*

A: Um, cause I didn't want to deal with them.

H: And did you ever see anyone around you role modeling, you know, coping with feelings or expressing feelings or taking care of feelings? *(Patterns; Paradigm)*

> Again, here, I asked about what she might have seen around her that contributed to her beliefs. Emotional avoidance is so common in our culture, and I wanted Abby to feel less alone in her experience and see that this pattern is not her "fault."

A: I never saw people in my life like expressing their feelings and working through problems together.

H: Well, it makes sense that this is what you learned then! How did you see them dealing with feelings? *(Validation; Paradigm; Patterns; Feelings)*

A: It was a lot of like bottling it up until they lashed out at somebody.

H: Definitely. That's really common. And do you ever have any thoughts about what you might need to help you? *(Validation; Skill)*

> This seemed like the right place to shift the conversation to what might help Abby support herself. We had reflected a lot, and she had explored a lot of layers of what was happening in her mind, so we had lots to draw on in terms of identifying what might help her.

A: Um, not really. I've never really known what I wanted, but I think someone who just like cared.

H: Yes. Absolutely. And what do you think would happen if you had someone who cared? *(Skill)*

A: Um, I don't know.

H: I really get that. And that's what you deserve, absolutely. I really recommend seeing a psychologist. I can give you a recommendation for someone I know because it really does make a difference. And that's the whole purpose of what a psychologist is there for. It's just to see you, to know you, to help you work through some things, to help give you some tools. And that can be really, really important and powerful. What do you think about trying to reach out, and have those kinds of conversations? *(Validation; Skill)*

> After our conversation, I made a referral to a psychologist for Abby. This is a great example of how self-reflection really opens the door for identifying a skill. It was clear to both me and Abby that bottling up her feelings was part of the problem, so the skill of reaching out to someone she could speak to about those feelings became a logical response. Sometimes when we refer a student to a psychologist, they don't truly understand *how this will help them*. Having the self-reflective conversation first allows them to really see the purpose, which means they will be much more motivated to reach out and ask for help. It is a great practice to build up a list of practitioners or organizations that you can refer students to. Your school should have some ideas, and I encourage you also to do your own research. Knowing that you are putting your student in good hands is extremely helpful for your own stress levels (because you will worry less about their well-being).

A: I would do it. I know that a lot of people would never talk to people, but I feel like I like talking to people. Um, yeah. So I think it'd be good.

H: That's so great. And how do you feel when you take actions to help yourself? Like what's an example of some of the things that you've done already? *(Validation; Feelings; Power)*

> I wanted to explore things that Abby already does to help her feel more confident in her ability to take this next step of reaching out to a professional.

A: Um, a lot of like, yeah. Um, I don't know.

H: So what are some of the things you do that make you feel good? Like you do draw, do you listen to music? What are the things you do? *(Power; Skill)*

> When I get the "I don't know" response (which is so common with teenagers), I usually respond in this way—with examples that can trigger their memory.

A: Go for a walk. Yeah. I used to like walk every day for the past couple of years, but now I work and stuff, so it's only a couple of days. And then I listen to music every day. I draw sometimes.

H: That's great! And how do you feel when you're by yourself walking, listening to music? *(Feelings; Power)*

> I wanted Abby to *identify how she feels* when she uses her support strategies as a tool for motivating her to use them again in the future.

A: I just, yeah, I feel just whatever emotion that I'm playing in my head, like if I'm imagining some like heroic scenario from a movie, I feel brave and, yeah.

H: Yeah. And what's that like to kind of feel that bravery? *(Feelings; Power)*

A: It's, um, well, I like it because, you know, this is, it's my thing. Yeah.

H: Awesome. And then what about drawing? Do you ever feel unmotivated to draw? *(Patterns)*

> I asked if she feels unmotivated to draw because she mentioned she does it "sometimes," and she also mentioned earlier that she gets unmotivated to do things she loves. I wanted to explore this pattern to see if we could uncover any ways that she could support herself to keep doing the things she loves.

A: Yeah. Or just like, I just can't think of anything to draw. I'll just like, sometimes I'll just look at my old drawings, like, "I can't even draw. Why am I bothering?" And then one day, like I can't like draw what I see in my mind, so I'm like, "What's the point? I can't put my images down on paper or whatever, so I can't draw." But then, um, a wave of ideas will come in, like, "Oh, I can actually do that." And then I just feel proud of myself.

H: Definitely. And so how do you feel, how do you help yourself, encourage yourself to draw anyways when you are stuck? *(Power; Skill)*

A: Mostly thinking back to other times where I have drawn and been really happy. So like "If I draw, I'll feel good, so I just gotta do it."

H: Awesome. And then how do you feel? *(Feelings; Power)*

A: And then I just feel just better, I guess. Like reliving a moment I guess.

H: Definitely. And what are some other the things that you love to do? That make you feel really good? *(Skill; Power)*

A: Um, I love my friends and I like being with them, and I really love making them laugh. Like, yeah, I'm just like a comedic relief with them.

H: Yeah. Awesome. And why do you like that? What's that like for you? *(Feelings; Power; Skill)*

A: Um, I'm not sure why I like it. Like, um, if there's like something I remember about a day, it'll always be like something I said to make someone laugh or like, yeah, just stuff like that. Like I'll always try and figure out what a person's humor is. So in like tough scenarios or like if they're anxious and stressed, I can say something to easily lift them up.

H: That's awesome. That's a really cool skill. So do you have any aspirations to like be a comedian or would that be interesting for you? *(Validation; Paradigm)*

> With students in high school, I like to point out a shift in thinking about how they can use the *skills they learned by overcoming adversity* to help them in a career path. I was hoping this could give Abby a bit more excitement for the future.

A: Um, yeah, I would like to be a comedian cuz I know that comedians tell a lot of stories and I have lots of stories, but I'm really bad at public speaking. So, yeah, I really wanna be an animator or like animators on like YouTube who just like animate the stories of their life cuz I like drawing, I like telling stories and I like making people laugh.

H: What a great idea! And how do you feel when you think about that as a possibility for what you can do? *(Validation; Power; Feelings)*

A: Um, it's always like half of my brain would be saying like, "Just do it." Like, "People always start somewhere." Like when I first wanted to do it, I would scroll down to the bottom of my favorite, um, animators, like YouTube channels to their first video, and I'd be like, "That's what I do. Like, it's like, not good, but like they're doing it and look where they are now."

H: That's such a good point. And so how does that help you be motivated, like to take the first step? *(Validation; Power; Skill)*

> I wanted Abby to identify *one small, practical step* she could take to move forward, that she can use when she is feeling unmotivated.

A: Um, it usually just like, it comes randomly like, like I wanted to do this like a couple months ago, but I don't have, like the tools I need to do it, so I'm like just waiting for the right moment to do it.

H: And what's the first step you can take? *(Skill)*

A: Probably like, um, just practicing what you want to do and just like getting it how you want it. And then you start getting the things you need and I just like do something simple. Like I made something for the first time, like last year and it was like a real; it was like four seconds of animation and I was so proud of it. And I always show it to people cuz, like, it's the first thing I've ever done, so it is not gonna be good. But yeah.

H: That's awesome! And then how do you feel about yourself when you do that? *(Validation; Power; Feelings)*

A: I feel a lot better about myself. Like I am actually good at something.

H: Definitely. And when you think of that, do you feel worried about the future or is that something that actually makes you feel excited about the future? *(Paradigm; Pattern)*

> This was a great opportunity to bring us back to Abby's pattern, so she could *use a new perspective* to help with her fears for the future and change.

A: Um, I think, um, excited and worried at the same time. Like excited, like "I can do this." And worried like, "What if I can't do this?"

H: Totally. We're always gonna have those worries. But it sounds like you've found something that yeah, the worries are still there, but there's also that excitement. And that's key. So how do you feel, like when you think of yourself being an animator, having that job doing this thing that you love? *(Validation; Feelings; Paradigm; Power)*

A: Yeah. When I think of myself being an animator, I think of all the times I've seen people who I watch, um, like going to big events and meeting people and showing off their work. And I'm like, "I wanna do that. Like, I wanna go to these places. Uh, I wanna travel and meet people and show people what I do."

H: Amazing. And why do you wanna do those things? *(Feelings; Paradigm; Power)*

A: Um, I think I wanna do it partly cuz I want to inspire other people. And um, it's not as, um, like uplifting, but I want people to know who I am and like, leave an impression. Like when somebody says, "Who's your favorite animator?" They'll say me.

H: I love that aim. There's nothing wrong with wanting to impact people! I think you totally have the ability to get there. *(Validation; Paradigm; Power)*

> It's so important to validate *any reasons* that help a depressed student feel motivated. Even if it seems like a shallow motivation, this can lead to a more profound motivation later. They need something to pull them out of their low mood, and it doesn't matter what that motivation is, as long as it works for them.

This type of conversation will help your students become more *open* toward their feelings, and remember the *courage* they have to take steps to help themselves. This will help them *shift patterns of emotional avoidance* so that they can connect to the joy and excitement of their life again.

Related Chapters

Chapter 12, "Supporting Students Who Self-Harm"; Chapter 13, "Helping Students Who People-Please"; Chapter 15, "Guiding Students Who Are Caught in Addictive Patterns"

15 | Guiding Students Who Are Caught in Addictive Patterns

This chapter will give you strategies for supporting students who are caught in addictive cycles (e.g., can't put their phone down, consume large amounts of sugar, party regularly, binge drink, etc.). You will learn tools for having conversations that can help students become more *open* to their feelings so they have less of a need to escape them through their addictive patterns.

WHY Do Students Become Addicted?

Students struggle with addiction because they are trying to *avoid* an uncomfortable feeling (e.g., insecurity, loneliness, sadness), and they are using a *substance* or an *activity* to keep this uncomfortable feeling at bay. (See Chapter 11 for a deeper explanation of *avoiding* behaviors.) The reason addiction is so challenging is that when our brain finds a way to escape difficult emotions, we get a hit of *dopamine*, which makes us feel really powerful and uplifted in the moment. This dopamine release is such a stark contrast to the discomfort of our low feelings that every time we feel those feelings, our mind will crave the escape of the dopamine and will signal us to do whatever it takes to bring that "high" experience back. This process is especially enhanced in pre-teens and teenagers because their brains seek more dopamine and they are less averse to risk-taking (both of which are necessary for their phase of life, which requires great risks and lots of change). This is how really dangerous cycles can manifest. A student's mind can become so focused on seeking the rush of dopamine that everything else that matters to them can be pushed aside. This, in turn, can cause students to see themselves in a negative light because they know they are acting against their values, which brings more low feelings, and increased dopamine cravings. Students with addictive patterns can appear to not care about the things that matter (e.g., friends, schoolwork, social issues), and it's important to remember that they probably do care, but their mind is so focused on their cravings that their values are taking a back seat.

WHAT Can I Do to Help a Student Who Is in an Addictive Pattern?

Students who are addicted to substances or activities need to be guided to reflect on *what it is they are avoiding* and how they can make choices to *reconnect to who they truly are* and make decisions that are in line with that, even when they are in painful or uncomfortable experiences. It's completely fine if you don't feel comfortable diving into a deep conversation about addiction. If so, this might be a great time to refer your student to support staff who can help with this. Even if you just focus on *normalizing patterns of addiction* (which we all experience), this can be a great place to start getting more comfortable with the subject (e.g., "It's really common to use things to avoid what we're feeling, but it usually ends up making us feel worse."). As always, if you suspect a student is being harmed by an addictive pattern, always refer to a mental health practitioner for follow-up.

HOW Will I Have a Constructive Conversation with a Student Who Is in an Addictive Pattern?

In my conversation with Sam, he disclosed that he was addicted to marijuana and that he had been addicted to harder drugs in the past. I chose to explore his past experiences first in order to give him the space to reflect on his patterns in a less confronting way (the past is always less confronting than the present when we are self-analyzing!). This allowed Sam to reflect on where his patterns came from and what helped him to change them. These reflections led to the identification of some skills that Sam could use to help him with his current challenge. Even though we didn't get a chance to explore his current experience in this conversation, a seed was planted for a future conversation where the same framework could be applied and be more focused on what he is facing right now.

The following is a transcript of my conversation with Sam, showing how the six steps of the learning cycle, shown in Figure 15.1 (validation, patterns, feelings, paradigms, power, and skills), can be used with students who are caught in addictive patterns. See Chapter 11 for a deeper analysis of using these steps with students who are *avoiding* their emotions.

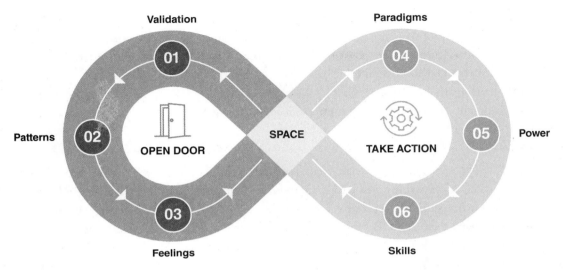

Figure 15.1 The learning cycle for building mental health skills.

Reproduced with permission from Open Parachute.

Interview with Sam (Age 18)

S: I struggle with addiction nowadays. I smoke weed. I'm chronic. Um, no hard drugs or anything like that. Uh, but I used to struggle a lot.

H: I'm glad to hear you're away from hard drugs! Do you want to tell me about how the addiction started for you? What was it that drew you to that? Cuz at the time, we don't realize what we're doing, right? *(Validation; Patterns)*

> I wanted to start the conversation with a validation about addictive patterns so that Sam knew I wasn't judging him, and I understood that there were reasons he got into this cycle. I used a few questions in a row here, which was partly to give Sam a few options of how he could answer (sometimes, this can help a student if they are not sure how to answer). However, sometimes too many questions at once can be off-putting for a student, so it's not always the best approach!

S: Well, it was, it was like these people, I was in this group, um, I was a part of this classroom and, you know, I didn't really fit in with all these people. And it was like, I wanted to fit in. I wanted to, you know, be friends with everyone. . . . And eventually I got asked, "Hey, do you want to come blaze with us?" So I was like, "Okay." I went and I smoked with them, and at the time, it was just kind of like, "Okay, cool, I'm chilling, like I'm hanging out, like I'm wanted here."

H: Yeah, that's really how it starts isn't it? We're using the substance to get a need met. When did you realize that it was a problem? *(Validation; Patterns)*

> I used "we" here because I can relate to this pattern. This is a great way to validate students without disclosing anything, just letting them know that we *get how it feels*. We can probably all relate to the pattern of emotional avoidance in one way or another (e.g., you might distract yourself from difficult emotions with work, relationships, food, social media, etc.). Drawing on these feelings helps students feel *less alone* in their experiences, so they are more able to self-reflect.

S: Well, eventually that thought process kind of changed and the thought was, "Oh, yeah, cool. I want to hang out with these people." But the underlying thought was, "Oh, yeah, let's go smoke weed in a group." And when you're thinking about going and hanging out with people and then you put something above them, if you put a reason to have to go hang out with the people, then you shouldn't be hanging out with those people because obviously that's not genuine and you're taking something from them that you probably shouldn't be.

H: I love the way you put that. That's so powerful. We're just in it and we just wanna feel something different. We want to feel like we fit in. And so then what happened? How did that then lead to, you know, more partying or more drugs? *(Validation; Patterns)*

S: Well, it went from okay, we were smoking and, you know, doing drugs after school and maybe like a little bit during school. Well, now, every day we're linking up and we're drinking and my friends are drinking and driving. And then the next day it was like, wow, now they're taking acid and they're driving and running around graffitiing like cars and houses. And it was just like, it just felt like all of it digressed . . . like it's easy to laugh something off. It's easy to laugh something off until somebody gets hurt or something happens. . . .

H: Totally. And so did you have an experience where something bad happened? *(Validation; Patterns)*

> Sometimes just a simple word like *totally* or even nodding can indicate that we understand where they are coming from, and we are *accepting them,* even if we don't agree with their actions. I also wanted to ask about a specific situation so that Sam and I could explore his experiences and find exactly what skills he could use to support himself.

S: There was, um, there was this one time, so I smoked, it was in winter. I smoked two bowls and I was throwing up in a toilet for like an hour and I basically passed out on the toilet. Because my lungs weren't able to handle that or nothing like that. It should have been a sign that I shouldn't been smoking. And my friends ended up going, "Okay, well, we gotta go, we gotta go. So let's pick 'im up." They carried me about a block or two and they're like, "Okay, well, you know, he's throwing up. We can't keep carrying him around, so we're just gonna leave him." And I didn't have a jacket or anything like that, so I was just left on the side of the road. And I was lucky enough to have someone, you know, come pick me up, throw a blanket over me and like call the ambulance, call my mother, all that. And you know, I was okay, but you know, I could've been left out there and you know, people could've just been like, "Oh, that's a crack head," you know. And like, you know, I could've lost fingers or something like that. You know, you just don't know. . . . It's just, yeah, it's brutal. It's just wild. It's wild.

H: Wow, that sounds really hard. How old were you at the time? *(Validation; Patterns)*

S: Uh, I was 15 or 16, I think it was. Yeah.

H: And how did you feel when you woke up and kind of realized that this is what your friends did? *(Feelings)*

> I wanted to explore Sam's feelings about this negative outcome from doing drugs to see if we could uncover his *motivation to change* his past addictive patterns (which could help him change his current patterns too).

S: Oh, I was like, "Oh, yeah, like F this person, F this person." Like I wasn't cool with it. People were like, "Oh, yeah, I'm so sorry, blah, blah, blah." And I was like "You know, don't hit my line. Don't ring me up. Don't talk to me." But like, it's so easy to forgive and forget. I guarantee you that the next two, three days I was smoking with the same group of people, like hands down. And that's wild.

H: Yeah, it's crazy how we just let go of what matters, hey? Why do you think you just let it go so fast? *(Validation; Patterns)*

> Again, talking in "we" terms helped Sam feel like I was *joining* him in this reflection, not *judging* him in it. (I have also definitely made choices that are not in line with my values, and I was drawing on that experience, even if for me that didn't relate to drugs specifically.)

S: Like, because you can think something, but you can also be addicted to something and you can decide that your philosophies and what you believe in are nothing compared to your wants. And that's what people do all the time. They'll just throw away their beliefs, their philosophies because, "Oh, I want to drink, or I want to get a little high."

H: Totally, totally. And you speak so well about this and you know, I love what you're saying about like you trade your own morals or your own beliefs for something. Do you know what you were trading? Like were you trading your sense of, like, respect or boundaries with friends for, you know, the desire to be, you know, a part of the group or the desire to feel just, you know, get high or whatever it was. What were you trading? *(Validation; Patterns; Paradigm)*

> Sam already had a great deal of insight into this, so I was able to just probe into what he already said to go deeper with his understanding. If he hadn't brought this up, then the focus of the conversation would have been to help him make this paradigm shift to see that he was sacrificing his values in order to fit in.

S: I think what I actually gave up was friends and, um, my social standing, the way that people viewed me because at first people thought that I was a pretty cool person, but after a while people just kind of thought I was a bum and which I was, you know, like I definitely was. I don't think for most of the year I spent, I probably spent less than $300 on any other person. I probably spent less than $300 on myself that year. And like, you know, I was smoking every day, like twice, three times a day.

H: Yeah. It's so hard to see those patterns in ourselves, hey? But it's amazing that you have this insight! I'm so grateful for you sharing this with me. I know this from my own experience too. It's actually really common, it's like it's normalized to treat each other badly. *(Validation; Patterns)*

I could tell that Sam was feeling uncomfortable with this self-reflection, and he was sharing some really powerful insights, so I wanted to make sure that he knew I was *with him* in this. It can be easy to feel worse about ourselves when we start seeing our patterns, but actually seeing ourselves clearly is a massive step forward, so I wanted Sam to really feel that. I could have also explained this more explicitly to Sam (e.g., "Seeing yourself clearly is a really important skill that really helps us make changes in our lives, even though it can feel pretty awful in the moment"), and that would have helped him feel even more validated.

S: Yeah. Basically. No, it is, it really is. In a society where it's like, full of competition, it is super like common, or super praised upon almost to be pushy. I mean, it's true for every gender, but I think guys especially experience this, all this pressure to be like manly and to be tough and, and basically to be an asshole. It's like "Chin up, you know, hold your own, don't talk to other people. You talk to other people, they're gonna hurt you."

H: You speak about this so well. That really ties into addiction. It's like something's hurting in us. Something's hard, and because of society, we don't understand the human mind, at all. So none of us know what to do with that. So all we're doing is avoiding. Most people are walking around just avoiding. You obviously have an incredible amount of insight and you have made changes in your life. Like, how did you start to realize and make those changes? *(Validation; Patterns; Paradigm; Power)*

Talking about the cultural patterns that lead to our own personal patterns is a really great paradigm shift for students, so they can reflect on the fact that these patterns don't say anything bad about them *as a person* (we are all a product of our environment).

S: Basically, I just lost and lost and lost until I realized that it's not everyone else that's, you know, causing me to lose people. It's more so that, you know, I keep making the same or similar mistakes. I keep pushing people away and being like, "Okay, well it's their fault." You know, "They just don't want to be around me," or this and that. And not being like, okay, well maybe "What did I do that irked them or made them not want to be around me?" Like, and that reflection alone, is the only thing that really, I think that without being able to reflect, I wouldn't have been able to get here.

H: Amazing. And so did you consciously sit down and come to these realizations? Like do you have a practice where you think of things, or how does it happen for you? *(Validation; Power; Skill)*

> I wanted Sam to identify *exactly what he did* in the past to help himself make a change, so that he could use the same skill in the present.

S: It's more so like if you are doing things and you are self-sabotaging yourself and sabotaging others around you and just futzing around being stupid, and then other people around you start doing the same things that you do and you start seeing them reflecting that, the way that you used to act being like, okay, wow. Like people around me really look at my actions, and be like, "Damn, he does that. I should go do that too." It's like, "Well, shit, I have to kick up. I have to start, you know, being better."

H: Yeah, absolutely. Seeing your actions reflected in other people makes it a lot clearer! And so do you remember what triggered you starting to change and starting to care and starting to notice, "Hey, this isn't good for me"? *(Validation; Power; Skill)*

> I kept probing here because I wanted Sam to identify a *specific skill* that he used.

S: Uh, I can't think of like a key time, but I remember I was, I was sitting alone at a bus stop. I ran away from home cuz I was having a really bad time and I biked for like several hours. I didn't know where I was. I just biked in a straight line and I was sitting and it was raining. I was just kind of thinking and I was like, you know, like "In the past two years I've been like doing so poorly." And like all my grades were poor and I just kept making all the wrong mistakes. So I was like, you know, like I was literally like, I might as well walk into the street and lay down. It's dark enough that a car could run me over and that would be that. And I was like, like I might as well. And I sat there for like several hours and like, I was sitting there and like eventually I was just like, you know, "Thinking like this, being up in the rain is just self-destructive." Like "I could be doing something better with my time. Like even sleeping might be better than sitting out here just telling myself that I'm a piece of garbage." So I went home and I went to bed and like in the morning I wrote this note and I have this note stickied on my desk and it's a quote from a movie, I think it was, uh, Samuel L. Jackson who did the quote.

H: That's really powerful. Sometimes it has to get really bad for us to realize that we deserve better. I'm really glad to hear that you aren't in that place any more. So how did that quote help you? *(Validation; Patterns; Paradigm; Skill)*

> I wanted Sam to know that I saw his pain and also that I saw the effort it took on his part to make changes. This is a really powerful realization that he shared, a huge paradigm shift from *feeling bad about himself* to *wanting to make better choices*, and I wanted to honor that, as well as help him figure out a skill that he could repeat in the future. A further note here— Sam shared a past suicidal thought, and so later on in the conversation I circled back and asked if he had any of those same thoughts now to see if he was in danger of hurting himself. He said "no," but I referred him to a psychologist anyway so that he could be supported with everything he had faced in the past and was facing now.

S: I don't know, just like looking at that, like, it's just thinking about that note, it's just like every morning if you wake up and you're like, "What did I do yesterday that I can do today better?" And you pursue that regardless of if it helps anyone. If it doesn't help anyone, you're still pushing to be better. Just as long as you live out what you are, you know, pushing for, or even if it doesn't affect anyone, as long as you know that you are better, you are better. And that's where it starts.

H: Amazing. And it's incredible that you made those changes in your life. That's such a powerful thing to realize! So how do you feel now about not being in that party scene anymore? *(Validation; Feelings; Paradigm; Power)*

> Again, Sam already had such powerful insights, so I was trying to help him explore *how good it feels to make those changes* so that this could motivate him to use this perspective with his current challenge of marijuana use.

S: Um, not being in the party scene is like, it's nice, it's good because, you know, it's peaceful.

H: Totally. And how do you think those same skills could help you with your weed addiction now? *(Skill)*

S: Yeah, I probably need to think about that more. . . .

The conversation turned to a few other things here, and we never got to explore this more deeply. This will, of course, often happen in conversations with students! The great thing is that the seed was planted. This gave Sam something to think about and reflect on. If I had the opportunity to talk to him again, I would simply pick back up by saying something like "I loved all the insights you shared the other day. It would be awesome to see how those insights could keep helping you now . . . have you had any more reflections since we last spoke?"

This type of conversation will help your students notice their patterns of *avoidance* in the form of addiction and learn to be *courageous* in *opening up* to the feelings that they are seeking to escape from, so they can learn to make choices that are more in line with who they want to be as a person.

Related Chapters

Chapter 10, "Talking to Students about Unhealthy Eating Habits"; Chapter 12, "Supporting Students Who Self-Harm"; Chapter 14, "Encouraging Students Who Are Depressed or Apathetic"; Chapter 21, "Helping Students Stand Up to Peer Pressure"; Chapter 22, "Supporting Students Who Are Bullied"

16 | Communicating with Students Who Have Faced Loss

This chapter will give you strategies for supporting students who are grieving or who have lost someone they care about. This chapter deals with loss by suicide, which is sadly relatively common, and is, of course, an incredibly challenging experience for educators as well. The focus of this chapter is to give you tools to help students open up to their feelings of loss so that these feelings don't get bottled up and become more intense and overwhelming.

WHY Do Students Struggle to Cope with Loss/Grief?

Everyone struggles with grief, but young people can be especially impacted by losing someone because they are less familiar with the feelings of loss. One of the most damaging outcomes of the *patterns of emotional avoidance* in our culture is that we as adults don't want to say things that upset children, so we don't bring up topics like grief even if we know a student is grieving. But the reality is that this only reinforces the pattern of emotional avoidance in students, which is already a very typical response to grief. The emotions are so intense that a student's mind is trying to do whatever they can to *get away from these feelings*. (See Chapter 11 for a deeper explanation of *avoiding* behaviors.) The more they avoid their feelings of grief, the more intense and confusing these feelings become because their mind has less and less perspective on *why they feel the way they do*. For example, many students will keep themselves distracted all day so they don't notice their feelings of sadness. These feelings then build up, and when they are in a quiet room going to bed at night, all of their feelings will come rushing back in. There are so many emotions coming at them at once that it's too overwhelming to understand what each one means. This adds confusion, which makes the experience even more intense. Often students who are grieving have big angry or overwhelmed reactions, and often they will appear completely "fine." It's important to remember that every student will be impacted by losing someone, whether they are showing it on the surface or not. As always, if you are concerned that a grieving student is in danger of harming themself, always refer to a mental health professional and encourage students to do the same. It is often very hard to see the signs, so any hunch should be followed up immediately. In addition, if you are supporting students through a loss that you have also experienced (e.g., the loss of another student), it is vital that you are also supported to care for your own feelings as well.

WHAT Can I Do to Help a Student Who Is Struggling with Grief?

Students who are struggling with grief need to be given a safe space to find the *courage to open up* to their true feelings so that those feelings can *move through them* rather than staying bottled up and coming out in other ways (e.g., self-harm, people-pleasing, addiction, or any other pattern that arises as a result of emotional avoidance).

HOW Will I Have a Constructive Conversation with a Student Who Is Grieving?

I knew going into my conversation with Casey that there had been a suicide at her school in the recent past, which came after a devastating forest fire that caused many people in her small farming community to lose their houses, jobs, and livestock. I chose this interview because student suicide is such a challenging (and devastatingly common) experience to deal with. The steps are similar for any loss, so this conversation can be used as a guide for losses that are not a result of suicide as well. Sometimes students bring up these challenges directly, and sometimes they are waiting for a place where they are brought up for them. If a student doesn't feel safe enough to speak about the situation directly, we can also have these conversations by talking about "hard things" and exploring the same steps. During our conversation, Casey was able to reflect on the way she felt as a result of her experience of loss and how she was able to break her patterns of emotional avoidance in order to begin the healing process. If she had been less far along in this journey of reflection and healing, I would have focused on just making a safe space to reflect on any parts of this that she wanted to speak about. Sometimes we just need to plant the seed that we are here and that it's okay to talk about these things, and that opens the door for a student to have a deeper conversation when they are ready.

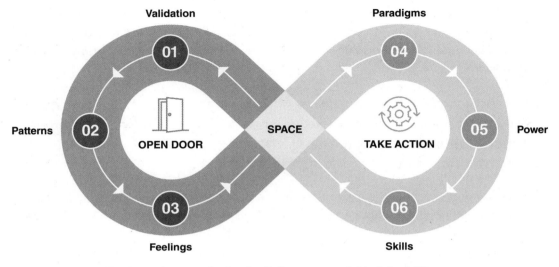

Figure 16.1 The learning cycle for building mental health skills.

Reproduced with permission from Open Parachute.

The following is a transcript of my conversation with Casey, showing how the six steps of the learning cycle, shown in Figure 16.1 (validation, patterns, feelings, paradigms, power, and skills), can be used with students who are struggling with a loss See Chapter 11 for a deeper analysis of using these steps with students who are *avoiding* their emotions.

Interview with Casey (Age 14)

C: Um, at our school, there was a guy who took his own life.

H: Oh, gosh that's so hard. I'm so glad you brought that up, I would really like to hear your experience of that. Do you remember when you found out about it? *(Validation; Patterns)*

> I asked how Casey found out about the situation as a way to begin speaking about her experience of it. Usually, the moment we find out about a sudden loss is a powerful memory, so it can be a good place to start the self-reflection process.

C: I remember coming to school, getting off the bus, and the teachers were just, they were all sad. We didn't know, nobody had any idea about what was wrong, why the teachers were acting like that. None of us had any idea. And the kids that did have an idea, they didn't want to tell anyone. And then the teachers brought us into a classroom at like nearly the end of the day cuz they thought we should know, like we should find out why they were all acting a bit strange. And they told us and everyone was shocked.

H: Yeah, I bet. And what were some of the thoughts that you had during that time? *(Validation; Patterns)*

Asking about *thoughts* and *feelings* is another way to help focus the reflection on how the student is impacted by their experiences of loss.

C: Um, confused cuz soon as they said his name, I thought "that can't be right." Like he was such a happy person at school. I have older siblings who were friends with him. Um, as soon as they told us, I immediately just thought of like the people who were real close with him, like my siblings and people in that room at the time, like classmates who were close with him, people who played sports with him, did after school activities with him, things like that.

H: Yeah . . . It's so hard. And how did you feel about that? *(Validation; Feelings)*

It is very common for students to appear happy or completely fine before taking their own life. Sometimes this is because they have made the decision to end their life and are relieved that their pain will be over soon, and sometimes this is because they are simply very good at hiding (avoiding) their feelings. I didn't address this here, but it would have been a great opportunity to let Casey know that this is a common pattern. Understanding that suicidal thoughts can be completely hidden can help students feel less guilt about not being able to stop a suicide from occurring.

C: It was a big shock and pretty much nearly everyone like was in tears, and like turning up to school and just seeing the teachers in tears in hallways. And then if a student came around the corner, they would try and hide it from us. Like they didn't want us to see them crying, like they would try and hide it. And then when you found out you didn't really want to go anywhere except with your friends, so you're like kind of just stuck and like not sure what to do anymore. Yeah, because you're not, as a kid, you're not really exposed to that as much.

H: Yeah, it's really intense and overwhelming. So why do you think that this boy was so down? What do you think was happening for him? *(Validation; Paradigm)*

I chose to ask about why this boy took his own life because when it comes to suicide, the unresolved question of "why someone would do that" can be really unsettling for students. If they can understand on some level *why a person would take their own life*, this can help them feel less scared about this happening again. We don't have to have an answer for this "why" question, but simply reflecting that *they must have been in a great deal of pain that they didn't know how to deal* with is a powerful paradigm shift.

C: A lot of people did speculate because it was pretty much after the fires. He worked for, or volunteered for like a firefighting crew, um, forestry, I think it was. And I think he might have been exposed to a lot of things like that [people losing their houses and livestock], and maybe it just pushed him over the edge, but he was too good at hiding it, and so, yeah. Um, yeah, it's not like good to hide that because like people can't, if you are good at hiding it, people can't tell what you're going through and it'll be harder and harder and harder to seek help.

H: Absolutely. And so what was the impact of hearing about this, hearing about someone your age or a little bit older that has taken their life. Like what are the thoughts and feelings that come up for you when you hear about this? *(Patterns; Feelings)*

C: Um, it just makes you really like paranoid and it's always in the back of your head, like whenever you're talking to someone or someone's feeling down, or even if they're feeling happy, you just think, "Are they actually happy?" Or, um, like you're always paranoid about how someone is really feeling.

H: Mm-hmm. Absolutely. Yeah. *(Validation)*

Sometimes just validating what a student is saying and pausing is enough to help them keep exploring their thoughts.

C: So it just sticks there for ages and ages, and you just think, "Why would they do it? How would they even know how to do it?" And like "What's going through their head?"

H: Absolutely. And one of the big things that comes up with suicide is that feeling of hopelessness, feeling like it's never gonna get better and, like, you know, when you are hearing about someone doing that, it makes you feel hopeless. When I feel, when I hear about that, it makes me feel down. Did you feel that at all when you heard about what happened? *(Validation; Feelings)*

> This was a true statement about what I was feeling in the moment, and I wanted to share it as a way to make it safe for Casey to explore any similar feelings that she felt as well. I often try to open the door to an exploration of feelings by sharing my own in this way. As long as you are not taking over the conversation with your own story, *but using your experience as a way to encourage further inquiry*, this can be a really helpful tool.

C: Yeah. Well, you're just like, "Oh, could I have helped this person?" Like at the funeral. Because you're so quiet, your thoughts are just going and going. So you're thinking, "Oh, could I have helped him or could I like have found someone to help him or something?" So, yeah.

H: And that's a really, really normal reaction. And so what are the ways that you help yourself in this? How do you, how do we come out of it? What are the things you do maybe to connect with people or speak about what you're feeling? *(Validation; Skill; Power)*

> Giving Casey the space to say these thoughts aloud and letting her know that they are *normal thoughts to think* is a really powerful tool to encourage her to open up and reflect about what she's feeling to other people in her life as well. This also gave me an opening to ask about a skill—because we had identified one of her patterns, now we could identify a skill to help with that pattern.

C: After a while I did like start opening up like about death and all that, like just because a few of my family did pass away, like after, because of old age and stuff. And when I talk to my cousin, we just like let everything out. Like we'll be on the phone for a while, but that's because he's like grown up and he's an adult now, so he's like going through a lot more than I have.

H: That's really good that you have someone to talk to about it. That's a really brave thing to do. What does it feel like to share? *(Validation; Power; Feelings)*

> I asked about Casey's experiences of sharing her feelings so that she could reflect on how helpful this action is, which would hopefully motivate her to do this more in the future.

C: Yeah, it's good to like, just get it out because it is hard with like immediate family, the ones you live with, because they'll like check in 24/7 if you do tell 'em something. Whereas if you can do it over the phone or like talk to another family member, um, you can just let it out and they'll like check up on you like once a day or something like not, come into your room all the time, say, "Are you okay?" And that, and you know, you can trust them and like feel safe with them being your family still.

H: Yeah, I get that. So, and what does it feel like when you let it out? Or what is, what is the impact on you? *(Power; Skill; Feelings)*

C: You get a lot better night's sleep and like a better mindset during the day because you've been able to let it out and just have a clear head and not have to worry about it for so much longer. And just have a happy day and a good day.

H: Awesome. So it impacts how you feel about the day. It impacts your thoughts. What else does it impact when you're able to sort of share? *(Power; Skill)*

C: You get better learning out of it. Just being able to come to school with a clear head and like not have to worry as much about it and like just have a good mindset on the day. You get your learning a bit better. Whereas if it was just pondering in your head, you weren't focused on work or anything and you could fail some subjects, which is not good.

H: Absolutely. And did that happen for you? Did you struggle to concentrate at school? *(Patterns)*

> Often students will talk about patterns in other people or in the third person, and when this happens, I try to bring the conversation back to a personal reflection so that we can explore *exactly what happens for this student* and therefore, what can specifically help them.

C: Yes. I was like, "Oh, I can't concentrate," and I, like, had to leave to have drink breaks or go to the bathroom or something, and not be able to concentrate. It got better through the year, but it was still hard sometimes, like if it was ever brought up or like people would say like, "Oh, it's been four months without you," and it would like click back into your head. So it'd be like hard after that for a bit.

H: Yeah, absolutely. And when you talk about it, it's a bit of a weird question, but like, what happens? Like, cuz almost when we don't talk about it, the feelings are still there, it's still bottled up. But when we talk about it, it's like, it's not that it's not sad, it's not that we don't feel it, but it's almost like it can move through us. What's your experience with that? *(Power; Feelings)*

> I said "It's a bit of a weird question" because it was the third time I asked basically the same thing, and I didn't want her to think that she wasn't answering it "correctly." I kept asking because I wanted to lead Casey into a deeper exploration of *what actually happens in her feelings, in her body, and in her experience* when she speaks about her feelings, so that she could identify an even deeper way that her actions helped her.

C: Yeah, so, um, [my cousin] always makes me look on the bright side of it and like, helps me look on the bright side . . . and sometimes he would make like jokes about his ones that he's had to deal with, like, just make me feel better or something

H: Absolutely. And how do we look at it on the bright side? Is it that we look at like, you know, the connection we have with them or do we look at what we can learn from it or we look at, "Oh, it brought us closer as a community." Like what is the way that we can look at it in a positive way? *(Paradigm; Skill)*

> Casey didn't go into the deeper exploration of her feelings that I was fishing for, but she went into her own exploration of what helps her, so I followed that train of thought instead. This was a fantastic opportunity to explore the *change in how she was thinking about the loss,* which is a really important part of healing.

C: Yeah, like the community's a lot closer, and yeah, the connections and stuff and like all the good memories and just joking about it sometimes. Like, it's definitely the humor has changed in our school. Like there's a lot more people like talking about it now, like, not as much when it first happened, but a lot more now. So, yeah, it's finally opening up to like, "Oh, people will talk about it now." And that helps when everyone's kind of talking, so you can feel like you can open up, so yeah. Not hide anymore.

H: And then what's the overall impact of that? *(Power; Paradigm)*

C: Everyone's gotta clear mind, good learning, especially for the older grades, because he was in a bit of an older grade to us, so they can finally have a clear mind and focus on school because it's their time at school that they want to focus on.

H: Awesome. And what about for you? *(Power; Paradigm)*

> Again, I was bringing it back to Casey's *personal experiences* here, so that we could reflect on what could help her, specifically.

C: Um, stress-free, you just, the weight gets lifted off your shoulders. You can concentrate more at school. And around friends. Um, yeah.

H: Absolutely. And did you have any experiences where you didn't want, like you were nervous to talk about it and had to kind of overcome that? *(Patterns; Power)*

> I was hoping that Casey could identify her own strength in breaking her pattern of emotional avoidance by talking about her challenges, *even when it was hard*, so that she could trust in her ability to do this again in the future.

C: Um, as like people first started getting the thought out of their head, you didn't really want to bring it back up in front of people. Like you didn't wanna talk about it, cuz you kind of just wanted to forget about it altogether. You didn't wanna bring it up and make everyone feel sad, but you didn't want to keep it bottled up at the same time.

H: And that's so huge cuz that's what keeps this whole cycle going, doesn't it? Nobody wants to bring it up. And even with this, like there are schools that are like, "Oh, let's not talk about teen suicide in the school cause we're gonna upset people." But what good does that do? So to you, what is the importance of talking about it? Even if it upsets people? What's the benefit of talking about it? *(Validation; Patterns; Power)*

> It is an excellent practice within a school setting to create spaces for students to speak openly about suicide or any other mental health concerns. This could be a specific room, or a group that meets regularly, or a practitioner coming into every classroom to have these conversations on a regular basis. These topics are very stigmatized, and unless we actively bring them up, most students will not share their feelings with anyone. The more we talk about it, the fewer students will suffer in silence.

C: Um, to normalize, like people talking to each other, opening up to people you trust, like not keeping it bottled up cuz that's what it leads back to those kind of extremes. Taking your own life. So the main thing is to definitely have someone in your life that you can open up to talk to.

H: You're so right. So, is there anything else you do to help yourself when you're feeling down about this? *(Skill)*

C: I definitely, like, after it happened, I was up at the pool like 24/7, like, in the afternoons, I would stay there till like seven o'clock or till it closed. Just swimming and chatting with people up there. And then I would like make myself go to school so I could be around my friends. And it would make me feel like good because after it you feel dull. You don't wanna go to school, you don't wanna wake up in the morning. But like having the mindset that, "Oh, I'll see my friends, yes, that's a good idea." Is just like a good situation to get yourself into. Like now it's a good thing going to school because you see your friends, you have good times and laughs. Like I think I laugh most of the day at school.

H: That's awesome. And that's so important. Right? And that's what we have to do to get ourselves out of that depressed state. We kind of have to push ourselves. Do you ever consciously notice, like changing your thoughts, like thinking a thought like, "I need to get up, I need to, you know, focus on something positive, or I need to let myself feel sad." Like you do anything where you kind of are sort of talking to yourself or changing your thoughts? *(Validation; Power; Skill)*

> I asked about Casey choosing her thoughts because I could tell she had, in fact, done this, but she might not be conscious of the fact that she had. *Identifying this as a skill* will help Casey make use of this skill again in the future if she is feeling unmotivated or low.

C: Sometimes, not really. You're just like in the moment.

H: Yeah. Cool. And what about the importance of letting yourself feel sad when things are hard? What's your experience with that? *(Feelings; Skill; Paradigm)*

> Casey didn't take this reflection where I was hoping she would, so I changed tacks and asked instead about the paradigm shift of not blocking out our feelings, but just letting ourselves feel them (as a tool for processing grief).

C: Um, it's just another way of letting it out. Like you can let your sadness out and try to forget about it and then be happy. Like, let it out to your friends and be happy with them. Or if you're by yourself you can just, you can be sad, like, yeah.

H: And why is it important to let yourself be sad? *(Feelings; Power; Paradigm)*

> I wanted Casey to identify why *she* thought this was an important skill, so that she felt motivated to use it again in the future.

C: Oh, cuz you can't be happy all the time. Sometimes you just have to be sad, but it's not a bad thing.

H: Yeah, absolutely. And are there benefits to letting those feelings be there? *(Feelings; Power; Paradigm)*

C: Um, it just like reassures other people, like, um, some people may think, "oh, no one probably wants to hear it. Or like, oh, no one really cares." But if you are like sad, they might start opening up because people won't want to open up to make other people sad or trigger other people. So, it's almost like we give them permission. We say "I'm sad." Then they're like, "Oh, okay. I can be sad too." Like you wouldn't judge them or anything because it's just a normal thing.

H: That's so amazing. You're exactly right. Wow. What a gift to give other people! *(Power; Paradigm)*

This was such a great reflection, and one that came entirely from Casey, so I wanted to make a point of validating her insight and encouraging her to keep thinking in this way. If I saw Casey regularly, I would bring this up again many times, just to check in and make sure she always knew that she could talk to me (e.g., "I am so grateful that you felt comfortable talking to me about your experiences with losing your classmate. I am always here if you want to talk," or "How are you feeling about everything after our conversation?").

This type of conversation will help your students *open up to their feelings of grief*, and reflect on their own courage in being able to do so. This will, in turn, help them shift patterns of *emotional avoidance* so that they can *move through* all of their feelings as they continue to arise.

Related Chapters

Chapter 12, "Supporting Students Who Self-Harm"; Chapter 13, "Helping Students Who People-Please"; Chapter 14, "Encouraging Students Who Are Depressed or Apathetic"; Chapter 15, "Guiding Students Who Are Caught in Addictive Patterns"

Following/Leadership (Remembering Identity)

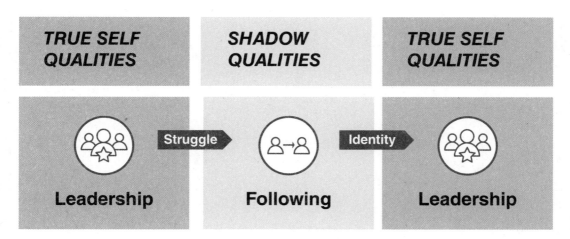

TRUE SELF QUALITIES	SHADOW QUALITIES	TRUE SELF QUALITIES
Leadership	**Following**	**Leadership**

Reproduced with permission from Open Parachute.

This section will provide conversation tips for students who have patterns of not listening to their own internal compass, who *follow others* (e.g., through peer pressure, social media, or gang involvement), who *follow external pressures instead of being attuned to others* (e.g., through violations of consent), or who have been made to feel "less than" and have *internalized the negative messages they have received from others* (e.g., through prejudice, gender norms, bullying, or body shaming). You will learn tools for helping students who are caught in these patterns to find their internal capacity for *leadership* by reminding them of their individual *identity* and ability to make their own choices.

17 | Finding the Words with Students Who Are in *Following* Behavior Patterns

Leadership is a skill that we are all trying to encourage in students. We know that young people have the capacity to create incredible change in the world. They often see things more clearly than we do as adults, and youthful energy has repeatedly led the world to a much healthier, saner, and more compassionate place. Watching one of your students become a leader in their peer group or community is one of the most rewarding experiences because you know that the values you have helped instill in them are having a ripple effect that touches so many others.

The reason a young leader is so powerful is because youth is often a time of great insecurity. The developing mind is primed to focus on *fitting in with their peer group* because, from a survival standpoint, their same-aged peers are the ones who will be available to assist them throughout their whole lives long after their parents and mentors are gone. This hardwired psychological tendency starts to cause problems when students feel strong feelings that overwhelm them (which is, of course, very common in childhood and adolescence). They do not yet have the foundation in themselves to know these feelings will pass or to have confidence in their own intuition. There is a sense of instability, and during times of instability, we all seek external sources of support.

This is why students are always looking to their friends, partners, and social media influencers to indicate the "right" actions to take. They follow the loudest voices because this *loudness* feels like *strength* when we doubt our own internal resources. Following someone who appears very confident *gives them the feeling of confidence* (even though that confidence is not their own). And this feels much better in the moment than their own experience of insecurity. This is how students learn to stop listening to their own intuition and focus instead on the guidance of others.

The challenge is that the feelings these students are experiencing are actually what *tells them what is okay and not okay for them*. So eventually, they become unable to think for themselves or even know what they like and what they don't like. This is why a group of students could be standing around watching a peer being cruel and unkind to another student and *do nothing*. In those moments, they will feel the sadness, anger, uncertainty, and confusion that naturally arise when we see someone being mistreated, and the *instinct to stop them* will naturally be present. But the second that instinct arises, their brain silences it because they have established a pattern of looking *outward* rather than *inward* for guidance. When this pattern is in full force in a student's life, they will always go along with the crowd, become susceptible to peer pressure, and not stand up for what they know is right. In order to change this, they need to strengthen their own *identity* so they can uncover their capacity for leadership. Their ability to make their own choices *based on their own internal compass*. Even when it goes against the group norm.

In general, what these students need is to be encouraged *to listen to themselves*. If you don't have the chance to engage in a direct conversation with students who are *following* their peers, you can simply focus on sending the message to your whole class that *they know what's best for them*. If they learn to listen to their internal voice, that is all they will ever need. You can give examples from your own life where this is true, and also point to other young people in the world who have accomplished great acts of leadership (e.g., Malala Yousefzai, Greta Thunberg) and the incredible *strength of personal identity* that this kind of leadership requires. All students have the capacity to build that strong of an identity, and the more they are reminded of this, the more likely they are to dig deep and find it.

If you have these general conversations with your students, you can open the door to a deeper conversation when the opportunity arises. This deeper conversation occurs when there is a safe space where they are reminded that they have what it takes to be a *leader*.

What Can I Do to Help Students Who Are Following?

Your goal is to make *space* for students to move through the six steps of self-reflection, shown in Figure 17.1, that will help them move away from *following* and toward leadership. These steps fall into the two categories explained next.

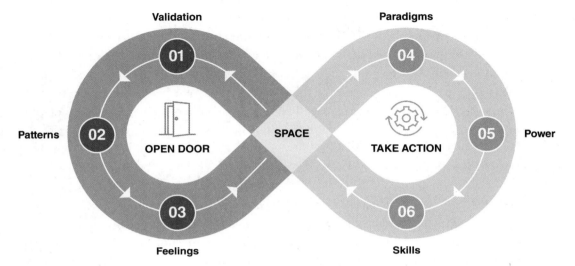

Figure 17.1   The learning cycle for building mental health skills.

Reproduced with permission from Open Parachute.

Figure Explanations

Category 1: Open the Door.

1. **Validating** them and their experiences.

   Validation means letting a student know that what they are facing is normal and that we understand where they are coming from. When a student is following, they need to be reminded that they are part of a community *that also feels the same way they do.* This helps them remember that they don't have to change themselves to be accepted (e.g., "I really understand that feeling," or "I know lots of other people feel the same way you do, even if they don't show it," or "I think anyone who went through what you did would feel that way!").

2. Helping them notice their own **patterns.**

   A *pattern* can be any behavioral reaction, way of thinking, or emotional response. When students are following, we want to help them notice that they are *not acting in their own best interests* (e.g., "Does it feel good when you do that, or not so good?" or "It's normal to want to fit in, but sometimes we go against who we really are when we do that. Do you think that ever happens for you?").

3. Encouraging them to relate directly to their **feelings.**

   Feelings are the physical and emotional responses that a student has to their experiences. When students are following, they are usually not listening to their own feelings and intuitions. If we can guide them to look inward and to trust their feelings, this helps them move past their insecurities so their own truthful voice becomes stronger than the voices of others. We can use language like "I know you have the answer inside of you" or "What do you feel deep down is the right decision?"

Category 2: Take Action.

4. Helping them shift their **paradigm**, or the way they are seeing things.

   A *paradigm* is a student's fundamental views about themselves and the world. Students who are following usually do not see themselves as having agency, power, or leadership. If we can help to shift their perspective of themselves, this can help them learn to trust themselves more (e.g., "You are showing so much wisdom right now" or "You really do know the answer").

5. Reminding them of their **power.**

   A student's *power* is their ability to act with agency in their own world—their ability to enact change and influence their experiences. When a student is following, we want to help them see that they are capable of doing hard things, and that they have already shown the strength to make their own decisions. This will greatly increase their confidence, and see themselves as a leader (e.g., "I have seen you make some really great decisions" or "It's really hard to do something different than what your peers are doing, and I've noticed that you have the ability to think for yourself in those situations. I know you can keep doing that more and more!").

6. Supporting them to use a **skill** that helps them move forward.

   Skills are anything a student does that helps them cope or change their physical and emotional circumstances. Students who are following need to know that they are capable of *doing something to help themselves* (it doesn't matter what the skill is, if they are taking actions that benefit them; they are remembering their own ability to lead themselves in a positive way). You can assist this with language like "Sharing what you're feeling is already a huge step toward helping yourself" or "I've noticed you are really good at speaking up. That's such a great skill that can help you in so many ways!"

These steps can help your students find their own internal strength, and overcome whatever is blocking them from making their own decisions. The chapters that follow will give you examples of putting these conversation points into practice in specific situations where students are *following*, so that you can guide them in looking inward rather than outward for guidance.

18 | Supporting Students Who Are Negatively Impacted by Gender Norms

This chapter will give you tools for responding to students who are negatively impacted by gender norms (e.g., they feel like they need to "be a certain way" or they are mistreated because of their gender). Students impacted in this way are *following* because they are influenced by a cultural belief system that limits them. You will learn the language to help them become a *leader* in their own lives instead of feeling like they need to follow a norm that is holding them back.

WHY Are Gender Norms Impacting Students?

When children are exposed to norms telling them that different genders *should* be, look, or act a certain way, this causes them to doubt themselves. They stop looking inward to their own intuition and start blindly following their peers in an attempt to "fit in" because they know on a deep level that if they fit in, they will be supported. This is a primal instinct that was vitally important when humans relied on a "pack" for survival, and this instinct still lives within our nervous systems today. When this instinct takes over, students look for *external* cues to guide their actions rather than their own internal guidance of what they like and don't like and what is okay or not okay for them, which causes them to move further and further away from their true selves. (See Chapter 17 for a deeper explanation of *following* behaviors.) Gender norms become really harmful when students start making choices based on what they *think* fits their gender, even if that goes against how they truly want to behave (e.g., a group of boys sexualizing a girl's appearance, with each of them ignoring their own impulses to stop, and the girl ignoring her impulses to stand up for herself, all because *this kind of male aggression has been normalized*). It is very challenging for students to step outside of gender roles, and when they feel like they simply don't fit into these categories, it can create a great deal of confusion and shame and lead to harmful decisions. Students who are struggling with gender labels can sometimes seem like they are intentionally trying to separate themselves from others (e.g., a boy who won't play games at lunch with the other boys) or overtly confident (e.g., a girl who dominates the boys in physical competitions). It's vital that we remember the internal struggle these students may be facing, given that they are going against the grain of societal norms.

WHAT Can I Do to Help a Student Who Is Impacted by Gender Norms?

Students who are negatively impacted by gender norms need to be supported to step into their own *identity* to become *leaders* instead of silencing their own voices and feelings. This will help them move from feeling trapped in a box of gender norms to a place where they can lead their peers toward more acceptance of themselves and each other.

HOW Will I Have a Constructive Conversation with a Student about Gender Norms?

In my interview with Tara, we uncovered that gender norms were an issue for her, and she felt she was limited by her gender. In our conversation, she realized that she does not have to be constricted by these norms and that she can also pass this same message on to her peers and become a *leader*.

The following is a transcript of my conversation with Tara, showing how the six steps of the learning cycle, shown in Figure 18.1 (validation, patterns, feelings, paradigms, power, and skills), can be used with a student who is negatively impacted by gender norms. See Chapter 17 for a deeper analysis of using these steps with students who are *following*.

Interview with Tara (Age 10)

T: I have short hair and I guess I look kind of like a boy. People mistake me for it. Um, and so I just let people call me a boy. I feel like the boys would treat me differently if they knew I was a girl because like they think girls might not be able to do things as well as they can, so they might not want me to play with them. . . . Then I say, "My name's Tom" because that's short for Tara, so it doesn't really matter. And then sometimes in the end I tell them [I'm a girl], and it doesn't make a difference, cuz by then they know that I can do things as good as them.

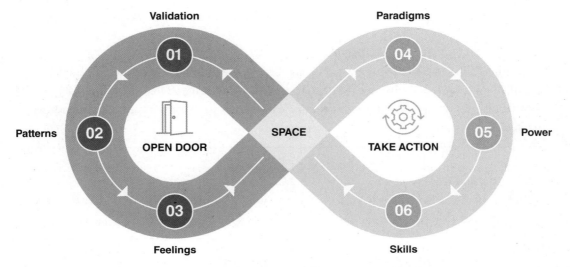

Figure 18.1   The learning cycle for building mental health skills.

Reproduced with permission from Open Parachute.

H: And why would anyone think that a girl can't do things that a boy can do? *(Patterns; Paradigm)*

> Often students will say statements like this about *the way things are*, and they have never considered *why* they are being treated a certain way. Sometimes the most helpful thing we can do is simply ask the question "Why do you think this is happening?" I was asking this question to begin a paradigm shift for Tara about her ability to be herself.

T: Uh, I don't know.

H: It doesn't make any sense, does it? That they would think that. . . . *(Patterns; Paradigm)*

> Simply saying "That doesn't make sense, does it?" can provide an opening for a student to feel safe to reflect on cultural norms.

T: Yeah. It doesn't make any sense that they would like, think that I can't do anything as good as they could because I can, I know I can. I can even do things better than they can.

H: And so does it feel fair to you that you get judged for being a girl? *(Paradigm; Feelings)*

> I introduced the idea that "it doesn't feel fair" because I could sense that this was how Tara was feeling. I wanted to give her the chance to *explore this feeling* so that she could *clarify her own thinking* (it is very challenging to think clearly when we have not fully identified how we feel).

T: No, it doesn't feel fair at all.

H: And do you ever wish that it kind of didn't matter if you were a boy or a girl? *(Paradigm)*

> I suggested this because, generally speaking, when a student feels like they are being put in the box of a norm, they *wish the box didn't matter* so they could just be themselves. Again, I was using suggestions here to help Tara feel safe to explore this perspective.

T: Well, yeah, I wish I didn't have to say that [I'm a boy]. I wish I could just say "I'm a girl" and they would think that I could do anything as good as them.

H: Yeah, absolutely. I had the same feeling as you when I was growing up. I felt left out with boys. And so what can we do to help change that? *(Validation; Skill)*

> I used my own experience and "we" language to help Tara feel less alone and more confident. If I had not had experiences like she had, I could have still related to her feelings in a less direct way (e.g., "I know what it feels like to be left out.").

T: Um, I don't know. What did you do?

H: Good question. I think I did the same thing that you did. I just sort of tried to fit in and tried to be a little bit like a boy. But now I look back on that and I go, "It's actually pretty cool to be a girl." I like being a girl now, and I kind of wish that I was able to like being a girl when I was younger cuz it's pretty fun to be a girl. *(Validation; Paradigm)*

I always find that honesty is the best policy when a student asks a direct question like this. I was trying to show her that I did struggle in the same ways that she is struggling, but that I found a new perspective, in order to show her that there was a pathway for to change her experience also. If I hadn't come to a resolution about this in my own life, I could have also said, "I don't really think I figured out an answer. Maybe we can help each other decide what to do about it!". Honesty is always okay as long as we are showing students that there *is a way forward*, and we believe they have the ability to find it.

T: Yeah. But then the boys think you don't like climbing trees and you don't like swimming, you just like baking or sewing. Well, I like doing all that stuff. I like climbing trees. I like swimming. I like baking. I like cooking. I like sewing. I like everything.

H: Yes! And there shouldn't be any reason why that should be! One thing shouldn't be for girls and one thing for boys, right? *(Validation; Patterns; Paradigm)*

T: Yeah. You should be able to climb trees and swim if you're a boy or if you're a girl. Like my parents don't say that you can't climb trees or swim.

H: Yeah. And I think what I've learned only as an adult, you're learning a lot younger than me, that actually we can do all those things. It just takes confidence, doesn't it? *(Validation; Skill)*

I use this phrase a lot with students as a way of validating them (letting them know that they are learning things at a much younger age than I learned them). This means they *have more potential to make use of these insights*, and being reminded of this can feel very empowering for them. I also suggested the skill of *confidence* because I wanted Tara to start seeing her own power to be herself in the situation, even in the face of these norms.

T: Yeah.

H: Like if we're confident and we say, yeah, "I'm a girl," or "I'm a boy," and "This is what I like," then people may go, "Oh, that's different." But then that's okay. They accept you, right? *(Skill)*

T: Yeah.

H: Is that an experience you've gone through where you just do your thing and then you say, yeah, I'm a girl, and then it's okay? *(Power)*

> I wanted to help Tara find an example of a time when she had already acted with some level of confidence about her gender to help her see that she could do this again in the future.

T: What do you mean?

H: Like, do you have friends who don't care if you're a boy or a girl? *(Power)*

> I was fishing here because I suspected that Tara had *positive experiences of being accepted* that she might be forgetting in this moment (which often happens when we are thinking about challenges—we only see the negatives!).

T: Like, I have friends at swimming, and there's separate change rooms for the boys and the girls. They see me coming out of there all the time, but they know I can swim. I can swim faster than all the boys there.

H: That's so cool. And do you ever try to teach your friends to see things differently? Do you ever say "Girls and boys can do the same things"? Do you ever say those kinds of things to your friends? *(Power)*

T: Um, I haven't said anything like that to my friends. . . . But there was someone who said, "Hey, you can't do that. You're a girl." So I was just like, "Boys can do anything girls can do; girls can do anything the boys can do."

H: Amazing. What did you feel like when they said that? *(Validation; Power; Feelings)*

> Now that Tara had identified something she had done to help herself, I wanted to explore how this felt for her to help motivate her to do it again in the future.

T: I felt angry, but I also felt calm because I knew I could do anything they could do.

H: Amazing. And that calmness, that confidence, right? That's how we can change things. I think you are the one that's gonna change things. I love that. You can teach the people around you, can't you? *(Validation; Power)*

> I wanted to *explicitly tell Tara that she could be a leader* so that she started to see herself that way.

T: Yeah!

H: And what does it feel like when you make your own choices about what you like to do, instead of listening to other people? *(Feelings; Power; Skill)*

T: It feels really good because I feel like "I can do this, I can do that. I can do like whatever I need to do."

H: Amazing. Is there anything you would want to say to other kids who might be struggling with some of the same things you struggle with? *(Validation; Power; Skill)*

> Asking her what she would say to another student was another way I was trying to help Tara see herself as a leader.

T: Uh, "Just be yourself." I always just say, "Just be yourself. What do you like to do? Just do it."

H: Love it. And how do you *know* what you like? *(Validation; Skill)*

> I ask this question to students a lot (*how do you know* what you like) because I am trying to help them to look inward, to their own intuition (body signals, thoughts, feelings) to make choices.

T: When I do the thing, I like it. Like I feel happy because I like drawing. I like reading. I like reading like the most ever, I love reading. So when I read, I really like it because I feel like involved in the story.

H: Amazing. And so that's a good signal, isn't it? When you feel happy doing something that tells you that you like it. When you feel angry or sad doing something that tells you that you might not like it. *(Validation; Skill; Paradigm)*

I wanted to reinforce this paradigm shift by reminding her that *she could listen to herself and be confident in who she is* in order to counteract harmful norms. The conversation ended here, but if I had a chance to speak to Tara again, I would check back in by asking her something like "Have you had any more chances to teach people that they can do what they enjoy, whether they're a boy or a girl?"

T: Right.

These conversations will help your students find strength and confidence in themselves to counteract the negative impacts that can arise as a result of gender stereotypes (e.g., consent violations, objectification, peer pressure, etc.). By making it safe for them to reflect on the impacts of the norms they experience, seeing their own power to change these stereotypes, and identifying the skills they can use to create a more accepting world, your students can learn to be true leaders for their peers in changing harmful gender norms.

Related Chapters

Chapter 13, "Helping Students Who People-Please"; Chapter 20, "Supporting Students with Low Body Image"; Chapter 21, "Helping Students Stand Up to Peer Pressure"; Chapter 22, "Supporting Students Who Are Bullied"; Chapter 26, "Minimizing the Influence of Pornography and 'Rape Culture'"; Chapter 28, "Helping Students Cope with Being Objectified"

19 | Guiding Students to Make Healthy Choices on Social Media

This chapter will give you tools for responding to students who are negatively impacted by social media (e.g., they feel shame or insecurity because of the content they see, they are posting things that are causing harm to themselves or others, or they are being impacted by harmful online messages). Social media creates a desire to *follow*, and you will learn strategies for communicating with students in a way that can help them remember their ability to make their own decisions, regardless of what they see online.

WHY Is Social Media Impacting Students?

Social media presents many opportunities for students to *follow* others and seek guidance from their peer group rather than listen to their own internal wisdom. (See Chapter 17 for a deeper explanation of *following* behaviors.) This is so appealing to students because following what they see online *takes them away from their own feelings of insecurity* for a brief moment in time. The trap they get caught into is that they feel insecure, so they look online at someone who *appears more secure than they do*. For a moment, this feels relieving because they are caught up in the emotion that is being portrayed on screen. But then they are immediately hit with a wave of even more profound insecurity when they inevitably feel that awful feeling that they *don't measure up*. But because they have established a *pattern of looking online to avoid feelings of insecurity*, they will dive

155

even deeper, scroll longer, and engage more with the online world, *even though that is actually making them feel more insecure.* The poison feels like the cure, and as long as they don't have other skills for relating to their feelings of insecurity, they will continue to look in harmful places to avoid these feelings. In addition to this, social media is often used to actively bully/harass others, and when this is happening, a student's feelings of insecurity are even more intense and overwhelming. Online abuse invades their private space, and it can feel like there literally is no escape. This is not to say that all social media interactions are negative. Far from it. Social media can help students feel connected and seen. But *the way they use it really matters*, and this is where they need the most guidance. Students who are negatively impacted by social media might be constantly distracted or withdrawn or talk incessantly about their experiences online, and it can seem like they don't care about the "real world." It's important to remember that these students are simply lacking other healthy forms of self-soothing and are usually not aware that their online experiences are harming them.

WHAT Can I Do to Help a Student Who Is Impacted by Social Media?

Students who are negatively impacted by social media need to be supported to *build their own identity* based on *who they really are* (not what they *see*) in order to become *leaders* for their peers. They need guidance to move away from seeking external validation and learn instead to feel confident in *celebrating their own uniqueness*.

HOW Will I Have a Constructive Conversation with a Student about Social Media?

In my interview with Emma, we uncovered that she was struggling with the impacts of social media, and was seeking to deal with her feelings of insecurity online in a way that was actually making things worse for her. In our conversation, Emma reflected on the fact that she does not have to use social media in this way, and that she can also pass this message on to her peers and become a *leader* in this area. I chose this interview because it shows ways to address the simple and often subtle ways that social media impacts students. Online bullying is also a significant concern, and I address the language to use in situations of bullying (whether in person or online) in Chapter 5, "Coaching Students Who Bully or Are Aggressive/Violent."

The following is a transcript of my conversation with Emma, showing how the six steps of the learning cycle, shown in Figure 19.1 (validation, patterns, feelings, paradigms, power, and skills), can be used in conversation with a student who is negatively impacted by social media. See Chapter 17 for a deeper analysis of using these steps with students who are *following*.

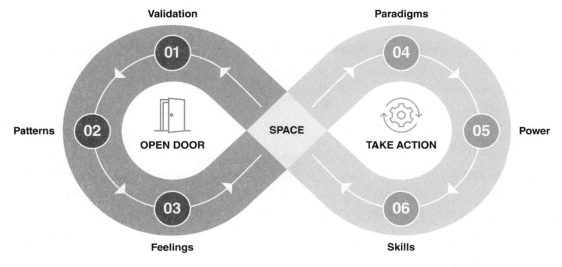

Figure 19.1 The learning cycle for building mental health skills.

Reproduced with permission from Open Parachute.

Interview with Emma (Age 13)

H: Do you ever feel bad about the images you see online? Like when people have perfect airbrushed images or images of girls only looking a certain way? That's something that's hard for all of us. *(Validation; Patterns; Feelings)*

> I often ask students direct questions like this, pointing out the challenges of social media and letting them know that we all struggle with these challenges in order to help them feel safe to reflect on their own experiences of this.

E: I really do feel bad cuz sometimes I wish I was like a skinny, perfect girl. I've seen images of girls in bikinis who are really skinny and like cute outfits and crop tops and shorts, and it's just made me wanna be skinny.

H: Yeah, that's really hard. It's normal to get negative thoughts and feelings when you see those images. Did you experience that? *(Validation; Feelings; Patterns)*

> I asked about Emma's *thoughts* and *feelings* to help her reflect more deeply on the impact of her experiences with social media.

E: Yeah, I get really negative and think, "Oh, I wish I was this, I wish I was skinny. I wish I was like them."

H: Yeah, I get that. It's super normal to think that when we see those images. They can be really damaging cuz they make us feel like we have to look like that. And what are some of the ways that you help yourself with online images? *(Validation; Feelings; Patterns; Skill; Power)*

> I moved into asking about how she helps herself quite quickly here without too much of an exploration of her feelings. This was at the end of a longer conversation, so I didn't have much time, but if I could talk to Emma again, I would ask more questions about her feelings in these situations to help her reflect even more deeply.

E: I talk to my girlfriend because she's like, "Just ignore it. They're probably fake. They've probably edited the photo. You're perfect the way you are. I don't want you to change at all."

H: That's great! And do you ever put it [phone] down or decide to look at different accounts? *(Validation; Skill; Power)*

> I wanted to suggest a few different coping strategies to Emma so she could reflect on times that she may have already used these, which would help her remember to use them again in the future.

E: Yeah, if I put it down and then talk to someone about it, it makes it just go away and makes me feel a hundred percent better.

H: That's so good. And do you try to think different thoughts when you see things online? *(Validation; Skill; Power)*

E: Yeah, like if I see a girl who I think is really pretty and is skinny, I'm just like, "Wow, they really look really good, but so do I."

H: That's awesome. That's such a good shift. Amazing. And so is there anything else you've learned about social media or online things? *(Validation; Skill; Power)*

E: Well about "fit checks."

H: What's that? *(Patterns)*

E: Basically I sent a photo on Instagram of what I looked like one day and thought I wanted to see what people thought of it.

H: Wow. That is a brave thing to do. So what, you posted and said, "What do you think of this photo?" *(Validation; Patterns)*

> I was taken aback when Emma said this. Even though I know this behavior happens regularly, hearing it said in such a matter-of-fact way always just feels so sad to me. I wanted to say "Why would you ever do that???" I had to dig deep to think about her strength here because it was in fact a courageous act, even though it was ultimately harmful. I wanted to validate her so that she didn't feel attacked or criticized, and felt safe to continue opening up to me.

E: Yeah.

H: And what did they respond with? *(Patterns)*

E: Only one person responded with, "It's one outta ten." And I'm like, "Why?" And they're just like, "Cuz I don't like it."

H: Oh, that's hard. What did that feel like for someone to say "One outta ten?" *(Validation; Feelings)*

> I was hoping that exploring Emma's feelings about this situation would encourage her to realize that this kind of a post can be really harmful for her.

E: I didn't like it. Like, it made me feel really bad because it was like, "Oh, why don't they like my outfit?"

H: Yeah. I get that. I would feel the same! It's a really hard part about social media. If we open up that door, sometimes people can be mean, can't they? *(Validation; Patterns)*

> I used "we" language again here to help Emma know that she was not alone in her experiences so that she felt safe to reflect on them.

E: Yeah. Because if I opened up and said, "This is me, I like my outfit, I don't care what you think," people aren't gonna comment cuz they're gonna be like, "Damn, I really wanted to like put someone down today and I can't." *(Laughs)*

H: Totally. Love it. And so did you learn it's better to not ask for other people's opinions? *(Validation; Power; Paradigm; Skill)*

I wanted Emma to identify *exactly what her thinking was* in this paradigm shift so that she could draw on it again in the future.

E: Yeah, I learned that it was better not to ask for other people's opinion because it could put me back down into the negative cycle that I went through before.

H: And now do you think maybe you would make a different choice in terms of asking for people's opinions? Like could you focus on what you believe instead of what other people think? *(Power; Paradigm)*

E: Yeah, now if I was doing a fit check, I could just put, "I love my outfit today. I think it's really cute."

H: Yeah, absolutely. And it's such a difference, isn't it, to say, "This is who I am," versus "This is who I am, do you like me?" And you only know that when you listen to yourself right? *(Paradigm; Power; Validation)*

I wanted to help Emma see that her change in perspective was an act of *listening to herself*. We didn't have time to explore this concept fully, but I planted the seed so that if I got the chance to talk to her again, I could refer back to this and help her reflect on it more.

E: Yeah, it is different for posting, saying "This is who I am, do you like it?" Compared to "This is who I am, I don't care what you think."

H: Amazing. Such a good message. It's so great you learned to listen to yourself like that. You have so much to teach other people about this! *(Validation; Power; Skill; Paradigm)*

Even though Emma was repeating back what I had just said, I treated it as though it was her own original thought. It doesn't really matter *where a thought comes from*; our power arises from *choosing to believe it*.

This type of conversation will help your students learn to look inward to decide what is *helping* or *hurting* them online, and know that they have the strength to guide others to do the same. When we help students see that it is *normal to feel insecure in online interactions*, they can identify the skills they can use to be more empowered online. This will help them form a personal identity based on their own uniqueness rather than trying to live up to unrealistic online standards.

Related Chapters

Chapter 8, "Supporting Students Who Are Worried, Anxious, or Stressed"; Chapter 13, "Helping Students Who People-Please"; Chapter 15, "Guiding Students Who Are Caught in Addictive Patterns"; Chapter 20, "Supporting Students with Low Body Image"; Chapter 22, "Supporting Students Who Are Bullied"; Chapter 28, "Helping Students Cope with Being Objectified"

20 | Supporting Students with Low Body Image

This chapter will give you tools for responding to students who feel negatively about their bodies (e.g., wishing they looked different, comparing their bodies to the bodies of others, feeling shame about their appearance). Low body image impacts most students at some point in their development, and you will learn conversation strategies to help them learn to see their own bodies in a positive light instead of thinking they need to look like anyone else.

WHY Does Body Image Impact Students?

It's natural for students to begin feeling insecure about their bodies if they are given messages from their peers, family, or the media that their body is different than the "norm" or the "ideal." Body image challenges are an example of *following* behavior because they are an indication that a student is looking for *external* sources to tell them how they should look. (See Chapter 17 for a deeper explanation of *following* behaviors.) Students then bury their feelings of shame and confusion about their bodies because they want to show the world the same confidence that they assume everyone else around them possesses. This creates a trap where *everyone feels secretly insecure and yet projects confidence to others,* creating more insecurity for everyone. Students who struggle with low body image can either appear timid and shy or else overly confident about their bodies. It's important to remember that most students will struggle with body image at some point in their development. Some of them deal with this by trying to hide themselves, and some of them deal with it by trying to pretend they don't care. Both of these reactions show the same internal feelings of insecurity and need a similar type of support to help them navigate this challenge.

WHAT Can I Do to Help a Student with Low Body Image?

Students who have low body image need to be supported to *feel their feelings about their body* (even the hard ones) so that they can move *through* those feelings. Acknowledging the natural feelings of insecurity and shame that are common for students to feel about their changing bodies helps them see their own bodies in a more honest way. This, in turn, allows them to develop a deeper appreciation for their own unique physical form.

HOW Will I Have a Constructive Conversation with a Student about Body Image?

In my interview with Layla, she mentioned being told negative things about her body. During our conversation, Layla was able to identify her feelings of shame and her pattern of burying those feelings, which enabled her to be honest about her body image (maybe for the first time). This allowed her to gain clarity and see a pathway toward a more loving relationship with her body.

The following is a transcript of my conversation with Layla, showing how the six steps of the learning cycle, shown in Figure 20.1 (validation, patterns, feelings, paradigms, power, and skills), can be used with a student who is experiencing low body image. See Chapter 17 for a deeper analysis of using these steps with students who are *following*.

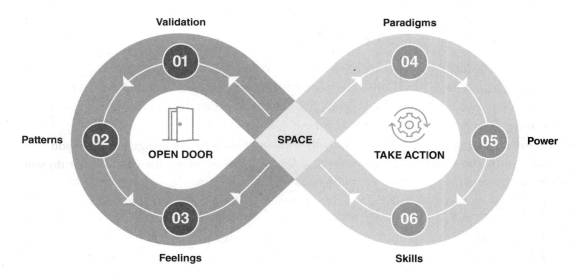

Figure 20.1   The learning cycle for building mental health skills.

Reproduced with permission from Open Parachute.

Interview with Layla (Age 16)

L: Basically, like, a group of girls kind of like started making fun of me and um saying things about the way I looked and my hair and my braids.

H: I'm so sorry you went through that! That's really hard. How did it make you feel? *(Validation; Feelings)*

> I started with a question about *feelings* so that I could help Layla identify how this experience impacted her, which would lead to finding tools for dealing with these impacts.

L: It kind of just felt unfair because it was like, "I can't do anything to change myself. There's literally nothing I can do."

H: A lot of kids going through something like that feel like there's something wrong with them. That's what makes it so hard! When we hear negative things, we can think it's our fault. Did you ever react like that? *(Validation; Patterns)*

> This is one of the most common thoughts students have when they are picked on by others, especially when it comes to their body image, so I wanted to suggest it to let Layla know that she was not alone if she had this response.

L: I was just angry and just sad. And, um, I guess I would kind of like isolate myself from even my family as well, cuz I was like a very, very quiet kid. So like I wouldn't talk to anyone, even like my family.

H: Yeah, I get that. So you sort of tried to bury it at first? *(Validation; Patterns)*

L: Yeah.

H: And did that work? Because often we feel like we can just bury things, but then, you know, they stay with us. Do you feel like that was a helpful thing for you to do or do you feel like it was not so helpful? *(Validation; Patterns; Paradigm)*

> I wanted to bring in the paradigm shift that *silencing our own feelings can cause harm, even if it feels better in the moment.* This is one of the ways that we continue to be impacted by painful experiences from the past. Anytime we block out our feelings, they remain unprocessed and stay with us for much longer than they would if we allowed ourselves to feel them in the moment.

L: Yes, it was very helpful. I mean, for me, because I'm someone, I'm very emotional. So like by just ignoring things, that's the best way that I can handle a situation.

H: So it helped you at the time. And how do you think that impacts you now, that you buried those hard feelings about your body? Do you think maybe the long-term impacts are different than the short-term ones? *(Validation; Paradigm)*

L: Um, I guess it impacted me a lot because I didn't confront those feelings back then. And so now I'm kind of dealing with it now because I feel so insecure in like my body. Like, it's hard for me to kind of gain a sort of self-confidence or self-love because I still have those issues that I haven't confronted. I guess it would've been probably helpful if I had just like dealt with it back then.

H: That's exactly right. You know, we think in the moment we just wanna feel better right now. But we don't realize that if we don't deal with it, then we have to keep feeling it later. So, when you're saying you feel insecure in your body, how does that show up for you? *(Validation; Paradigm; Patterns)*

> Layla just shared something quite vulnerable about herself, so I wanted to be really validating, and also ask a direct question about her experiences so that she felt safe to explore this issue with me head-on.

L: Well, I guess it was very subconsciously, like, I didn't actively think, "Oh, I'm like the ugliest person in the world." But like, every time I look in the mirror, like I'd like be like, damn, like "Why do I look this way?" And it's like, I guess their words slowly but surely kind of like impacted the way that I saw myself.

H: What I see is that you have so much wisdom in terms of what you've been through and now you're realizing, "Oh, I need to confront this and feel these feelings." What do you think helps you remember that you're beautiful? *(Validation; Skill; Power)*

> I wanted to help Layla find her own power in this moment because she was being so honest about her struggles. It's always a delicate balance between *giving space for feelings* (e.g., exploring the challenge) and *reminding a student of their power* (e.g., focusing on how they can help themselves). I chose to go for the power angle because I could see that Layla was quite raw with emotion in that moment already.

L: I don't think I fully think that I'm beautiful. I don't think I've actually thought that, like, "Oh, I'm really pretty." I don't think I've ever really thought about that about myself. Like I've gotten compliments, but it's just like, "Oh, they're just saying it to be nice." I don't think I've ever really. . . . Yeah, I don't think, I don't think I've actually thought of myself as pretty. Whoa, I didn't realize that. Yeah, I don't think so. I think I still face those issues. No, I haven't fully recovered from it.

H: Thank you so much for sharing that. I think that you will recover from that a hundred percent because what you're doing right now is exactly what's needed. Letting yourself feel all those feelings. Because when you let yourself feel all those feelings, then you realize, you don't get stuck in them. What do you feel right now when you sort of realize that? *(Validation; Paradigm; Feelings)*

> This was such a poignant moment, and my whole focus was helping Layla feel safe and validated in what she was sharing, and also to help her get as much learning out of the moment that she could by supporting her to just *be in the moment with what she was feeling.*

L: I feel ashamed. Oh. Like, I'm a very confident person, I would say, but I mean, oh, it's not, it's okay. Yeah. Um, sorry. . . . *(Layla started welling up with tears.)*

H: That's okay. Don't worry at all. I'm really grateful for you, for being so honest, because so many other girls feel the exact same way as you. And you being so vulnerable and brave is exactly what's gonna show others that they can be that honest too. . . . *(Validation)*

> Here, my whole focus was validation, and I also paused to give Layla space to just feel her feelings, or to continue talking if she chose.

L: Um, I think I have the "fake it till you make it" mentality, um, I keep telling myself that, like, "Oh, I'm confident, or like people's words don't affect me." Or like, "I don't really care what anyone says." Um, but I guess deep down I do care. That sounds so corny, but, um, yeah, I guess subconsciously, like, I do care, but I just want to make myself not care.

H: Thank you so much for sharing that because I would say that all of us are in exactly the same position. And what you're doing right now is exactly what will shift that cuz you're letting yourself feel it. That's so powerful! Doing this learning really gives you a lot of insight and empathy for others, doesn't it? *(Validation; Paradigm; Power; Skill)*

> I wanted Layla to identify the *power in her vulnerability*. One of the greatest things about self-reflection is that it allows us to help others, and I like to remind students of this when they are really emotional, to help them see a brightness within their struggles.

L: Oh, definitely. Like for me, I hate it when people are mean. I've actually been like, "Hey, like why are you talking about this girl behind her back?" Like, I'm actually very like proactive when it comes to that. So I feel like it's definitely helped me more like look at things from like other people's perspective and kind of like see other people's like point of view in situations.

H: That's so great. You can really help so many people with that! And do you think that lots of other people also feel body shame? *(Validation; Patterns; Power)*

> I asked Layla to reflect on *other people* because I wanted her to remember that she is definitely not alone.

L: Uh, I guess I think everyone feels it. I don't think anyone's a hundred-percent confident in themselves, and if they are, they're probably lying to themselves *(laughs)*.

H: You're exactly right. And that's the power of letting yourself feel those emotions! You see things so clearly now! So how can you use this to help yourself feel better about your body? *(Validation; Power; Skill)*

> I was so excited by this realization that Layla had. As soon as she was honest with herself about her own feelings of shame, she could clearly see that everyone else was probably exactly the same. If I had the chance to talk to her again, I would bring this up to keep reinforcing the power of recognizing our own vulnerability (e.g., "I loved what you said the other day that no one is really as confident in their bodies as they think they are. Have you thought any more about that?").

L: I feel like, um, the best way to kind of like move through those spaces is just like, just allowing yourself to feel those emotions.

H: Amazing.

This type of conversation will help your students *explore their true feelings about their body image*, and the patterns of emotional suppression that often keep these feelings stuck. When we open the door to this type of reflection, students feel supported to look inward, and can find their own clarity for what is needed in order to build self-love.

Related Chapters

Chapter 10, "Talking to Students about Unhealthy Eating Habits"; Chapter 12, "Supporting Students Who Self-Harm"; Chapter 13, "Helping Students Who People-Please"; Chapter 18, "Supporting Students Who Are Negatively Impacted by Gender Norms"; Chapter 19, "Guiding Students to Make Healthy Choices on Social Media"; Chapter 22, "Supporting Students Who Are Bullied"; Chapter 28, "Helping Students Cope with Being Objectified"

21 | Helping Students Stand Up to Peer Pressure

This chapter will give you tools for responding to students who face peer pressure (e.g., they are encouraged to do things they don't want to do by their peers, they struggle to speak up when people are acting in ways that make them uncomfortable, they go along with the crowd when teasing/bullying is happening, etc.). You will learn the language you can use to help students facing peer pressure *follow* their peers less and begin to find their own capacity for *leadership*.

WHY Does Peer Pressure Impact Students?

Being susceptible to peer pressure is one of the more obvious forms of *following* in students. (See Chapter 17 for a deeper explanation of *following* behaviors.) When students have not practiced the skill of *listening to their own emotions*, it can be very challenging to stand up to their peers. When their peer group is making harmful choices, a student will naturally feel uncomfortable and usually anxious or sad. If they listen to those feelings, they will decide to *do something in order to change the situation* (using their own personal identity to become a *leader* in some capacity). On the other hand, if they are used to burying their feelings, they will instead become numb to the situation or start to doubt themselves and think their feelings are an indication that *they are faulty* in some way (e.g., "What's wrong with me for feeling sad? Everyone else seems fine with that's happening."). This can keep students in a cycle of self-doubt and confusion, where they feel less and less sure of what they can do or say to make any positive changes in their peer group. It can be easy to misinterpret the behavior of a student who is impacted by peer pressure.

They might do things that are harmful to others or go against your instructions in class as a way to impress their peers. It's important to remember that usually, students will not feel good about these actions and will be able to make changes if they are given a chance to reflect.

WHAT Can I Do to Help a Student Who Is Impacted by Peer Pressure?

Students who are easily swayed by peer pressure need to be supported to build their own *identity* by listening to their *intuition*. Their intuition will help them find positive peers with common interests and join clubs or activities that make them feel inspired and supported. This will help them stop following along with the harmful behavior of others and learn to lead their peers toward making positive choices by noticing how each choice makes them *feel*.

HOW Will I Have a Constructive Conversation with a Student about Peer Pressure?

In my interview with Chad, he talked about an experience of peer pressure he had been through, where he struggled to listen to his feelings, and it started to impact him negatively. I chose this interview because I focused on peer pressure in the conversation, but Chad also brought up bullying and a lack of acceptance of differences. Often there are many layers like this when you are speaking to students, and I wanted to show how you can choose to focus on one angle at a time even when lots of different concepts are presented to you at once. In our conversation, Chad reflected on the power of *learning to listen to his feelings*, and making positive choices based on how he feels so that he can be a *leader* for others. I was asking Chad about a *past* experience in this interview, which can be a helpful tool. By asking about previous incidents, we can help students see how their past strength can be used in a current situation.

The following is a transcript of my conversation with Chad, showing how the six steps of the learning cycle, shown in Figure 21.1 (validation, patterns, feelings, paradigms, power, and skills), can help a student who is negatively impacted by peer pressure. See Chapter 17 for a deeper analysis of using these steps with students who are *following*.

Interview with Chad (Age 14)

H: Can you tell me about a time you faced peer pressure in the past? *(Patterns)*
C: Yeah, I was peer-pressured before. My friends were bullying other kids with disabilities.
H: That's hard. What were they doing? *(Validating; Patterns)*
C: They were saying, "Hey, look at you. You can't, uh, like do stuff," and they had a wheelchair and they say, "You can't walk."
H: And what did that feel like? *(Feelings)*

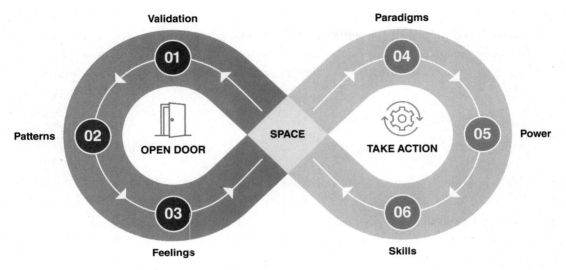

Figure 21.1 The learning cycle for building mental health skills.

Reproduced with permission from Open Parachute.

> I asked about Chad's *feelings* to help him learn to identify when something is okay or not okay (we always feel uncomfortable feelings when something is not okay for us).

C: Uh, inside it made me feel really bad because those people were born with it. They couldn't change it.

H: And did you feel uncomfortable? Did you feel sad? *(Feelings)*

Chad spoke in really short sentences and didn't show a lot of emotion, so I kept probing for more explanations of his thoughts and feelings, and made suggestions to help him explore and identify his own experiences.

C: I felt very anxious and uncomfortable.

H: That's really hard. What were the thoughts that you were thinking? Were you thinking like something negative about yourself or about them, or about the situation? *(Validation; Patterns)*

C: I was thinking I shouldn't be around these people because they make fun of people who are born with something they can't change.

H: And did you feel nervous to say something to them about it? Did you want to say something? *(Feelings; Skill; Power)*

> I wanted Chad to identify *how he overcame the challenge of standing up to peer pressure* in the past so that he could use that same skill in the future. If he could reflect on how hard this might have been for him, that would give him the courage to do it again (e.g., "I can do hard things.").

C: Yeah, I felt very scared and nervous to say anything against them because they were my friends.

H: That makes sense. What did you think might happen? *(Validation; Patterns)*

C: Uh, I thought they were going to like not be friends with me anymore.

H: Yeah, I get that. And so at first, did you not say anything? *(Validation; Patterns)*

C: Yeah, at first, I didn't say anything about the problem.

H: That's a really normal response. But it can really cause harm when we don't listen to ourselves, can't it? How did that impact you to not say anything about it? *(Validation; Patterns)*

> I asked how this impacted him in order to help Chad reflect on the fact that even though standing up to peer pressure is really hard, the alternative is worse.

C: It made me feel very sad inside.

H: It makes sense that you would feel that. When we aren't listening to ourselves, it can start to change how we act. Did you notice that it impacted how you concentrated at school or how you interacted with friends or with family? *(Validation; Patterns)*

C: Mm. It made me very sad around people. I was a bit more grumpy and [felt] less like speaking to people.

H: Makes perfect sense. You know, sometimes we actually have to get to that place in order to change. It can be helpful to look at it that way. . . . So then what happened? What helped you change this? *(Validation; Paradigm; Power)*

> I wanted to introduce the paradigm shift of seeing that *going through struggles can help us grow*, so that Chad didn't feel so much shame in reflecting back on this experience.

C: Uh, I made friends with other people that didn't do stuff like that, and actually helped the people with disabilities.

H: That's so good! And do you remember the first thing you did? *(Validation; Skill; Power)*

> I wanted to ask Chad *exactly what he did as a first step* to help him remember to take this same step in the future.

C: I was very nervous at the time, uh, but I tried my best to stop them.

H: Amazing. What did you do? What did you say? *(Validation; Skill; Power)*

C: I said, "Stop this guys. Uh, this isn't good. They are born with disabilities. They can't change it."

H: That's so brave. And do you remember what that felt like to do that? *(Validation; Feelings)*

> I wanted Chad to identify *how it felt to make this choice* to help motivate him to make the same choice again.

C: It made me feel very scared, but also brave at the same time.

H: I bet! Sometimes people don't respond that well to us when we stand up to them, which is what makes it so hard. What happened when you said those things? Did they get upset with you? *(Validation; Patterns)*

C: Uh, they were very angry and they were like, "You're no longer my friend. You cannot hang around me anymore."

H: That's terrible. How did that make you feel? *(Validation; Feelings)*

C: Made me feel very sad.

H: And it's really normal when those things happen that we start thinking we've done the wrong thing. Did you ever think that? *(Validation; Patterns)*

> I suggested the thought, "I've done the wrong thing" because this is a common thinking pattern in peer pressure—a student standing up to their peers will feel ashamed and think they have messed up when their peers respond badly.

C: Like, yeah, I felt like I was doing the wrong thing because I made other people mad.

H: Yeah that's hard. And so then did you choose at some point, "Those are not the kind of people I wanna be friends with"? Did you make that choice? *(Validation; Skill; Power)*

C: Yeah, when I realized the effect that they were having on the people with disabilities, I dumped them and made new friends.

H: That's huge. And how do you make choices about friends now? Like do you think about and decide what makes someone a good friend? *(Validation; Paradigm; Skill)*

> I wanted Chad to reflect on the paradigm shift of *consciously making choices about his friends* so that he could apply this learning to current situations.

C: Uh, I look at their actions and how like kind they are. I choose who my friends are by looking at their kindness and their actions.

H: That's so great. And how do you feel around people who are kind? *(Validation; Feelings)*

C: I feel really good around people who are kind because they help other people and I also get to help other people.

H: Awesome. And so now what do you do when you see someone like bullying someone or picking on someone? *(Validation; Skill)*

> I wanted to bring the conversation from the past to the present here so that Chad could reflect on how his past learning was being applied to his current life.

C: When I see anyone getting bullied, I tell the teacher immediately so they know, like, to help the person.

H: And so do you ever get that same feeling of like, "This is scary, I don't want to do this?" *(Patterns)*

> I wanted to help Chad see his own courage, and reflect on the fact that he stands up for others even though it probably still scares him. I wanted him to identify himself as a courageous person, to encourage him to use that courage even more in the future.

C: Uh, yeah, I sometimes get the feeling, "Uh, this is really scary and I don't want to do this."

H: And what helps you do it anyway? *(Skill)*

C: Uh, I think about what kind of person I want to be. I make choices, uh, because that's how I want to be, not like how other people expect me to be.

H: What a great perspective. And then what happens? What's the outcome of speaking up and doing it anyway? *(Validation; Power)*

C: Like the other person doesn't get bullied anymore and they feel better.

H: And so is it worth it? *(Validation; Power; Paradigm)*

> I wanted to ask Chad if it was *worth it*, as a tool for motivating him to continue making choices that are hard, but good for him. This, in itself, can be a big paradigm shift for some students!

C: Yes. I think it's worth it.

H: That's amazing. That's a huge amount of strength to do that. Do you feel that? *(Validation; Power)*

C: Yeah.

H: You earned that. You feel that because you made the hard choice. When you look back on that experience, what do you think you learned through that? *(Validation; Power; Paradigm)*

C: I learned that helping other people makes you feel better inside, and it also helps the other person as well.

H: Amazing. And so now do you think you could help other kids who might be going through something similar? *(Validation; Power)*

> Chad was displaying powerful leadership qualities, and I really wanted him to see this in himself and the power he had to influence others. If I saw Chad regularly, I would ask him about this as much as I could to keep reinforcing his view of himself as a leader (e.g., "Have you shown anyone lately how good it feels to help others? You're such a great role model—I want everyone to learn from you!").

C: Yeah, I can tell them to think positively about themselves instead of negatively because that helps a lot. If somebody makes them feel really bad, choose, uh, not to spend time with them.

H: What a great role model. *(Validation)*

This type of conversation will help your students reflect on their own feelings about what is okay and not okay. When we remind them of their strength to face hard things and normalize how hard it is to stand up for what we believe in, students can become stronger in their own identity so they are less swayed by pressure from others.

Related Chapters

Chapter 5, "Coaching Students Who Bully or Are Aggressive/Violent"; Chapter 13, "Helping Students Who People-Please"; Chapter 22; "Supporting Students Who Are Bullied"; Chapter 24, "Helping Students Who Face Prejudice"

22 | Supporting Students Who Are Bullied

This chapter will give you tools for supporting students who have been bullied (e.g., physically hurt, verbally abused in person or online, left out of social activities, etc.). Any behavior that causes harm and is done repeatedly to a student who believes that they cannot make it stop (e.g., there is a power imbalance) is considered bullying. You will learn ways of speaking with students who are facing these situations to help them see their own brilliance instead of listening to the perspective of the people who are causing them harm.

WHY Does Being Bullied Impact Students?

Bullying is repeated acts of harm, where the person being bullied doesn't feel like they can make it stop. This feeling of *disempowerment* is what creates a reaction of *following* in many chronically bullied students. (See Chapter 17 for a deeper explanation of *following* behaviors.) There can be a compulsion for them to believe the bully because it is easier to internalize the negative messages they hear than it is to fight a battle that feels impossible to win. Students who are bullied can get into a cycle of wanting to please their bullies (sometimes, this is conscious, and sometimes it is unconscious). This cycle keeps them trapped because they are always *reacting to the behavior of others* rather than *choosing their actions* based on their own internal compass. Students who are bullied can become overly passive or overly aggressive themselves, which both reveal a struggle to believe in their own worth that arises from listening to the words of

179

others. When we see these passive or aggressive behaviors in students, it's essential to pay close attention and ask questions to determine if they are being bullied.

WHAT Can I Do to Help a Student Who Is Being Bullied?

Students who are being bullied need to be reminded of their own power to create change in the situation. Even if they can't *make the person stop bullying them*, they can set small boundaries and talk about their challenges with people they trust. These empowered actions can make a hard situation feel a little bit easier and help students begin to move away from the influence of the bullying dynamic. It is also a really good idea to learn your school's policies on bullying so that you know the steps required of you in these situations. And, like any other situation of harm, you want to make sure you report any suspected bullying behavior to the support team at your school.

HOW Will I Have a Constructive Conversation with a Student about Being Bullied?

In my interview with Paige, she brought up an experience of being bullied. In our conversation, she was able to express her challenging thoughts and feelings and why it is so hard to speak up or set boundaries. She was also able to identify ways that she was, in fact, able to do both of these things. Most students have taken more empowered actions than they realize, and being reminded of this brings back their sense of *power* in the situation. Paige's bullying happened in person, but the steps to take in situations of online bullying are the same. Even when the perpetrator is unknown, students can still take steps to set boundaries (e.g., blocking accounts, putting their devices down) and support themselves by talking about their experiences.

The following is a transcript of my conversation with Paige, showing how the six steps of the learning cycle, shown in Figure 22.1 (validation, patterns, feelings, paradigms, power, and skills), can be used to support a student who has been bullied. See Chapter 17 for a deeper analysis of using these steps with students who are *following*.

Interview with Paige (Age 14)

P: He always calls me "fat" and he always shames me. He'd be like, "Oh, you need to get your hair cut, like you look sloppy."

H: Oh, wow, that's such a hard thing to go through! Usually when people are mean like that, it's because they are hurting. It's actually not about us at all. What do you think he's feeling when he does that? Why do you think he hurts you? *(Validation; Paradigm)*

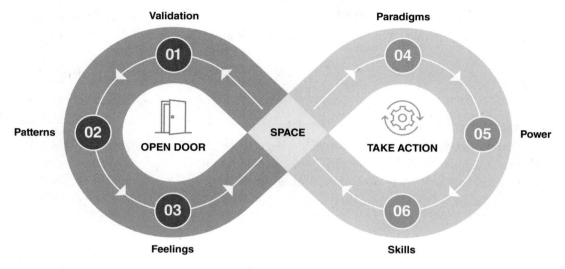

Figure 22.1 The learning cycle for building mental health skills.

Reproduced with permission from Open Parachute.

> I wanted to introduce the paradigm shift that "other people are unkind because they are hurting" so that Paige could see that this cruelty *wasn't her fault*, which is the first step to regaining our power when we are mistreated.

P: To make himself feel more powerful, because a lot of guys at our school, they pick on him, but I'm the one nice person. I let everyone have a second, third, fourth chance. You know, I try to make everyone feel included, but he takes advantage of that and twists my feelings to make me feel like it's my problem.

H: Absolutely. That's really hard. And it's so amazing you can see why he does that! Can you tell me about some of the ways this impacts you? *(Validation; Paradigm; Patterns)*

> I could see that Paige had already made the paradigm shift, so I focused instead on the *impacts of this abuse* so that we could find the right tools to help her cope.

P: It makes me super anxious and I used to go home and cry and, I mean cry for hours and my mom just thought, "Oh, she's being bullied at school." But I didn't wanna tell her the extent of it.

H: It's really normal to worry about telling. Why did you feel like you couldn't? *(Validation; Patterns)*

I wanted Paige to know there was *nothing wrong with her for hiding her experiences.* This is a common part of the cycle of being bullied—a student thinks it's their fault, and therefore doesn't tell anyone, which leads to even more abuse. The only way to change this is for them to get away from the thought that they are doing the "wrong" thing and explore why they might be holding back.

P: I didn't wanna speak up because I felt like if I did speak up and I lost that friendship, then I was the bad person. I was the person to blame. I'm the one who destroyed the friendship. I'm the one who made it all about me and ruined it.

H: I totally get that. But when we don't tell our parents what's going on, it impacts us a lot. Do you notice any of the ways this is impacting you? *(Validation; Patterns)*

P: It makes me cautious around a bunch of my guy friends. I don't have that many for that reason. I'm always cautious with who I make friends with, and I'm always scared that it's gonna happen again, or some person is gonna find a way into my emotions, trick me, and then I'm gonna end up 10 times worse than before.

H: I really get that. It makes sense to feel that way after being mistreated! Do you ever get angry? *(Validation; Feelings)*

I wanted to suggest *anger* because many students who are bullied have anger that they haven't been able to express, and this anger then gets turned on themselves or on others when they lash out.

P: I never get mad at anyone else. I just, I go home and I just, you know, scream into my pillow or cry for hours on end because I don't wanna take it out on anyone else. It's not their problem, it's mine.

H: That's such a common reaction. We think that they're right and we're wrong. That's how the cycle keeps going isn't it? *(Validation; Paradigm)*

> I explicitly stated this pattern to help Paige shift her paradigm in thinking that *any of this was her fault.*

P: Um, yeah, it makes me feel like I'm not worth any person's time. I felt like, I don't understand how these people even, you know, hang around me. I don't know how these teachers even get along with me, sometimes I think I'm such a bad person that no one could ever like me.

H: I'm so sorry you feel that way. And I want you to know that it's not your fault that you're mistreated. You are showing so much strength by talking about this! Those thoughts can really hold us back sometimes, can't they? *(Validation; Patterns; Paradigm)*

> When a student shares a really negative thought like this, I always make sure to focus on making them feel safe and supported in the moment. These thoughts are concerning, so if I hadn't already been speaking with her counselor I would report this to make sure Paige had follow-up support. If I had the chance to talk to her again, I would also want to explore these thoughts more to help her shift them (e.g., "Sometimes our thoughts can be really negative, and that is a really hard thing to go through. I would love to talk to you more about that, to see if I can help you change some of your hard thoughts.").

P: Yeah, like I wanna try and find out why he doesn't like me. Try and, you know, get him to stop or make him like me, you know? So maybe we can be friends. Cuz he's older and like, having an older friend would be great.

H: Definitely. It's really normal to react that way. That's exactly what keeps us stuck. Have you ever been able to set a boundary with him? *(Validation; Patterns; Paradigm; Skill; Power)*

> Given that Paige seemed caught in a cycle of trying to please her bully, I suggested the skill of boundary-setting to introduce a shift in thinking and help her see that she has more power in this situation than she realizes.

P: Well, actually, there was one time he came up to me and said "Hey, you wanna hang out?" And I'm like, "No, I don't wanna hang out with you."

H: That's amazing! How did you feel when you said that? *(Validation; Feelings)*

> I wanted to help Paige see *how good it feels to set a boundary* to motivate her to use this skill again in the future.

P: It was so scary, but it felt so rewarding after, I was like, "I can breathe."

H: That's amazing. What a huge step! And have you been able to talk to your parents about it since then? *(Validation; Skill; Power)*

> I was fishing for other skills, but I also wanted to make sure that Paige had told her parents about this experience. If she hadn't, I would suggest that we tell her parents together.

P: I was like, "I can't let this keep going. Like this has been happening for way too long." And so I told my dad and he felt so bad that it was happening for me.

H: I'm so glad you were able to do that! That's really brave. How did it feel to start finally being honest? *(Validation; Feelings; Power)*

P: It was very hard, but it felt so rewarding. I felt like I could finally talk, like I wasn't trapped in a box anymore. I felt like, you know, I could tell my friends what's going on too. Like, I trust these people.

H: I'm so glad to hear that. You are showing such great strength! That is exactly what will help you get through this. *(Validation; Skill; Power)*

This type of conversation will help your students remember *the power they have to change their circumstances*, by changing their levels of support and the way they feel about themselves in bullying dynamics. This shift in perspective is the support that bullied students need to lead themselves toward more positive friendships.

Related Chapters

Chapter 4, "Supporting Students Who Face Abuse and Domestic Violence"; Chapter 5, "Coaching Students Who Bully or Are Aggressive/Violent"; Chapter 8, "Supporting Students Who Are Worried, Anxious, or Stressed"; Chapter 12, "Supporting Students Who Self-Harm"; Chapter 13, "Helping Students Who People-Please"

23 | Guiding Students Who Violate Consent

This chapter will give you tools for supporting students who have violated the consent of others (e.g., touched someone, spoken about someone in a sexual way, or engaged in any sexual act with someone who did not want these things to occur). You will learn some language you can use to help students who are exhibiting these behaviors to *listen to their own moral compass* instead of following along with cultural norms that perpetuate violations of consent.

WHY Do Students Violate Consent?

Students often don't uphold the boundaries of others because of the pressure they feel to engage in sexual acts "since everyone else is doing it." Many teenagers have sex before they are ready and in situations where they are not truly comfortable because they are *following* outside influences rather than paying attention to their own body signals and noticing what is happening between them and another person. (See Chapter 17 for a deeper explanation of *following* behaviors.) When teenagers make a decision that is disconnected from what is okay for them or their partner, they feel an incredible amount of shame and self-doubt. Because they do not have practice listening to themselves, instead of using these feelings as a guide to making better choices, they often cause further harm to each other to try to make those feelings go away (e.g., "I'm ashamed, so I will spread a rumor about you instead of expressing how I'm feeling.").

185

WHAT Can I Do to Help a Student Who Has Violated Consent?

Students who struggle to uphold consent for themselves or others need to be reminded that they have the wisdom within them to *notice if something is okay or not*. When they start paying attention to their own internal compass, they are able to make decisions about sexual acts that cause no harm. If you ever suspect a consent violation has occurred, it's vital that you immediately report this to the support team at your school. I included this chapter so that you could get a glimpse into how a conversation like this could play out, even if you won't be engaging in it yourself. Having a framework in the back of your mind can really help if this topic comes up at a moment when you have the opportunity to make a difference and you really want to say something to guide a student in the right direction (either before or after you have made a referral). Sometimes students throw out comments in class about consent violations, and your response can really help that student and/or others who are listening.

HOW Will I Have a Constructive Conversation with a Student about Consent Violations?

Michael told me about a situation in which he violated the consent of a partner without realizing it or intending to. In our discussion, Michael had a safe space to explore his feelings and what he learned from this experience. Whether a student is speaking about being violated or being accused of violating someone else, the same steps can help them regain their own internal wisdom to process what happened and move forward in a more empowered way.

The following is a transcript of my conversation with Michael, showing how the six steps of the learning cycle, shown in Figure 23.1 (validation, patterns, feelings, paradigms, power, and skills), can be used with a student who is talking about violations of consent. See Chapter 17 for a deeper analysis of using these steps with students who are *following*.

Interview with Michael (Age 18)

M: There was this girl in my friend group, and we had some like awkward sexual tension. And anyway, we all ended up at my place playing like stripping games and stuff like that. And I was a virgin. And none of them were. I felt like, somewhat pressured, not like, pressured by them, more like by myself, you know, I'm almost 18. Like I haven't lost it. And like, she was hesitant, but I never, ever forced anything on her. And then she kept getting more comfortable and stuff ended up happening. And after the fact she told me that I wasn't allowed to tell anyone. And like, that was my first time. It was a big deal for me. You know, like I was gonna tell a friend at least. So I did, and word spread. And then because word spread, she started telling people that I did it without her permission. She

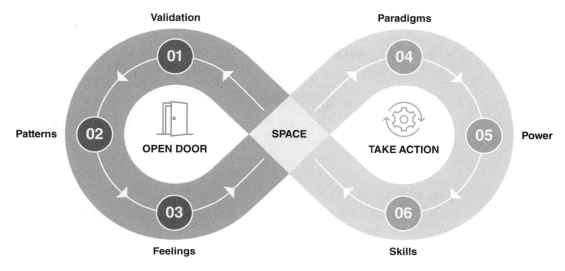

Figure 23.1   The learning cycle for building mental health skills.

Reproduced with permission from Open Parachute.

basically like reneged the agreement after the fact, which made me feel very kind of like, "Am I a rapist?" You know?

H: I'm so glad you shared that because I think a lot of men find themselves in that situation and they don't want to talk about it, but that's what keeps the problem going. So what did it feel like for you when that happened? Like, did you feel shame? Did you feel anger? Did you feel confused? *(Validation; Patterns; Feelings)*

> I wanted to make sure that Michael felt like he could talk about his harmful actions without being judged, so my first response was to *validate* and be *curious* about his experience.

M: It was like self-disgust, you know, like she said some real awful things to me. And from my perspective, all that had happened was that like we'd had sex and like, whatever, and it was fun and it was great and it was my first time, so it was memorable. But I remember one night she called me, she was drunk, and she said some stuff to me that still hurts to think about. And it was really, really painful like "What the fuck have I done? Like, have I actually done the wrong thing? Or is this me overthinking?" There's nothing worse than feeling like you violated someone. . . .

H: It's so hard to feel like you've done the wrong thing! But those feelings are actually so valuable because they teach us what we want to do in the future. Most people bury those feelings, which means they never learn from them. What did you learn from going through that? *(Validation; Power; Paradigm)*

> I wanted to introduce the paradigm shift that *feeling bad about our past actions is actually a helpful thing* (because it gives us the power of insight).

M: Well, I like just sat with myself for a while and was kind of like, "Consent is a thing that is very, like, it's not a 'yes' or 'no,' like it is, but it's also not, you know. It's not like a 'maybe' because a 'maybe' can be reneged. And it's also kind of a blurred line because emotions play into decision-making."

H: Definitely. And so now looking back on it, it sounds like she didn't want to and kind of convinced herself into it, is that something you can see now? *(Validation; Patterns; Paradigm)*

> This is a really important mental shift for students to make—that someone could give verbal consent, but not actually want to do it deep down, and that it's a *partner's responsibility to pay attention to the undercurrent of what's really going on.*

M: Yeah, like at the time I was like . . . a part of me was kind of like, "I don't know if she wants to do this, but the fact that she's going along and saying 'yes' means 'yes,' but like, you need to kind of work around more than that." You know, you can't, it's not just words, it's actions, it's body language, you know.

H: Exactly. It's so incredible that you learned that! And looking back on it now, what can you see? What were the signals that told you that she didn't really want to do it? *(Validation; Skill; Power)*

> Because Michael had already realized this concept, I wanted to help him explore the *skill he used to notice his partner's emotions* because that is the skill that will help him navigate consent in the future. Note that making the space for this kind of honest reflection requires us to withhold our own judgment (like most women, I have experienced consent violations and so hearing about them makes me incredibly angry, but I needed to put that anger aside and validate Michael's perspective in order for him to reflect and learn).

M: It's a hesitancy and it's a kind of slouchy body language. It's kind of like a turtle going back into their shell, you know?

H: That makes sense. Like their body is saying "no" even if they are saying "yes." So what did you learn from that experience? Like how do you apply that learning *(Validation; Paradigm; Power; Skill)*

M: Going into my next relationship, I was very like, "I've really gotta be careful because shit can go south real quick. After the fact, during the fact, before the fact," like, you know, and I was very like, I had to wait, you know, as much as I, you know, wanted to kiss her and like I had to kind of like slow down because you don't have control of the other person's body. It's their body; it's their choice. And like if you push those boundaries, then good luck to you, you know?

H: Wow, that is so powerful! You have so much wisdom about this. How do you navigate that? What do you do to like slow yourself down or take a breath to remember that? Like what do you actually do in the moment? *(Validation; Skill)*

I wanted Michael to explicitly explore his helpful actions so that he consciously remembers and can call on these actions again.

M: You just distract yourself. I remember like we were making out and then like, I wanted to go further, but I kind of had to stop myself and be like, "She might not want to." So I like went to the kitchen to get a drink or like, kind of change it up a bit, you know?

H: That's such a good strategy! And how did breaking the moment help? Did you have more perspective when you weren't so caught up? *(Validation; Skill; Power)*

I asked *how this helped*, but I wanted Michael to see the power in his actions so that he would be encouraged to do it again in future sexual encounters.

M: Yeah, well, if you're able to kind of look at something and be like, you know, "What are the pros and cons of this situation? What are the consequences of this action, of this decision? Where is this going to put me in an hour, a week, a year?" It's about looking at things from a perspective.

H: And so what does that feel like when you take a moment to step back? Cuz that's so powerful. *(Validation; Feelings)*

M: It's like an intuition, like a gut sense.

H: Like what do you feel? It is a nervousness or do you start to feel like a questioning? *(Feelings; Skill)*

> I wanted Michael to identify *exactly how his body talks to him when he has a "gut sense"* so that he could keep listening to it, even in the face of strong emotions or impulses.

M: It's interesting; it's interesting. It's almost like the calm before the storm. It's like nothing's actually happening, but you can tell something could come.

H: Right. And what do you physically feel like? *(Feelings; Skill)*

M: Uh, well, I don't know if this is normal, but like I have a very strong pulse. Um, usually when I feel something's off, my heart can stop. I can't feel it beating anymore, which kind of triggers my brain into thinking like, not fight or flight, but like, you know, "wake up to the situation."

H: That's incredible that you have such an awareness about your own body signals! That is such an important thing to listen to. It's more important than listening to what other people are doing, isn't it? *(Validation; Skill; Paradigm)*

> I circled back to the mental shift of *listening to ourselves, not to other people* because Michael mentioned at the beginning of our conversation that he had sex because "everyone else had done it." I also wanted to validate his insight because that insight is what will help him make helpful choices in intimate relationships in the future. If I could talk to Michael again, I would bring up this concept as a way of reinforcing this learning and applying it to other contexts (e.g., "You really seem to be good at listening to yourself. You are such a great role model for that! How do you think you could use that skill to help others?").

M: Yeah, like listening to too many different perspectives kind of can make you forget about what you feel. And obviously like it can help you make an informed decision, but it depends on who you ask. And it depends on what experiences they've had. Like, if you listen to that, you're not actually able to make your own decision. You're influenced by everyone else.

H: That's so true! And what about talking to your girlfriend? Is that a helpful conversation? *(Validation; Skill)*

> I always like to suggest open dialogue about sex between partners because it's something that not a lot of teenagers feel comfortable doing, and reinforcing that this is a really helpful tool can encourage them to have these conversations more.

M: Yeah, I remember I asked her, I said like, "Have you, you know, have you ever slept with anyone?" You know, it's a weird conversation to bring up and I don't think it's something that you just bring up out of the blue. I think you have to consciously think about the chain of conversation and how to bring that into conversation naturally.

H: Totally. That's such powerful learning! So what's the benefit of having conversations like about consent and sex and awkward topics? *(Validation; Skill; Power)*

M: I think just talking about it makes it so much easier to kind of, the more you talk about it, the more you can talk about it, you know?

H: Definitely.

This type of conversation will encourage your students to listen to their own body signals and notice what is okay and not okay for themselves and others. Digging into the question "What did you feel when it wasn't okay?" will help students tune into their own intuition, and will enable them to learn from their past harmful experiences, and make positive decisions about sexual intimacy in the future.

Related Chapters

Chapter 4, "Supporting Students Who Face Abuse and Domestic Violence"; Chapter 5, "Coaching Students Who Bully or Are Aggressive/Violent"; Chapter 13, "Helping Students Who People-Please"; Chapter 26, "Minimizing the Influence of Pornography and 'Rape Culture'"; Chapter 28, "Helping Students Cope with Being Objectified"

24

Helping Students Who Face Prejudice

This chapter will give you tools for supporting students who have experienced prejudice (e.g., treated "less than" others on the basis of a characteristic like gender, race, age, weight, ability level, etc.). You will learn how you can communicate with a student who has faced these experiences so they can learn that their differences provide them with qualities of *leadership* that they may not realize they possess and that they do not need to listen to the voices of those who oppress them.

WHY Are Students Impacted by Prejudice?

Students are impacted by prejudice because, when we are treated differently, we naturally feel like *we need to change to fit in and be like everyone else*. Whether this prejudice is about their race, gender, sexuality, ability level, neurodivergence, or any other form of difference from their peers, the experience for students is similar. The more pervasive and consistent this treatment is, the more intensely they will be impacted. Students who are treated differently feel confused about their uniqueness and misinterpret it as a fault, so they often try to *follow* their peers in a way that is impossible, attempting to hide their true selves and therefore, their brilliance from the world. (See Chapter 17 for a deeper explanation of *following* behaviors.) Students who are negatively impacted by prejudice can appear to be defiant, self-focused, or constantly complaining. It's important to remember that these actions are a reaction to repeated and consistent mistreatment, and these students need to be supported to process their experiences before they are able to act in harmony with the people around them.

WHAT Can I Do to Help a Student Who Is Impacted by Prejudice?

Students who are impacted by prejudice need to be reminded of the *power of their own uniqueness* and helped to find ways to follow their own path rather than feeling like they need to fit into the framework of others who are different from them.

HOW Will I Have a Constructive Conversation with a Student Who Is Impacted by Prejudice?

In my interview with Abby, she mentioned that she stood out in family photos because of her skin color. During our conversation, I aimed to help her explore the impacts of being singled out or treated differently and to remind herself of the power of the things that made her different. This is an example of subtle prejudice, which is often a bit harder to speak about than blatant cruelty or aggression, and it is vital to help students explore this so that they can understand the ways that they are impacted and can begin the process of helping themselves.

The following is a transcript of my conversation with Abby, showing how the six steps of the learning cycle, shown in Figure 24.1 (validation, patterns, feelings, paradigms, power, and skills), can be used to support a student who has experienced prejudice. See Chapter 17 for a deeper analysis of using these steps with students who are *following*. Another part of my conversation with Abby can be found in Chapter 14, "Encouraging Students Who Are Depressed or

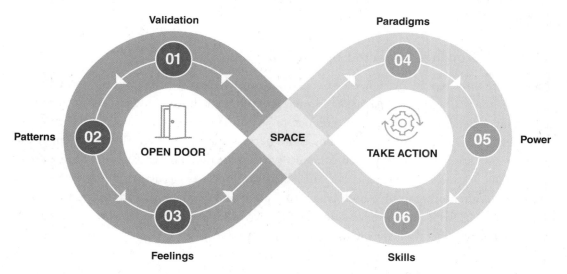

Figure 24.1 The learning cycle for building mental health skills.

Reproduced with permission from Open Parachute.

Apathetic" (there were other factors involved, but there is a strong link between experiencing prejudice and symptoms of depression).

Interview with Abby (Age 15)

A: My dad, he's African and all my family who are darker are all with him and I'm the only one over here. I would always stand out in family photos. Um, and you know, when I would mix in the family, the first thing they would like say is like, "Wow, like your skin is so beautiful." And I'm like, "Uh. . . ."

H: And how does that make you feel when you're singled out in that way? *(Feelings)*

> I wanted to encourage Abby to identify her feelings so that she could find the tools she needed to help with those feelings.

A: Definitely just like really different from the rest of them. Um, I think a lot of my family at family gatherings would assume that I was just really sad all the time and I wasn't, you know, I was usually just there for the food. Like, I don't really care.

H: And how did it make you feel? *(Feelings)*

A: Um, I mean, the attention was nice at first, but like, eventually there's like a hundred other cousins and stuff to go and pester and, yeah. It was just, I felt like it was getting annoying.

H: And so say more about feeling annoyed. Like, did it make you feel different? Did it make you feel like, like singled out? Like, where did your mind go? *(Feelings; Patterns)*

> I suggested the thought about being "different" because it is a very common response to being treated differently, and I wanted Abby to feel safe to explore thoughts like this.

A: Definitely feeling different. Um, yeah.

H: Definitely. And what do you wish they would've done? *(Validation; Patterns; Paradigm)*

> I asked this question to help Abby make the paradigm shift that *she could ask for something different*, that she didn't have to be treated the way she was being treated.

A: Um, just treated me like the rest of them.

H: And why did you want that? *(Patterns)*

> Asking "why" questions can help a student get to the core of what is really going on for them.

A: Well, cuz that's what everybody else had and I wanted to be like everybody else.

H: And that's such a normal desire. Why did you wanna be like everyone else? Like what did you hope, did you wanna feel like you belonged? Did you want to feel like part of the family? *(Validation; Patterns)*

A: I think it was cuz I'm so different. I wanted to be like everybody else. Like I used to always dress like everyone else and I would act like everyone else. And then like as I got older I'm like, "Yeah, it doesn't matter."

H: Definitely. Those thoughts come when we feel different. And so tell me a bit about that. When you were younger, tell me about that thought pattern of wanting to just be like everyone else. Can you describe that? Like was it with friends, was it at school, was it family? *(Validation; Paradigm; Patterns)*

> I wanted to take more time exploring how this challenge impacted Abby before moving on to her change in perspective because I wanted to help her identify what she might still need support with.

A: It would always be like when I would see photos of myself with other people and my mom or other people would always point out like, like, "Look how much taller you are than these other kids." Or like, "You're like the only brown kid here." I'm like, "Yeah, I know, but don't really need to point it out cuz it's obvious."

H: And so what did that make you feel like? *(Feelings)*

A: So that thought of like everyone who's seen that photo now knows who I am.

H: And what was it like to feel like people know you? *(Feelings)*

A: Just like, definitely uncomfortable. Um, yeah, it made me feel very uncomfortable.

H: Yeah. And that's so interesting because some kids are a little bit invisible and all they want is to be seen. But if you're seen, all you want is to be invisible. *(Validation; Paradigm)*

> I wanted to drop in the perspective here that being different or "seen" might also have positive aspects to it.

A: Yeah.

H: I was really tall, you know, I didn't have different colored skin than my peers, but I was really tall. And so I can really relate to that piece of it, of just like, I always wanted to shrink. *(Validation; Patterns)*

> I chose to say a bit about myself here because I thought it might make Abby feel more comfortable and less alone. She was giving short answers and talking in a flat tone, and I wanted to open the door for her to reflect a bit deeper about her experiences.

A: Yeah, exactly. And people are like, "Oh, you're so tall." And it's like, well, you know, you just like, it's almost like the things that make us stand out. We don't, we don't want 'em pointed out. Yeah.

H: Definitely! And so can you talk a little bit about that? So you'd see this photo, someone pointed out, then you'd think, "Oh, my gosh, everyone's seen that." Then what would happen? What would you start doing? *(Validation; Patterns)*

> I was trying to get to the pattern of Abby *thinking she had to be like everyone else* (and the impacts of this), so that we could talk about how she could change this for herself.

A: Um, probably when I was younger, just like, I would try and like first forget about it. Um, but then the next time I would go somewhere where I know there would be photos taken. I would try my best to look like everybody. Like obviously I can't, but just like dress the same and act the same or I would just avoid photos.

H: And then how did that impact your self-esteem, like when you were kind of trying to fit in and be like everyone else? *(Patterns)*

> I asked about self-esteem here as a way to help Abby reflect more on the impacts of trying to fit in.

A: Um, it definitely impacted it a lot cuz, yeah, I just, um, for a while I didn't wanna be in any photos and, uh, yeah, I just didn't really know what to do with myself.

H: And what were the, some of the negative thoughts you started thinking? *(Patterns)*

A: Just like, you know, I wish I was like everybody else. I wish I had pale skin and blonde hair or blue eyes, you know.

H: Those are really hard thoughts. Does anything help you feel differently about yourself? *(Validation; Skill; Power)*

> Now that Abby had shared some really honest truths about herself, it seemed like she was open enough to explore how she can truly help herself.

A: I draw, watch movies.

H: Awesome! How do you feel when you draw? *(Feelings; Skill)*

> I chose to ask about drawing, not watching movies, because creativity can often help us relate to and process our emotions, whereas movies can be soothing but can also be an *escape*, which doesn't ultimately change anything.

A: It's like, you know, this is, it's my thing. Yeah.

H: And what's that like to have your thing? *(Feelings; Power; Paradigm)*

> Abby's comment helped bring the conversation back to the paradigm shift I was hoping to get to earlier, which is that *being different can be a really positive thing* so I wanted to explore this so that she was encouraged to use it as a way to support herself. If I had the chance to talk to Abby again, I would bring up her drawing and the positives of her uniqueness to help her continue to grow in this learning (e.g., "I loved what you were telling me about your drawing the other day. Can you show me some of your style?").

A: Um, it feels good cuz you know, everyone has their thing and I've always followed what everybody else has. So my own thing. It's cool.

H: Awesome. That's great. And so, when you were younger, you didn't wanna stand out. But with your drawing and having your own thing, you are seeing how cool it is to be different. Does this feel like you stepping into your power a little bit? *(Validation; Paradigm; Power; Feelings)*

A: Like it's okay, it's definitely recently I've like realized that I wanna stand out. Not too much, but enough. Definitely a lot more than I would've wanted when I was younger.

H: And so do you think that you are actually seeing the positives of standing out? *(Paradigm)*

A: Yeah, I guess I realized that standing out was better for me. Like I'm not ever gonna fit in, so I gotta accept that I stand out and just do it better.

H: Yeah. Own it, right? What a great skill! *(Validation; Skill)*

A: Yeah. I wanna own being different than everybody else.

H: Amazing. It takes so much strength to realize that! *(Validation; Skill)*

This type of conversation will encourage your students to reflect on the challenge of being treated differently, and how it can make them look outward *to fit in with others*. When we explore this challenge, we can help students remember the power of their own uniqueness, and how valuable it is to appreciate the things that make us different.

Related Chapters

Chapter 6, "Helping Gender Diverse Students Feel Included"; Chapter 13, "Helping Students Who People-Please"; Chapter 14, "Encouraging Students Who Are Depressed or Apathetic"; Chapter 20, "Supporting Students with Low Body Image"; Chapter 22, "Supporting Students Who Are Bullied"

Repeating/Freedom (Remembering Clarity)

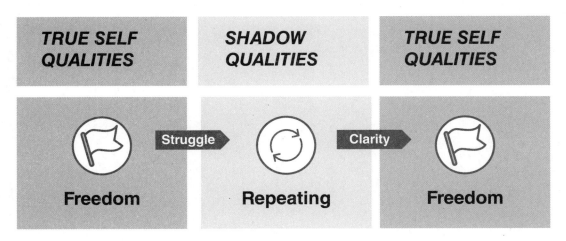

TRUE SELF QUALITIES	SHADOW QUALITIES	TRUE SELF QUALITIES
Freedom	Repeating	Freedom

Struggle → Clarity →

Reproduced with permission from Open Parachute.

This section will provide conversation tips for students who are repeating the *patterns they have experienced in their families* (e.g., through intergenerational trauma or parental conflict/separation) or who are repeating the *cultural patterns of sexualization they have been exposed to* (e.g., perpetuating the mentality of "rape culture" found in pornographic content, or objectifying themselves as a result of being objectified by others). You will learn strategies for supporting students to find the *freedom* to break these repetitive cycles by providing *clarity* about their own behavior.

25

Finding the Words with Students Who Are in *Repeating* Behavior Patterns

Any harmful behavior you see in students could be a *repeat of behavior they have seen before* or ways that they have been treated. However, there are some specific examples that are worth noting so that you have some language to draw on if you are caught off-guard by something a student does that seems to have come from somewhere else.

Young people are always taking in their surroundings and are heavily influenced by the things they witness and experience. Their brains are still forming, and they are figuring out who they want to be. Some students don't yet have a defined set of *values they have decided to live by*, and it can therefore be easy for them to repeat the things they see without realizing the harm they are causing. You see this every day when young students hit each other or use slurs or when older students start smoking or vaping (behaviors that they have clearly witnessed from others or online).

The reason students repeat the harmful actions they see or have experienced is because they lack the clarity to see what they are doing and the impact it is having. This lack of clarity is a protective mechanism, a survival instinct that is designed to keep them safe. When a student repeats patterns based on trauma or harm they have experienced/witnessed, *their mind is trying to protect them from the truth* because the truth is too painful. When someone close to a child betrays their trust and hurts them, often their mind cannot see this person as "bad" because that is too scary of a concept. ("If my parent is cruel and unkind, does that mean the *whole world* is cruel and unkind?" is a very painful thought.) Repeating the cruelty that has been shown to them actually helps a child's mind *normalize* the ways they have been treated (e.g., "What happened to me wasn't so bad because it happens to everyone.").

When students are repeating patterns that they have witnessed in peers or online, this same dynamic is playing out in their minds. It is too overwhelming to think that their peer group or the world (as represented by social media, etc.) has darkness in it, and so by repeating what they see, they unconsciously *block out the harshness of reality by normalizing it*.

This is, of course, a very unhelpful pattern, and while it does provide some emotional protection in the moment, it leads to devastating impacts in the long run. When students repeat harmful behavior, on some level, they know that it is not okay (a *sense of right and wrong* is always there, deep down in all of us). They realize on some level that *they are part of the problem*, which leads to low self-esteem and getting caught in cycles of negativity (e.g., "I know I'm a bad kid, so I might as well keep doing bad things.").

Students who are repeating behaviors need to develop *clarity* so they can see their choices and *understand the freedom they have to choose a different path* than the one that has been laid down before them. If they can be helped to see what pattern they are repeating, understand that this behavior is *not representative of who they really are*, and connect to their own values and the *freedom they have to live those values*, students can move away from harmful, repetitive patterns, and make choices that do not cause harm to themselves or others. If you can have conversations with your students about values and how hard it can be to live in line with our values when there is so much harm happening in the world around us, this will set the stage for diving deeper into conversations with students when the opportunity arises.

What Can I Do to Help Students Who Are Repeating?

Your goal is to make *space* for students to move through the six steps of self-reflection, shown in Figure 25.1, that will help them move away from *repeating* and toward freedom. These steps fall into the two categories explained next.

Figure Explanations
Category 1: Open the Door.

1. **Validating** them and their experiences.

   Validation means letting a student know that what they are facing is normal and that we understand where they are coming from. When a student is repeating, we want to approach them with *curiosity about their actions without judging them* so that they feel safe to self-reflect (e.g., "I know you had a reason to do what you did, I wonder what caused

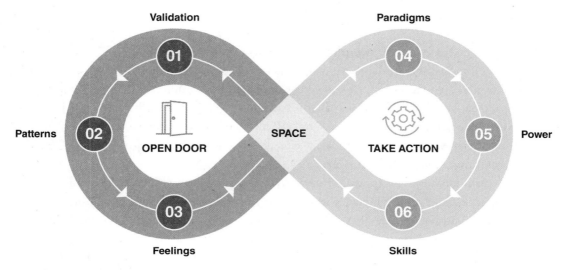

Figure 25.1   The learning cycle for building mental health skills.

Reproduced with permission from Open Parachute.

you to act that way?" or "I really get why you reacted that way. Do you want to talk to me more about it?").

2. Helping them notice their own **patterns.**

   A *pattern* can be any behavioral reaction, way of thinking, or emotional response. When students are repeating, it's vital that they identify the actions they are repeating (and where they learned this pattern from) so they can start to see a pathway to changing things (e.g., "We all learn behavior from somewhere. Do you think you've seen other people doing this same thing?" or "My family has a habit of hiding what they're feeling, so I know I do that sometimes too. Do you have any patterns like that in your family, too?" You never have to use yourself as an example if you don't feel comfortable, but if you do, it can help normalize repetitive patterns, which can help students feel less ashamed, and therefore, more able to reflect.

3. Encouraging them to relate directly to their **feelings.**

   Feelings are the physical and emotional responses that a student has to their experiences. When students are repeating, they need to *feel the impacts of their actions*. This is challenging, and must be done gently and with a lot of empathy because this can be a very painful reflection (e.g., "I know it's hard to reflect on this, but do you notice how you feel after you act that way?" or "It's really easy to feel bad about ourselves because of the things that have happened to us. Do you ever feel that way?").

Category 2: Take Action.

4. Helping them shift their **paradigm,** or the way they are seeing things.

   A *paradigm* is a student's fundamental views about themselves and the world. Students who are repeating to be *reminded of their own freedom,* and helped to see that *they are more than how they are acting* (e.g., "You have done things that are harmful, but I can see you're not that person deep down" or "We all do things we're not proud of" or "Seeing the pattern we are caught in means we're already partway to changing it!").

5. Reminding them of their **power.**

   A student's *power* is their ability to act with agency in their own world—their ability to enact change and influence their experiences. When a student is repeating, we want to help them see that they have *already made their own positive choices.* This will help them see that they have more freedom than they realize (e.g., "Have you ever made a different choice than the choices your parents/friends have made?" or "I have seen you start to react, and then you stopped yourself. Do you remember that?").

6. Supporting them to use a **skill** that helps them move forward.

   Skills are anything a student does that helps them cope or change their physical and emotional circumstances. Students who are repeating need to reconnect to what they truly believe in and who they want to be in order to have the self-esteem necessary to make choices to change harmful patterns. You can help them with phrases such as "Who do you want to be in this situation?" or "Tell me what matters to you the most."

These steps can help your students gain clarity about their experiences and actions, and reconnect to their own freedom of choice about the way they respond to the struggles they have faced. This reflection will help them stop repeating the harmful actions they witness or experience. We want to use gentleness and curiosity to help students question their own actions and see the connection between their actions and challenges they have been through. The following chapters will give you examples of how you can support students in various repeating patterns so that you can find the words to say when you notice a student is repeating behavior that is causing harm.

26

Minimizing the Influence of Pornography and "Rape Culture"

This chapter will give you tools for supporting students who are exposed to pornography or "rape culture" (e.g., the normalization of sexual violence perpetrated against women). You will learn conversation strategies for helping students learn to stop *repeating* the patterns they witness.

WHY Are Students Impacted by Pornography and Why Does "Rape Culture" Exist?

When students watch a lot of pornography, they often want to *repeat the acts they witness*, which is part of what contributes to "rape culture" (e.g., condoning sexual assault and the objectification of others). (See Chapter 25 for a deeper explanation of *repeating* behavior.) In recent years, more and more students have a great deal of access to pornography (based on greater internet access, less parental supervision, and more time on social media), and this often desensitizes them to this type of content. A lot of the pornography that is readily available for students involves sexual violence and domination, and this can create confusion in their minds about what is acceptable and desired by their potential partners. In addition, sex has historically been used as a weapon of domination, and sexual violence toward children is still a devastatingly

207

common abuse of power in our world. Students are exposed to all of this, and so it is natural that they might see sex as an act that involves a *victim* and a *perpetrator*. This leads many students to seek sexual domination *in order to ensure they are never the victim*. Students who are participating in "rape culture" (e.g., making derogatory comments, grabbing/touching inappropriately, or laughing along with someone else who is doing those things) will likely appear to enjoy this behavior in a way that is cruel and even sadistic. It's important to remember that this perceived enjoyment is usually only a reflection of how they think they should respond or an indication that deep down they are worried they could be mistreated in the same way.

WHAT Can I Do to Help a Student Who Is Impacted by Pornography and Involved in "Rape Culture"?

Students who are playing out patterns of sexual domination need to be given a space to reflect on these behaviors so they can gain the *clarity* to understand their own *freedom* to make different choices that acknowledge the vulnerability of intimacy and therefore, respect that these experiences require.

HOW Will I Have a Constructive Conversation with a Student Who Is Impacted by Pornography and Participating in "Rape Culture"?

In my conversation with Raymond, he mentioned being in situations where nonconsensual acts occurred. This led to a discussion about common cultural pressures, which enabled him to express some of his feelings, gain clarity on things that have influenced him, and connect to his own values and ability to make different choices. Even students who seem completely caught up in these cultural patterns usually have much more of an ability to reflect than we realize, when they are given the chance to speak openly and reflectively about the dynamics they are a part of. This is why creating intentional conversations about this topic is so beneficial (even when it feels uncomfortable). It's very important that you are also supported in having these conversations by support staff at your school, and that you make a referral to ensure students have more in-depth conversations and guidance around this topic. However, when you have the opportunity, you can also reinforce helpful messages by following the steps laid out in Figure 26.1.

The following is a transcript of my conversation with Raymond, showing how the six steps of the learning cycle, shown in Figure 26.1 (validation, patterns, feelings, paradigms, power, and skills), can be used with a student who is exposed to pornography or "rape culture." See Chapter 25 for a deeper analysis of using these steps with students who are *repeating*.

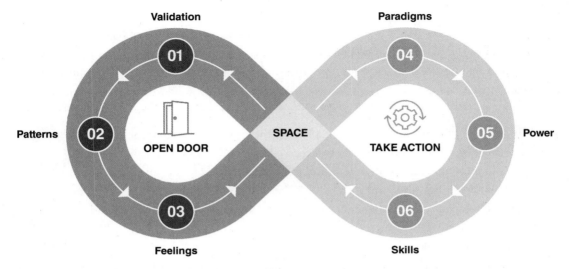

Figure 26.1 The learning cycle for building mental health skills.

Reproduced with permission from Open Parachute.

Interview with Raymond (Age 18)

R: I've definitely seen situations that aren't very pleasant to be in, um, especially with drugs and alcohol mixed together. Um, or nonconsensual acts.

H: I'm glad you brought this up, issues around consent. Do you want to talk about some of the things that you've seen or been around? *(Validation; Patterns)*

> I expressed curiosity and openness here because I could tell Raymond was uncomfortable bringing this up, and I wanted to make sure he felt safe to explore this topic with me.

R: Uh, we used to have competitions. Oh, how many can you hook up with in a night? Or how many have you hooked up with? And we used to, I mean, I don't wanna put myself in the group, but I was part of the group. We made lists of the girls we used to go out with, and then we would show each other. Like, "See, I've got more than you have." And for me it wasn't a conquest kind of thing, it was more of just, you know, um, "She's nice. Maybe it worked out and then it didn't. So try the next one."

H: Yeah, I hear about that a lot. What contributed to you going along with it? Where does that come from? *(Validation; Patterns; Paradigm)*

I asked "Where does that come from?" because I wanted Raymond to reflect on the paradigm shift that *he has been influenced by the patterns he has seen in the world around him*, which can open up the door to more compassion for himself, which will lead to honest self-reflection and change.

R: I think most men, we just want to be a part of the group and seem cool. Uh, like, "Be a dick. Be cool." You know? And it's not the right choice. You don't wanna do that, but. . . .

H: That's literally the culture in a snapshot, right? Isn't it? Like that's the message we give guys. "You're a dick and you're cool." *(Validation; Patterns; Paradigm)*

R: Yeah. It's like you measure your success on how many girls you've dated. And that was also a big insecurity for me starting high school.

H: Yeah, I get that. And you obviously shifted this in your own head because you can reflect on it, which is so cool. So what does it feel like as a guy to be in these situations? Does it feel like "If I don't play along with this, I'm not gonna be accepted?" *(Validation; Patterns; Feelings; Power)*

I wanted Raymond to see that *he has already started to make the change by seeing the pattern*, which can be a very empowering realization.

R: Yeah. Um, I think this toxic masculinity comes from different places. It comes from stereotypes from culture, um, social media, even like movies and music songs, and I feel like, uh, there's a lot from like older generations.

H: Absolutely. And do you think that porn plays a role in that too? Like when, you know, a lot of what we see in porn is these guys dominating women and you know, guys are exposed to this at a younger and younger age. Do you think that representation of what sex is and like women being there to please men, do you think that plays a role? *(Validation; Patterns; Paradigm)*

I brought up pornography because it is an important paradigm shift to see the role that porn plays in our understanding of sex, and most students won't know that it's okay to talk about this unless it is brought up first, in a safe and respectful conversation. I definitely felt awkward bringing this up, especially with a male student. Feelings of discomfort are a really normal and natural part of opening the door to deeper conversations, so it's a great skill for us to practice to sit with those feelings!

R: Yeah. Um, porn being on the internet and so easily accessible. Um, there's people, I've seen like little kids talking about it. . . .

H: Definitely. Have you watched porn or have your friends watched porn? *(Validation; Patterns)*

> I asked about his *friends* because sometimes it's easier for teens to talk about someone else at first when reflecting on sensitive topics like this. I usually bring the conversation back to focusing on themselves instead of others, but when it comes to topics like sex that a student might never feel comfortable opening up about to an adult, I don't push so much for "personal" reflections.

R: I mean, I have, yes. Um, I remember being little and kind of just searching it up the first time. Um, I didn't like it the first time, to be honest. I thought it was weird, so I just deleted it.

H: Yeah, that makes sense. So, what did you feel when you watched it that made you not like it? Like, did it seem wrong to you? Did it seem like graphic? Like were you young and it was like a shock? *(Validation; Patterns; Feelings)*

> I wanted to *suggest options* of how Raymond might have been impacted by seeing porn at a young age, so that he knew he could express these potentially uncomfortable feelings to me. I said a lot of things at once here, which does also have the potentially of confusing a student, so I could have probably slowed down and suggested these things one at a time.

R: Um, I think I felt maybe confused or even disgusted, maybe like not because I understood the complexity of what porn was, um, but like, "Oh, something is going inside of her. That's just weird," you know?

H: And so was that the first place you learned what sex was? *(Patterns; Validation)*

> Here, I was leading back to the paradigm shift of the *impact that porn has on our understanding of sex.* If porn is our first introduction to sex, this can have a massive impact on our perspectives.

R: Um, I don't recall, but I'm gonna say "yes." Yes, I think so.

H: What impact do you think that had on your young mind and other guys in your peer group to have seen this you know, a sexualized kind of male dominance version of sex.

Like how do you think that influenced the way you all saw women and saw girls? *(Patterns; Paradigm)*

R: For most men, uh, for most boys it's generally hard to separate these things. You see something at home, you wanna repeat it and you bring it to school and you talk to other guys about it. I remember when I was like grade two, my friends would bring some stuff home and like bring stuff to the class and I was like, "What are you talking about?" And then maybe that's even what made me go on the internet for the first time. Um, cuz I wanted to seem cool and be talking about the same things they were talking about, right.

H: Absolutely. And so coming from this, and like it's cool to hook up with girls, it's cool to be a dick. How did you change that? What did you do? How did you start, you know, seeing that actually, wow, this is disrespectful to girls. I need to change that. What changed for you? *(Patterns; Validation; Power)*

> I made the assumption that Raymond *had made this change* because he was able to reflect so deeply on these patterns. I wanted to help him find examples of things he had done differently so that he could see his own power to break free from this cultural norm.

R: Um, like I had a list of the girls I had made out with and once these topics come out, like BLM and like the Me Too movement and whatever, you kind of say, "Yeah, this is wrong." Um, I need to change. So you kind of just delete the list. You delete pictures of girls you have saved, "She looks pretty" and whatever. Because boys have those group chats and they say, "Oh, look at this girl. She's so hot." And then you just kind of delete them and you say like, "This was wrong."

H: That's so awesome. You're obviously a very incredible person, deep thinker, really principled. What has helped you know who you want to be? Like to become the person you are? *(Validation; Skill)*

> I wanted Raymond to identify the *specific steps he took* in order to change his behavior so that he could continue using the same skills going forward. Making a change like this is a huge deal for a teenager, so by validating it and exploring it I was hoping to encourage more of the same actions from him in the future. If I had a chance to talk to Raymond again, I would bring up his process again, so he could explore it even deeper (e.g., "I love what you said about the 'in between' and how you reflect on things. Can you tell me more about what that means to you?").

R: Uh, that's a deep question. Uh, I think I just have the sense of what is right or what is wrong. Like, it's not always black and white, you have to be able to look in the between and, yeah, I just feel good about myself.

H: I love that. And you're so right. It's not black and white, and it all comes from within, right? And so I would say what's true for me, and it sounds like what's true for you, is that the more time I spend looking at my own decisions, my own life, my own feelings, that helps me make more helpful decisions. *(Validation; Power; Skill)*

> I brought in my own experience as a tool for validating Raymond's process of self-reflection and really looking at what is okay and not okay based on how it makes us feel (knowing that an adult they respect uses the same tools of personal development that they do can help a student see their own wisdom and power).

R: Yeah, definitely. Um, the more I talk about these, subjects, um, the more I feel like I'm in the between of things and, um, I feel like kind of, like a bit of responsibility and, uh, independence of like just kind of growing up, you know?

H: Totally. The world is lucky to have you! *(Validation)*

This type of conversation will help your students find clarity about where their ideas of sexual intimacy come from, and the harmful impacts of cultural norms of sexual domination on themselves and others. This helps them remember their freedom of choice and ability to break free of the patterns they are exposed to.

Related Chapters

Chapter 5 "Coaching Students Who Bully or Are Aggressive/Violent"; Chapter 13, "Helping Students Who People-Please"; Chapter 18, "Supporting Students Who Are Negatively Impacted by Gender Norms"; Chapter 21, "Helping Students Stand Up to Peer Pressure"; Chapter 23, "Guiding Students Who Violate Consent"; Chapter 28, "Helping Students Cope with Being Objectified"

27 | Supporting Students Who Experience Intergenerational Trauma

This chapter will give you tools for supporting students who have experienced intergenerational trauma (traumatic patterns that are repeated throughout generations of their family). You will learn the words you can use to help students understand that they do not have to *repeat* these patterns in their own lives and that they have the *freedom* to become whomever they choose to be.

WHY Are Students Impacted by Intergenerational Trauma?

Students who experience intergenerational trauma often *repeat* the harm that was caused to them by their parents (who are repeating the harm that was caused to *them* by *their* parents). (See Chapter 25 for a deeper explanation of *repeating* behavior.) They feel so hurt by the trauma inflicted on them that it's easier to start acting out in ways that cause a similar trauma to others, so that it *normalizes* this behavior and protects students from feeling the full sadness of what has happened to them (e.g., "What happened to me isn't so bad because it happens to everyone."). Students who are caught in cycles of intergenerational trauma are often misidentified as "problem" kids because they can act erratically, aggressively, and disrupt learning. It's important to reflect on where students learned this behavior from and whether they are repeating something they have witnessed or experienced at home. This does not excuse harmful behavior, of course, but it provides context so we can communicate with them more effectively.

WHAT Can I Do to Help a Student Who Has Experienced Intergenerational Trauma?

Students who are in cycles of intergenerational trauma need to be shown a great deal of empathy so that they can *connect to the pain of their own experiences*. This helps them have *clarity* about what has happened to them and also the ways that they may be repeating these patterns, which creates a sense of *freedom* to do things differently.

HOW Will I Have a Constructive Conversation with a Student Who Has Experienced Intergenerational Trauma?

Caylen disclosed some really painful traumatic patterns in his family. By having a chance to speak about this openly, he was able to reflect on his patterns and also see the positive choices he had already made to change the cycles of trauma in his family. He was also able to express the kind of man he wanted to be, which is different than what he witnessed in his father. This helped him remember his freedom and *feel clear about his sense of self*. Patterns of intergenerational trauma are some of the hardest to shift because our family history is so instrumental in shaping our view of the world. It's important to keep in mind that students who face these patterns need the most consistent compassion and forgiveness that we can offer, and as many opportunities as possible to engage in respectful self-reflective dialogue. Change can happen at any time, and *when we see their potential for change*, this helps students to see it in themselves too. With any form of trauma, it's important that you look for signs that harm is being caused. If you suspect there is harm that has happened or is happening to your student or anyone in their family, make sure you refer to a mental health practitioner or the support staff at your school for further follow-up (you can do this before or after you speak with them, and you can keep reinforcing the steps below alongside any professional help they receive).

    The following is a transcript of my conversation with Caylen, showing how the six steps of the learning cycle, shown in Figure 27.1 (validation, patterns, feelings, paradigms, power, and skills), can be used to support a student who has faced intergenerational trauma. See Chapter 25 for a deeper analysis of using these steps with students who are *repeating*.

Interview with Caylen (Age 17)

C: Um, I did see a lot of violence and dad never really did hurt me or my sister. He was never like that. He was just really messed up on like drugs and stuff like that, alcohol, all

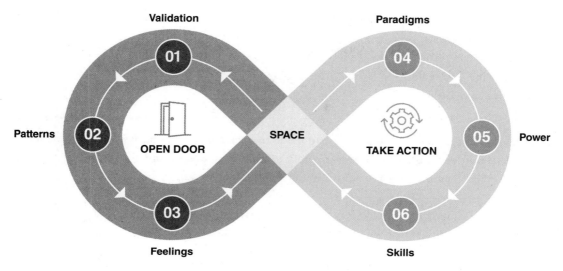

Figure 27.1   The learning cycle for building mental health skills.

Reproduced with permission from Open Parachute.

that stuff and like that, that's just clouded his mind to the point where, you know, he'd be in and out of jail half the time. The only way I could see him was to go to jails and visit him, and I've been through like four different jails, maybe five.

H: That's super hard. How did that impact you? What were the thoughts and feelings you had? Did you feel sad? Did you feel different? *(Validation; Patterns; Feelings)*

> Hearing about really sad experiences like this always feels like a bit of a shock. The thing I always try to remember is that if a student discloses something like this, they really want to talk about it. If I'm caught off-guard, *getting curious about it* is a good way to help me connect with them even if I'm feeling a bit overwhelmed by what they have said (which I was here). I suggested that he might have felt "different" because this is a common painful reaction to having an absent parent, and I wanted Caylen to feel safe to express his pain to me, by showing him that I understood.

C: I felt a lot different. You know, seeing other kids with their dads and stuff like that, father figures and that, I guess when I got to probably like 13 and that, I started more resenting dad and like, you know, that's the reason that I lash out a lot. I got really bad anger issues and that, and like I started saying like, "It's his fault," and this and that. And like over time I've matured myself up a lot.

H: Yeah, that's so great you can see that, that your anger might come a lot from your dad. What were you feeling underneath the anger? Were you feeling lost? *(Validation; Patterns; Paradigm; Feelings)*

> It was incredible that Caylen already had made the paradigm shift that *his anger was a result of pain.* Because of this, I was able to explore it a bit more deeply, and ask direct questions so he could benefit the most from his understanding of himself.

C: Uh, I was feeling like I gotta put on this, this show of like, strength.

H: And what were you feeling? Like, were you feeling sad? Were you feeling isolated? Were you feeling like. . . . *(Feelings; Paradigm)*

> Note that I asked the same question about his deeper feelings again. I often do this because it is hard for many students to reflect on these more vulnerable feelings right away, and it takes a bit of prompting to get there.

C: I felt, well, I felt pain and sad and that on both sides. Cuz like I said, I have my dad, which was the past, but he also could be in the future. And like that's really, that clashes in my mind like "What's it gonna be like in the future? Will I ever be connected with him? Will I ever talk to him?" And like, that like really digs into my heart and brain and like really gets me scratching and like scared, "What's gonna happen?"

H: Yeah, all that's going on in your brain and then you just lash out cause it's too much . . . I really get that. And so how do you make a different choice when that's happening? Is there something different you can do? *(Validation; Patterns; Power; Skill)*

> Because Caylen was so honest in his expression of feelings, I knew the door was open for him to also reflect on *how he could support himself with these feelings,* so I shifted the conversation to helping him find his power.

C: Um, I used to look at my great grandpa and he's a boxer. And I like to punch and like do boxing training and that. So I got to high school and I just jumped straight into it.

H: That's amazing. I love that you started finding your passion and finding things you care about to release your anger in a different way. That's more who you are right? And how did it feel to be acting more like who you wanna be? *(Validation; Feelings; Skill; Power)*

> I wanted Caylen to see that the choice to do boxing was an incredibly positive one because he was *turning toward things he cared about*, rather than repeating the patterns of his past.

C: It felt releasing. I wasn't even thinking about my father. . . . When I first started doing it, I thought of my dad, just hitting him. But then I felt the, the full like, potential of it and like the point of it. And then I sort of just got into that, not thinking about like the bad stuff that could anger me, but like the stuff that I want to focus on and that's where, you know, I've gotten to the point where I want to focus on what's best for me at the moment.

H: Amazing. So you really realized you want to focus on the future, not the past? Is that more who you want to be? *(Validation; Skill)*

C: Yeah.

H: And so how did you get out of that cycle? Like what different choices did you make? *(Validation; Power; Skill)*

> I probed more here because I wanted Caylen to keep reflecting on *things that he had already done* to make different choices so that he could see his own power to change his family patterns.

C: Uh, a lot of the time I try to stay gentle to myself in school when we have sports, I try to stay as gentle as possible.

H: I love that. How does it help you to be gentle? Does that help you not get aggressive with others? *(Validation; Skill; Power)*

C: Um, you know, it helps me put a different emotion onto other people like, um, for example, if I was rough, I'd be saying like, just swearing, like a really aggressive tone. But I like to speak a bit slower like in a more gentle tone.

H: That's so good. And how does that help you when you do that? *(Validation; Skill; Power)*

C: Um, it helps me like understand the people around me and like who I'm dealing with, what they're like, what their trauma's like as well.

H: Amazing. I can see that you really care about other people. And what do you do differently with those feelings about your dad now? *(Validation; Skill; Feelings)*

> I brought his dad up again here to help him see that his amazing level of insight was helping him change his patterns of intergenerational trauma. I didn't explore his insight into the trauma patterns of other people because I was focused on helping him see the link to his dad, but if I had the chance to speak with him again, I would bring this up (e.g., "You mentioned that you learn a lot about other people's trauma. What do you notice about that?"). This is a really powerful reflection for a student to have (that other people are often acting from a place of pain based on their personal histories), so the more we can help them explore it the better!

C: Well, I'm growing up now and I've now seen that he's in a dark place and it's not my fault. I think positive and like he still cares about me. I know that he does. He has a bloody hard way of like trying to, you know, show that love so, yeah, it's hard, but I just take it one day at a time. I know he does, and as much as I want him as my father, again, there's nothing I can do. But the least I can do is keep moving on with my life to keep supporting those that are in need, to have people move on with me and stuff like that, to move forward more to the brighter future.

H: Absolutely. And that's so wise. How does it feel to be focusing on the person you want to be? To do things differently than your dad? *(Validation; Power; Feelings; Paradigm)*

> This was such an incredible paradigm shift that Caylen had already made, so I asked *how it felt for him* so that his positive feelings could motivate him to continue thinking in this way.

C: It feels amazing because I wanna be that one person for other kids to look up to.

H: Amazing. And you are! *(Validation)*

This type of conversation will help your students gain more clarity about the trauma they have experienced within their family, and their ability to make different choices. Even if they only see a *glimpse of their potential for change*, every conversation that provides a space to reflect on *how they are connected to their own values* will have an impact on their cycles of intergenerational trauma.

Related Chapters

Chapter 4, "Supporting Students Who Face Abuse and Domestic Violence"; Chapter 5, "Coaching Students Who Bully or Are Aggressive/Violent"; Chapter 22 "Supporting Students Who Are Bullied"; Chapter 24, "Helping Students Who Face Prejudice"; Chapter 29, "Responding to Students Who Share Stories of Parental Conflict and Separation"

28 | Helping Students Cope with Being Objectified

This chapter will give you tools for supporting students who have experienced objectification (being treated like a sexual object or being talked about in a sexual way without their consent). You will learn strategies for having conversations that help students see the *freedom* they have to treat themselves with respect, even if that is not the pattern that is being *repeated* around them.

WHY Are Students Impacted by Objectification?

Objectification is *degrading a person to the status of an object*. In our culture, this often takes the form of sexual objectification, which prioritizes the importance of sexual attractiveness over other attributes. Students who are objectified often *repeat* the messages they hear by, in turn, objectifying themselves (thinking that their worth is based on their attractiveness to the people who are objectifying them). (See Chapter 25 for a deeper explanation of *repeating* behavior.) They feel overwhelmed by the shallowness and cruelty of being objectified, but if they repeat these messages to themselves, it *normalizes* this behavior, which makes it feel like the world is less unkind (e.g., "It's normal to treat people like this, so I'm not really being harmed."). This feels like a relief in the moment but causes a lot of confusion about how they should be treated and their own sense of self-respect. Often, students who are objectified appear not to care or even make similar comments about their peers. It's important to keep in mind that any student who "goes along" with being mistreated is, in fact, being impacted in a profound way, even if it's not visible on the surface.

WHAT Can I Do to Help a Student Who Has Experienced Objectification?

Students who are objectified need help to reflect on the harm of these patterns and gain clarity on the fact that they may *have internalized what they have heard*. This creates a sense of *freedom* to see themselves with the respect they deserve.

HOW Will I Have a Constructive Conversation with a Student Who Has Been Objectified?

Julia talked about her experiences of being sexualized by boys at her school. In our conversation, she was able to explore the impact of this experience and how it causes her to think of herself in a more negative way and repeat these messages in the way she sees herself. This clarity helped her to find options for how she could respond differently and see her own freedom to break free of this pattern.

The following is a transcript of my conversation with Julia, showing how the six steps of the learning cycle, shown in Figure 28.1 (validation, patterns, feelings, paradigms, power, and skills), can be used to support a student who has been objectified. See Chapter 25 for a deeper analysis of using these steps with students who are *repeating*.

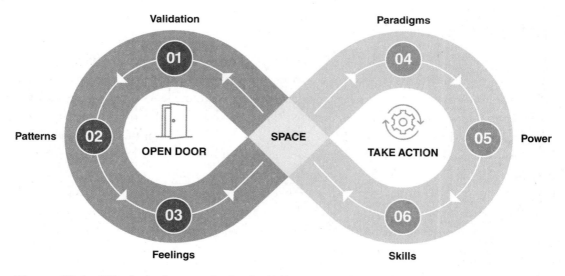

Figure 28.1 The learning cycle for building mental health skills.

Reproduced with permission from Open Parachute.

Interview with Julia (Age 18)

J: I remember it starting in middle school at our dances. It was a competition for the guys. How many girls could you get to dance with you. So you have all these guys going around asking every girl to dance, and I remember I had danced with this one guy, not knowing what it was, but then found out that you're just part of a game.

H: So brutal. And does anything like that happen now that you're in high school? *(Validation; Patterns)*

> Because Julia was talking about the past, I wanted to bring the conversation into the present so we could explore the many layers of this cultural pattern and how pervasive it might still be in her life.

J: I've heard guys make comments, um, saying that like "They're asking for it" if they're dressed a certain way. And they make comments about the way girls look.

H: Yeah. Yeah. That's really hard. And that has a big impact on us, doesn't it? How does that impact you? Does that change how you see yourself or feel about yourself? *(Validation; Patterns)*

> I asked Julia directly how this impacts her because just because we see patterns like this doesn't mean we realize how much they might be causing us harm. I also wanted to introduce the paradigm shift that *when we experience objectification, it can cause us to repeat this pattern by objectifying ourselves.*

J: Yeah, it's just kind of like, almost like a feeling of not being good enough and knowing that you will never be good enough.

H: Yeah. Where does that thought come from? *(Validation; Patterns)*

J: Uh, well, guys prefer, you know, wider hips, a bigger chest, stuff like that. And for me, I know that I would never, I mean, I have a smaller build and I just won't ever look like that. Um, not that I would like to, you know, be objectified by a man, but just like even for them to just think that you look nice. Like you have to fit a certain body shape for a boy to think that you look nice.

H: Isn't that just so frustrating that that's our sense of worth? Because it's like, "Does a guy find you attractive?" As a woman like that is a way that we measure ourselves. So how do we change this? Can we do anything differently? *(Validation; Patterns; Paradigm; Power)*

I used "we" language to help Julia feel less alone in her struggles (as a woman, I can relate to the challenge of objectification). Because she was able to reflect so clearly on her thoughts and feelings, she seemed ready to find her own power to help with those thoughts and feelings. I could have also explored her feelings a bit more before jumping into her empowerment. If I had a chance to speak with her again, I would ask more questions about this (e.g., "Tell me more about that feeling of wanting to not be objectified, but also wanting to be noticed. That's a really tough one, isn't it?").

J: We really have to learn and start to hold them accountable. So that they can recognize that this kind of stuff isn't okay. You just don't say certain stuff, you don't do certain things. Um, you know, just break the chain.

H: Yeah. Beautiful. You're so right. And do you have an example of when you've done that? Cause I know that's not easy. It's sort of the little steps, isn't it? Like maybe calling someone out in front of everyone is like, "Whoa, that's too far." But like, have you ever had a situation where you just said, you know, "That's not cool"? *(Validation; Power)*

I was trying to help Julia see that *she might have done more than she realizes.* I probably could have led with a more open-ended question, but I was trying to show her that it's okay if she hasn't been all that bold with this yet (it is incredibly hard for students to go against the grain of a cultural pattern like this).

J: Well, like one of my friends, a boy at our school had said something so offensive, and she had called him out on it and she's like, she's a more quieter type. And she called him out.

H: That's so brave! What does it feel like for you to, to see role models or see that other people are speaking up? How does that inspire you? Is that something you care about too? *(Validation; Feelings; Power)*

If a student doesn't have an example of their own actions, helping them identify *how good it feels to see the empowerment of others* is another way to motivate them to take similar actions themselves.

J: Um, I think it's really powerful to see that these women are finally taking a stand and they're finally recognizing that they are able to speak up. And I just wish that I could have been like that for somebody else.

H: Well, you can be, absolutely. Talking about it now is a huge first step! Do you think that having these conversations with your friends can help you support each other in this journey of, you know, creating a world that feels safer, that you can be yourself in? *(Validation; Power; Skill)*

> I wanted Julia to know that *speaking about this issue and reflecting on it* is actually a really powerful skill that will help her take the next step of action when she is ready.

J: Yeah. I think it's way easier when you have someone else to talk to, and I wish that there was more outlets for people who might not be comfortable talking to anyone, or they might not have friends at high school cuz kids suck.

H: Yeah, absolutely. And that really is the way forward, isn't it? We talk to each other, we support each other. You know, the more you realize, "Oh, we're all feeling the same way." You know, that's what turns those social systems on their head. *(Validation; Power; Skill)*

> Julia was still talking pretty negatively at this point, and it would have been really useful to explore her feelings a bit more, but I sensed that she could talk in circles about this and our conversation was ending, so I was trying to finish on a positive reframing of the situation to remind her of her power to do things differently. If I had a chance for a follow-up conversation, I would definitely explore her patterns of *internalizing the messages she hears* a bit deeper because that would help her see the power she has to *change how this experience is impacting her.*

This type of conversation will help your students see the impacts of the cultural patterns of objectification that are all too common in our culture. It will also help them remember that no matter how ingrained a pattern is, they always have the power to make small changes, and these changes can mean that they don't have to see themselves the way that others see them.

Related Chapters

Chapter 13, "Helping Students Who People-Please"; Chapter 18, "Supporting Students Who Are Negatively Impacted by Gender Norms"; Chapter 20, "Supporting Students with Low Body Image"; Chapter 22, "Supporting Students Who Are Bullied"; Chapter 23, "Guiding Students Who Violate Consent"; Chapter 24, "Helping Students Who Face Prejudice"; Chapter 26, "Minimizing the Influence of Pornography and 'Rape Culture'"

29 | Responding to Students Who Share Stories of Parental Conflict and Separation

This chapter will give you tools for supporting students whose parents are in conflict or have separated. These experiences are most impactful when students perceive aggression, resentment, or a lack of respect between parents. You will learn ways of communicating with students experiencing these situations so that they can understand that they do not have to *repeat* the dynamics they are witnessing in their own peer groups.

WHY Are Students Impacted by Parental Conflict and Separation?

When students are in households where there is conflict, or there are changes in how much they see their parents, they often *repeat* the frustration and sadness they feel at home by *creating situations that cause them to feel a similar way*. (See Chapter 25 for a deeper explanation of *repeating* behavior.) It is so challenging for a child to think of their parents as being imperfect or being the cause of harm, and if they create situations where *they themselves are creating harm*, it can help their minds to feel like their home life is less "faulty." This relieves stress in the moment but can cause *confusion* about whether or not the students themselves are to blame for their parents' behavior (e.g., "I know I am acting badly, maybe that's why my parents are fighting."). Until they realize that their actions are a result of the struggles they are experiencing at home, they will often make this unfortunate assumption. Often when students are acting out or getting into conflicts with peers, there will be similar patterns playing out in their family. It's important to remember this so that we don't assume these students are simply troublemakers.

WHAT Can I Do to Help a Student Who Is Struggling with Parental Conflict or Separation?

Students who are struggling with parental conflict or separation need a safe space to reflect on their own actions and be reminded that their actions are coming from a place of pain because of what they have experienced at home. This enables them to see the *freedom* they have to make different choices.

HOW Will I Have a Constructive Conversation with a Student Who Is Struggling with Parental Conflict or Separation?

Aiden shared with me some of the challenges his parents faced in their relationship. Often kids pick up on way more than we realize and don't have many opportunities to reflect on what they see. It was helpful for Aiden to be able to dig deeply into his experience of what happened between his parents so that he could also have a bit more *clarity* about where his own unhelpful behavior was coming from.

The following is a transcript of my conversation with Aiden, showing how the six steps of the learning cycle, shown in Figure 29.1 (validation, patterns, feelings, paradigms, power, and skills), can be used to support a student whose parents are in conflict or have separated. See Chapter 25 for a deeper analysis of using these steps with students who are *repeating*.

Interview with Aiden (Age 9)

A: Um, with my parents it was really hard because all the money involved. And they were arguing a lot cuz they probably didn't love each other anymore. And I was mad at him for a while, my dad. But after that, um, things were okay. After they broke up, we were all happy again and I got to see him and I really liked seeing him cuz I didn't get to live with him and I only got to spend a couple nights with him sometimes.

H: That's a really important challenge to talk about, isn't it? Cuz so many kids go through that and we don't necessarily know how to talk about it. How old were you when your parents separated? *(Validation; Patterns)*

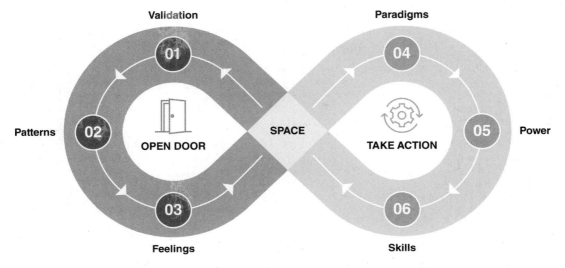

Figure 29.1   The learning cycle for building mental health skills.

Reproduced with permission from Open Parachute.

> I wanted to ask Aiden a few specific questions about what happened because I could tell by his comment that the whole experience with his parents was a bit overwhelming for him. Breaking things down into simple memories or facts can help students to feel more clear and less confused about their experiences.

A: Well, I was a lot of ages when they separated. They separated like five times in my life maybe, or something like that. The most recent one is probably when I was just eight and I think, I can't really remember anymore.

H: Got it. So they got back together and broke up lots of times. Yeah. That's hard. And what was it like for you? What did you feel? *(Validation; Feelings)*

> I asked about feelings here again to help Aiden understand his experience more clearly and simply.

A: Um, I felt like I was heartbroken because I need my dad in my life. . . .

H: Definitely. I get that. And what do you do now when you miss your dad, to help you feel better? *(Validation; Skill; Power)*

> I went straight to asking about *how Aiden could help himself* because he looked really sad in that moment, and I wanted to help him feel a bit more empowered. I circled back to exploring his feelings later, but I could have also done that here instead.

A: Oh, I FaceTime him on my iPad a lot and I text him.

H: That's awesome. And does that help you feel better? *(Validation; Power; Skill; Feelings)*

A: Yeah, I feel better because we get to talk, and sometimes I'm stressed and I need to talk to him about stuff.

H: So he's a good resource for you to talk to. That's awesome. What are the things that make you stressed? *(Validation; Power; Patterns)*

> I started asking about the challenges again as soon as I could tell that Aiden was feeling a bit more light-hearted and able to reflect without becoming overwhelmed.

A: Oh, not that much. It's just some kids kind of were rude sometimes, but I kind of was rude back cuz I didn't wanna stand down and stuff. So then we just got really mad at each other. But in the end we kind of became friends because that's what we needed to do.

H: That's great. What did they do that was rude? Can you tell me the story of what happened? *(Validation; Patterns)*

> Aiden jumped straight to telling me how *it all turned out okay*, and I wanted to help him unpack and explore the challenge more so he could reflect on ways to really help himself with what he was facing.

A: One time, like me and my best friend, we started playing, um, soccer and then some of the kids there were kind of rude and they were really cool and we wanted to be like them. Basically, we just kind of got mad at them and then they got mad at us. And we kind of felt sad after that. But luckily our friends are good friends and they stuck up for me and, and then I stuck up for them.

H: It was okay in the end at least. Good. What did they say that was rude? *(Validation; Power; Patterns)*

A: I don't like that question.

H: Okay. You don't wanna answer it. No problem. Do you wanna say just generally what happened? *(Validation; Patterns)*

> Aiden was setting a boundary here, and a part of me wanted to just end the conversation if it made him feel uncomfortable, but I also really wanted him to be able to reflect, so I rephrased and gave him another opportunity. This is always a fine line, but if you know you are creating a safe space for reflection, it's okay to push a little in a respectful way, to help a student move into the discomfort so they can connect to what's true for them. This was the first time I had met Aiden, so it's natural that he needed a little extra reassurance that this was a safe space, which is why I kept opening the door to more reflection here. If he pushed back again, I wouldn't have gone any further with this line of questioning. If you know a student better, there will usually be a sense of trust built up between you, so you can communicate about their boundaries and who they might feel more comfortable talking to (e.g., "It's totally fine if you don't want to talk to me about that. I want to make sure that you have someone you are talking to though. Do you have someone you feel comfortable to speak to about this?").

A: It's just, they were aiming for me a lot and one of them was kicking my legs when I had the ball and one of them was really rough, but then, well, we were fine after cuz I kind of started to ask them why they were doing that.

H: Got it. That's really important, it sounds like you stood up for yourself, which I love. How did it make you feel when they were being rough and kicking your legs? *(Validation; Power; Skill; Feelings)*

> I circled back to his *feelings* because Aiden was glossing over the challenge again, and I wanted him to know it was okay to feel whatever he was feeling.

A: Well, when I had the ball, I, I felt a lot of pain, especially since it was the start of when my dad was going away, the first day I was rude. I'm sorry. . . . *(Aiden started crying.)*.

H: It's okay. Take your time. That's a tough one, hey? It's so hard to miss your parent. It's totally fine. That feeling when they first leave, my mom also left and had to go move somewhere else, so I know what that feeling's like. It's really, really, really hard. Do you wanna get a glass of water or something? *(Validation; Feelings)*

> I brought up my own experience of parental separation because I wanted Aiden to feel less alone. It's always tricky when a student gets upset, and in those moments, we want to focus purely on making them feel safe, and let them know that their feelings are okay, in any way we can. You don't need to bring up your own experiences (and only do so if you are comfortable sharing and have previously talked about it with your own peers). You can also say general things like "Being left is such a hard experience," and this will also help students feel validated in their emotional experience.

A: My whole face turns red when I cry.

H: Me too. It's all good. You're doing so well. I'm really proud of you for sharing this. Why don't we move around. Shake it out. Shake it out. Do a little shake out . . . *(we both stood up here and shook out our bodies)*. Do you want to tell me what happened? *(Validation; Patterns)*

> I wanted to shift Aiden's energy so that he could feel empowered to keep reflecting. Sometimes moving our bodies physically can help us feel stronger in the moment. It was important that I *validated his feelings first* before doing this so that he didn't get the message "your feelings are unacceptable."

A: Um, I just kind of got mad at them and I said, mean stuff and like, like other stuff I don't really wanna talk about. That's all.

H: That's fine. You don't have to talk about that. Do you think that because of what was going on at home that made you feel extra stressed? *(Validation; Paradigm; Patterns)*

> I introduced the paradigm shift that *his actions were a result of the challenges he was facing at home* to help Aiden feel less ashamed of his own behavior, and start to see the situation more clearly.

A: Mm–hmm. (Aiden nodded.)

H: Yeah? What do you think was happening? *(Patterns; Paradigm)*

> I wanted Aiden to put this into his own words so that he could reflect on *what this paradigm shift means to him.*

A: Because of what was happening at home, that made me feel even more stressed out. But I saw a video on something to always be the bigger person, and I tried doing that and it definitely worked.

H: That's awesome! It sounds like that's more who you are, hey? What did you do specifically when you were the bigger person? *(Validation; Power; Skill)*

> I wanted Aiden to *identify exactly what he did to help himself,* so that he could do this action again in the future.

A: What did I do? I started to be nice and yeah, it was just funner to be in school if I wasn't, um, being like, if I wasn't being mean.

H: Totally. And that's what happens when things are hard at home, of course it makes us extra stressed, but it sounds like you've learned so many amazing things about how to make changes for yourself. You must be really proud. Is there anything else that you do to help yourself when you're feeling stressed? *(Validation; Power; Skill)*

A: Um, if I'm stressed out at school, I talk with the counselor and then I'm not as stressed out cuz we're talking about all this stress stuff and I get it out of my body, and then we do calming activities and it's just better. And sometimes what I do at home is I talk to my mom or I lay down or I play with my dog, or, yeah.

H: Awesome. Those are really good skills. It sounds like you're really figuring out how to cope with a super hard situation! *(Validation; Power; Skill)*

This type of conversation will help your students uncover their true feelings about challenges happening at home, and be able to link the stress of this with their own reactions. This clarity can also help them see that they have the power to make different, more helpful choices.

Related Chapters

Chapter 4, "Supporting Students Who Face Abuse and Domestic Violence"; Chapter 5, "Coaching Students Who Bully and Are Aggressive/Violent"; Chapter 16 "Communicating with Students Who Have Faced Loss"; Chapter 27, "Supporting Students Who Experience Intergenerational Trauma"

30 | What's Next?

In these chapters, you have heard from students across the United States, Canada, and Australia bravely sharing their thoughts, feelings, and experiences. These conversations have been transcribed along with specific guidance for you as an educator on what to say to students who are struggling with their mental health in various ways. There are many circumstances where a referral to a mental health practitioner is necessary and incredibly important (e.g., Chapter 4, "Supporting Students Who Face Abuse and Domestic Violence"; Chapter 5, "Coaching Students Who Bully or Are Aggressive/Violent"; Chapter 12, "Supporting Students Who Self-Harm"; Chapter 13, "Encouraging Students Who Are Depressed or Apathetic"; Chapter 15, "Guiding Students Who Are Caught in Addictive Patterns"; Chapter 16, "Communicating with Students Who Have Faced Loss"; Chapter 22, "Supporting Students Who Are Bullied"; Chapter 23, "Guiding Students Who Violate Consent"; Chapter 26, "Minimizing the Influence of Pornography and 'Rape Culture'"; Chapter 27, "Supporting Students Who Experience Intergenerational Trauma"). However, even in these circumstances, you still might find yourself interacting with a student and wishing you could find the words to make even a small positive difference to their well-being. The strategies found in this book are designed to give you a place to start and a framework to guide you.

You might have felt confident in diving into some of these conversations as you were reading through the chapters that are relevant to your current class. You might also like to gather all of the information first and decide to read through the book without practicing yet in real life. If you are feeling hesitant or uncomfortable using the conversation tools for any of the topics, I encourage you to go at your own pace and practice this language with your family, friends, colleagues, and even yourself as a first step. For example, you might have a friend who has recently lost a parent, and the language in Chapter 16 on loss and suicide can help you provide them with support. You might have a child who gets anxious sometimes, and you can use the tips from Chapter 8 on worries, anxiety, and stress to help them cope. You might have a colleague who experiences prejudice, and you aren't sure what to say, so the conversation strategies in Chapter 24 will give you a place to open up that dialogue. You might also find that you yourself have tendencies toward some of the patterns found in these chapters (e.g., people-pleasing is a pattern that applies to many of us in helping professions! [Chapter 13]), and you can read through the conversations, imagining these words being said to you.

As with any skill, it will take time to build confidence in talking to students about their mental health. I am so grateful that you are willing to dive in and face the discomfort of learning this new skill in order to *create generational change* in our world. Every student deserves to know that there are adults who understand them and can support them to reflect on their experiences (*open the door*) and help themselves (*take action*). We don't have to be perfect at this, we just have to *try*. Every attempt we make has the potential to *change the course of a student's life.* If we all tried a little bit each day, imagine the ripple effect we could create! My hope is that by using some of these tools, you will grow to feel more fulfilled, inspired, and invigorated by the critical work that you do because you will know on a deep level that you are truly *helping your students learn to thrive.*

About the Author

Dr. Hayley Watson, a clinical psychologist specializing in children and adolescents, has a Ph.D. in school bullying interventions along with four further academic degrees in the field of mental health. She has been creating and delivering youth and school-based programs globally for the past 20 years and has worked across a range of sectors, including police victim services, non-profit organizations, private psychology practices, hospitals, schools, and universities. She trains educators and parents worldwide on holistic well-being practices and is the founder of Open Parachute—an online school mental health program using documentary stories of real students sharing their experiences of overcoming struggle, which is being delivered in schools across the United States, Canada, and Australia.

Index

Page numbers followed by *f* refer to figures.